Is Your Jesus the Bible Jesus?

MARIE (FOWLER) YORK

WESTBOW
PRESS
A DIVISION OF THOMAS NELSON

WestBow Press books may be ordered through booksellers or by contacting:

WestBow Press
A Division of Thomas Nelson
1663 Liberty Drive
Bloomington, IN 47403
www.westbowpress.com
1-(866) 928-1240

ISBN: 978-1-4497-4756-5 (sc)
ISBN: 978-1-4497-4757-2 (e)

Library of Congress Control Number: 2012906456

Printed in the United States of America

WestBow Press rev. date: 05/04/2012

TABLE OF CONTENTS

DEDICATION

I want to dedicate this book to everyone who has claimed the promise of Acts 16:31, our text Scripture for this book, which reads, "Believe on the Lord Jesus Christ, and thou shalt be saved."

As you read the following pages, may your faith in this promise, and indeed, every promise in God's Word, be enriched and deepened. If, however, these pages reveal that your faith has been misguided, and placed in false, unscriptural, promises and assurances, my earnest prayer and burden for this study are that you may find what God intended for you when He made this promise.

Next, I want to dedicate this effort to the glory and honor and praise of my precious Lord! How sweet is His Word, His truth. How sweet is His love and His Presence. From my heart, I thank God for God, for Who and What He is, as well as all He does!

I also want to dedicate it to my former pastor, Bro. Emerson A. Wilson, and to my present pastor, Bro. Roger L. Decker. These two men have, by the grace and power of God, given immeasurable help and encouragement to me in my walk with God and truth.

Then, I want to lovingly dedicate this book to my husband, James York. What an inspiration, support, and all-around treasure he is!

Finally, I want to dedicate this work to the tearing down of Satan's deceptions and devices. May God use it in a mighty way to do just that, is my earnest prayer!

ACKNOWLEDGEMENTS

No book of this kind is ever produced by one person. A lot of assistance with this one was needed from, and generously given by, a number of wonderful people. All of these deserve heartfelt thanks! To express this gratitude is the reason for these acknowledgements.

I want very much to thank Bro. Earl Borders, pastor of the Church of God in Summersville, West Virginia, and author of a number of books on Bible studies, as well as a series of books explaining the Revelation, for answering a number of questions for me as I strove to be sure I had the right interpretations on certain points. He also supplied me with a number of arguments used by those who promote the doctrine of "eternal security," enabling me to give more focused Bible answers to refute this false doctrine.

I also want to thank Julia Hobbs, an associate editor for *The Gospel Trumpeter*, for giving this book an "independent" edit. Her help has been indispensable.

I am indebted to my son, Dan Fowler, for his financial support in bringing this book to reality, as well as for his encouragement.

A special thanks also goes to Sister Joyce M. Cramer, of Cuyahoga Falls, Ohio, for her generous contribution toward the expenses of this book.

I owe a lot of thanks to my husband, and to my pastor, Brother Roger Decker, along with a host of friends and relatives, for their help and encouragement along the way. May the Lord bless all of you, and if this book helps anyone, you may be sure that you will receive your rewards.

Finally, but actually most of all, I want to pour out a heart full of praise and adoration to my precious God! It is through Him, and only through Him, that my feeble efforts have resulted in this Bible study. How I love His law! How I appreciate His seeking and saving *this* soul that was lost! How I long for the day when I will fall at His feet and give Him thanks and honor and glory, released at last from the restraints of human flesh and the constraints of time.

May God's richest blessings abide upon every one of you!

AUTHOR'S NOTES

A) In this book I will be using the masculine pronouns *he, him, and his*, in most cases, when referring to the generic third person, since referring to third person with "his or her," "he or she," etc., is rather awkward for both the writer and the reader. I humbly ask you to give attention to the substance of this book and not the mechanics. I heartily thank you for your understanding.

B) I sometimes repeat Scriptures and comments throughout this book because a Scriptural text often applies to more than one of the sub-topics addressed in these chapters. At other times it is simply for the sake of emphasis. The subject we're dealing with, here, is highly controversial and has many opponents, and I felt it necessary at times to "tell 'em what I'm gonna tell 'em, then tell 'em, and then tell 'em what I told 'em." I want to indelibly stamp God's truth on your mind, by God's grace, and I pray that you will allow Him to do so in your heart.

C) All Scripture references, unless otherwise noted, are taken from the *Authorized King James Version* of the Bible.

CHAPTER ONE

We Have a Dilemma

God has given a wonderful promise to mankind: "Believe on the Lord Jesus Christ, and thou shalt be saved" (Acts 16:31). Another look at this promise is found in John 3:16, which says, "For God so loved the world, that he gave his only begotten Son, that whosoever believeth in him should not perish, but have everlasting life."

Everlasting life as opposed to perishing—what a gift! And God is so generous with it that He commissioned His followers to travel the world with this Good News. More than two thousand years have passed since Jesus died to save the world, and many have taken this news to the far reaches of the earth. The West, especially, has had widespread knowledge of this promise. The United States was actually founded as a Christian nation (this is fervently denied by many today, but all you have to do is check our historical documents, and I urge you to do so[a]). Although things have changed in recent years, at one time nearly everybody in "civilized" societies had heard about the Lamb of God, Who takes away the sins of the world. And many today have claimed this promise for their own. They have heard about it, they have believed it, and they have received the gift of everlasting life.

Or have they? Does everyone who professes Christianity really have it? Probably many would say, "Certainly not. A lot of people are hypocrites." What is a hypocrite? *Webster's New World Compact School*

---

[a] A good reference for studying America's godly heritage is *America's God and Country Encyclopedia of Quotations*, by William J. Federer. You can find this book by going to Mr. Federer's web site store at www.amerisearch.net/store, or, if this link no longer works, searching "William J. Federer" on the Internet. Check also at your local library or bookseller.

and Office Dictionary defines the term *hypocrite* as "one who pretends to be pious, virtuous, etc. without really being so."[1] But I am not writing about pretenders. I am writing about sincere believers. I am concerned about these believers because, as shocking as it may be, many of them do not have real salvation. The reason for that is that not all faith is saving faith.

Are you a believer? Have you come to Jesus for redemption? Has His blood covered all your sins? Do you have that everlasting life and the hope of going to Heaven? Because you are reading this book, I assume you are interested in your soul's welfare. That's wonderful. Jesus gave another promise in John 7:17 that says, "If any man will do his will [the Father's, verse 16], he shall know of the doctrine, whether it be of God, or whether I speak of myself." So, if we're willing to obey God's will, He will show us what that will is. It is my sincere, heartfelt, desire that I may, by His mercies, help you find a portion of God's will through this book. I want you to take a close look at *your* faith. If it is *saving* faith, it will stand the close scrutiny, but if you should find that it is not, be assured that it is God's mercy that revealed this to you so that you may "make your calling and election sure" (2 Peter 1:10).

When we consider the thought of true, or real, saving faith, it brings us face to face with the fact that there is a false faith, one that does not save. This is something very few people like to think about, but, again, if your faith is real, examining it will only make it gleam. It is tested and proven faith that causes the heart to rejoice. You may wonder why I would try to convince anyone that his faith isn't real. Well, let me assure you that it is only so he can have the chance to trade the false for the real thing. I can think of nothing more devastating than to come before God's Judgment Throne with a hope of Heaven, and then find out my faith was in the wrong thing! That is why I asked you the question, in this book's title, "Is your Jesus the Bible Jesus?" Not everyone's is.

The Bible Jesus, Himself, said, in Matthew 24:24, "For there shall arise false Christs . . . and shall shew great signs and wonders; insomuch that, if it were possible, they shall deceive the very elect." Think about those words for a moment: "they shall deceive." Not, "they may," but, "they shall." Jesus is telling us that everyone *but* the very elect *will* be deceived. That's scary. It means a lot of believers will believe in a false Jesus and be lost. If you are one of them, I pray this examination of your faith will reveal this to you. Never is truth more precious than when you discover that you had believed a lie—especially when that lie would have cost you your soul for eternity.

Is your Jesus the Bible Jesus? If not, believing in him will not save you. You will not be able to claim the promise of Acts 16:31 or John 3:16. You may marvel at the thought that some people actually believe in a false Jesus, but the Bible Jesus clearly said they would. Matthew 24:5 says, "For many shall come in my name, saying, I am Christ; and shall deceive many." If there are so many false prophets and false Christs, and so many deceived hearts, where are they all? Have you ever wondered about that? Well, the reason they are so hard to find is because they are so terribly *deceptive.* Once I was deceived by false prophets myself (not *cultists,* but *"Christians"*), and God mercifully opened my eyes, so I have a real burden for others in that condition. It is my earnest desire to help you make sure *you* are not one of the deceived. The cost of being mistaken about this is just too high. *It is beyond comprehension!*

Will it surprise—and maybe shock—you if I tell you that the vast majority of professed Christians, today, believe in a false Jesus? *Wait!* Don't shut the book. I know that's "radical," but please let me show you why I say it. I can prove that statement is based in fact. Come with me on a bold, brave, honest, examination of saving faith. And while we conduct this examination, keep two important things in mind:

First, be aware of what Jesus said in John 5:39: "Search the scriptures; for in them ye think ye have eternal life: and they are they which testify of me." Paul added, in 2 Corinthians 13:5, "Examine yourselves, whether ye be in the faith." A search of the Scriptures to be sure you have eternal life was actually commanded by Jesus. What we are doing in this book is nothing more or less than following Christ's command. Many religious leaders are saying a lot of things about Jesus, but Jesus said it is the *Scriptures* that correctly testify of Him.

Second, the Gospel is *simple;* the Apostle Paul spoke of the simplicity that is in Christ, and how he feared that people's minds would be corrupted regarding that simplicity (2 Corinthians 11:3). People's minds have, without a doubt, been corrupted today concerning the simplicity of saving faith, so as you read this book, remember that the Gospel is not complicated. When the Bible *simply* says something, it means it.

Now, then, I've set the dilemma before you: many are believing in false Christs, and we need to make sure we are not among them. Before we commence our search of the Scriptures, to examine saving faith, may I humbly suggest that you pause for a word of prayer? Honestly, friend, I do not want anyone reading this book without having earnestly prayed first. Ask God to help you shed all prejudices and preconceived ideas that don't line up with the Scriptures and to give you Judgment Day honesty. Friend, God's Word tells us that the heart is deceitful (Jeremiah 17:9). We human beings really do want to have things to our liking. It's easy, when reading the Bible, to try to mold what we read around our cherished beliefs, rather than to shape our beliefs around the Word of God. I admit that I have done that in the past. I had a very cherished belief, and I had to work, once, at making the Bible support it (more on this in a later chapter). When I came to understand what I was doing, and that what I believed and cherished was actually contrary to Scripture, I learned a great lesson: keep an honest heart, and be willing to let God show you when you're wrong. Build your beliefs and spiritual loyalties on the Word of God alone; then, if He shows you that you are mistaken along some line, you'll go with the truth rather than insisting that the truth upholds your beliefs. Another way to put it is, don't try to make the Scriptures support your beliefs; study them with an open mind and make your beliefs support the Scriptures.

From time to time, we all need to ask God to search our hearts and show us whether there's any trace in us of reading our pet theories into the Scriptures, and if He finds it, to cleanse us from it. He will. Remember, He has promised that, if we will draw nigh to Him, He'll draw nigh to us. So pause for prayer. Then, with an open heart, embark with me on this thrilling *Bible Adventure*.

CHAPTER TWO

What Does Believing in Christ Produce?

Multitudes of nominal Christians believe in a "Jesus" who overlooks their sins, one who cannot truly deliver them from sin, but what does believing in the real Jesus produce? Again, Acts 16:31 says, "Believe on the Lord Jesus Christ, and thou shalt be saved." What is being saved? *Webster's Compact Dictionary* says to *save* is "to rescue or preserve from harm or danger." Then, under the category "*Theol.*" for *theological*, or pertaining to the study of God, it adds that it means "to deliver from sin."[1]

Strong's Greek Dictionary of the New Testament says the word rendered *saved* in this text is *sozo* (sode'-zo), which means, "to save, i.e. *deliver* or *protect* . . . preserve . . . (make) whole."[2]

These definitions line up with what the angel who announced Jesus' birth told Joseph in Matthew 1:21: "And she shall bring forth a son, and thou shalt call his name JESUS: for he shall save his people from their sins."

All right, *Webster's* says to *save* is to deliver from sin, and the Greek says to *save* is to deliver and preserve, protect and make whole. The promise God gave, then, is that the Bible Jesus would save—deliver, preserve, protect, and make whole—*from sin.* Holiness fighters may contend that to *protect* us from our sins does not mean complete deliverance from sin; perhaps not, but to *deliver* most certainly does. And to *preserve* means to keep us that way. Remember what I said about keeping in mind the simplicity of the Gospel? This is so simple that the vast majority of believers fail to grasp it. Therefore, let me reemphasize what being saved actually means: being *delivered* and *preserved* from sin.

The devil likes to complicate this matter of being saved, this matter of believing on Jesus. Although the Word of God says Jesus would save people *from* sin, multitudes think instead that Jesus came to save people *in* their sins. Tragically, many follow such a "Jesus" today, but this is not the Bible Jesus. Can you save someone *from* drowning and save him *in* his drowning? Can you save someone *from* a fire and save him *in* the fire? Of course not, and neither can Jesus save people *from* sin and save them *in* their sins. It is impossible, friend. The very statement doesn't make sense.

Impossible! That's what the masses of believers cry today about being saved from sin. For some reason difficult to understand, they believe Christ can save from the really bad sins, but not from the "everyday" variety. Shouldn't it be harder to save from the vile sins than to save from the "mild" ones? It seems they have it backwards—but wait. The truth is that Jesus saves from *all* sins. Look at 1 John 1:9, which says, "If we confess our sins, he is faithful and just to forgive us our sins, and to cleanse us from all unrighteousness." How much unrighteousness is left after we are cleansed from all of it?

Someone may say, "That means that, as we commit sins from day to day, the blood of Jesus cleanses us. It keeps cleansing us, so it cleanses all." That may sound good in theory, but the Bible does not support the theory. It will not stand up under the scrutiny of Scripture. Please allow me to help you in studying what the clear Word of God says about saving faith.

I want us to look, here at the beginning, at three immutable Bible principles that make it impossible—yes, *impossible*—for the anti-holiness teaching to be true. First, people say that this world is so corrupt that no one can live in it and not sin. However, the Bible says, in Romans 5:20, that "where sin abounded, grace did much more abound." Friend, it doesn't matter how strong sin may be in this world, or how hideous, or how prevalent. It does not matter, because grace outdoes it. Not just barely, either; grace *much more* abounds than sin, wherever sin abounds. I ask you, in all honesty, if grace much more abounds than sin, right where sin abounds, how can sin overcome those who are filled with grace? Please reflect on this for a moment or two.

The answer is, it cannot. In fact, while the Apostle John acknowledged that "the whole world lieth in wickedness" (1 John 5:19), he said, in 4:17, "that we may have boldness in the day of judgment:

because as he [Christ] is, so are we *in this world* [emphasis added]." How *is* Jesus? He is holy, friend; He is totally without sin. He does always those things that please God (John 8:29). So, *we* can be holy, totally without sin, and doing always what is pleasing to God. See 1 Peter 2:21-22, 24.

Look at Jesus' own words, in His prayer for His followers. John 17:15 records, "I pray not that thou shouldest take them out of the world, but that thou shouldest *keep them from the evil* [emphasis added]." No one, dear reader, knows God's plan and His will more than Jesus, His Son, does. Here Christ clearly lets us know that God does not have to take us out of this world before He can make us holy. *He is able to keep us from the evil in the world right while we are in it.* And this was not only for the early church, as some claim, but also for us today: "Neither pray I for these alone, but for them also which shall believe on me through their word" (verse 20). That means you and me, dear one. May I say it again? God does not have to take us out of the world to keep us from the evil that's in the world. That's because, where sin abounds, grace much more abounds.

Paul believed this and taught it; look at his words in Galatians 1:4: "Who gave himself for our sins, that he might deliver us from this present evil world, according to the will of God and our Father." This deliverance from sin, in *this present evil world*, is God's will. Do you believe, have you been taught, that Paul was talking about when God takes us to Heaven—that it's then that He delivers us from this present evil world? Not so, friend. I just quoted Jesus' words about this. Our Lord said, to our Heavenly Father, that He did not want us taken out of this present evil world, but that He definitely wanted us kept from its evil! Dear one, I'd rather believe Jesus, the Jesus of the Bible, than *any* preacher or teacher, and I pray that you would too! So, the first principle we studied from God's Word that makes it impossible for anti-holiness teaching to be true is that *where sin abounds, grace doth much more abound.*

The second principle is found in 1 John 4:4, which says, "Greater is he that is in you, than he that is in the world." Again, no matter how black and ugly and powerful Satan and sin are, Christ-in-us is greater. Christ is greater than Satan, and Christ is in the true believer. Remember, Jesus said that His followers would be filled with the Holy Ghost (John 14:16-17, Matthew 3:11, Acts 2:4). How can Satan possibly overcome someone who is filled with the Holy Ghost? Let me say it again: Christ-in-us is greater than Satan and greater than sin, no matter how great and prevalent they are. These sin-you-must teachers may rant till doomsday about how impossible it is to live like Christ in such a sin-ridden world, but they can't change the truth of this second principle—*no matter how sinful this world is, He that is in us is greater than he that is in the world.* God is greater than Satan! Satan is in the world, *but God is in His people!* Friend, please take heed. To say that Satan's power is too great for God-in-us is *dangerous!* If Satan's being in the world makes the world evil, how can God's being in His children do anything but make us holy?

Second Corinthians 10:3-5 gives us our third principle:

3 For though we walk in the flesh, we do not war after the flesh:

4 (For the weapons of our warfare are not carnal, but mighty through God to the pulling down of strong holds;)

5 Casting down imaginations, and every high thing that exalteth itself against the knowledge of God, and bringing into captivity every thought to the obedience of Christ.

Wow! Did you grasp that? *The weapons of our warfare are mighty through God to the bringing into captivity of every thought to the obedience of Christ.* Reread it; that's what it says. So, if we can bring every thought into obedience to Christ, how is it that we must sin? "Well," some sin-more-or-less preacher may say, "certainly we need to try to bring our thoughts into obedience, but after all, this flesh is weak." Please read those verses again. It says our weapons are *mighty.* Mighty how? *Through God!* It's true that our flesh is weak, in and of itself, but this Scripture says *we do not war after the flesh.* We war with mighty weapons that enable us to *bring every thought into obedience* by that greater One Who is in us. Paul did not say, nor did he in any way infer, that "we should *try* to bring our thoughts into obedience, but we will probably fail."

Furthermore, these nominal Christian leaders' persistent emphasis on the *strong hold* sin has on the world, only enhances the victory this text promises. How is that, you wonder? Well, Paul said *our mighty weapons pull down strongholds!*

Because people "believe in Jesus" without gaining this deliverance from, and victory over, sin, they feel there is no such experience. But there is, friend. There really is. The reason their faith fails to secure it

8

for them is because they've been taught a false concept of what Bible believing really is. That false concept is taught, today, throughout nominal Christendom. Nearly all clergymen, as well as Sunday School teachers, youth leaders, etc., tell their people that, although they "believe," they cannot obtain complete deliverance from sin. Since they do not expect deliverance when they "believe," their faith cannot save them.

Do you realize that these holiness deniers don't glorify God? They glorify sin. They glorify Satan when they say that God cannot quite banish sin's power over us. What they teach is nothing less than an insult to Christ. But I, like Paul, am set for the defense of the Gospel! I exalt God by telling others that God doesn't have any trouble handling the devil. My Lord is the Almighty. He speaks today, just as He did more than two thousand years ago, and Satan has to flee. Friend, these teachers don't have a biblical leg to stand on, and if you will stay with me in this study, I will fully back up that statement by God's holy Word. What the Bible *does not* say is a very flimsy basis to build a doctrine—or one's belief—on.

To sin requires two things: knowledge and will. James 4:17 says, "Therefore to him that knoweth to do good, and doeth it not, to him it is sin." Also, the Apostle Paul said in Romans 7:9, "For I was alive without the law once: but when the commandment came, sin revived, and I died." In other words, Paul had not died spiritually, because of sin, before understanding of God's Law came to him. When that understanding came, however, disobedience to that Law was sin. Before the understanding came, he did not sin, though he might have done something that broke the Law. *Knowledge.* In order to commit sin, we have to know something *is* sin.

In the Garden of Eden, God gave Adam a commandment. He had also given Adam a free will for choosing whether to obey it or not, so both elements, knowledge and will, were present. When Adam chose to break a commandment that he understood, his act was sin. In Deuteronomy 30:19, Moses told the children of Israel, "I call heaven and earth to record this day against you, that I have set before you life and death, blessing and cursing: therefore choose life, that both thou and thy seed may live." And in Joshua 24:15, Joshua said, again to the children of Israel, "Choose you this day whom ye will serve . . . but as for me and my house, we will serve the LORD." We all have this free will; to sin, we must have knowledge and then choose to do what we *know* is wrong. The verse we quoted from James refers to both knowledge and will when it says "to him that *knoweth* . . . and *doeth* it not." *Doing it not* is an act of the will, and it is disobedience, it is sin, when knowledge is present. To commit sin, I repeat, takes both knowledge and will, or choice.

Surely a sinful *act* cannot be committed without it having been a *thought* first. In Eden, Satan got Eve to think about the forbidden fruit before she chose to eat it. If we can bring every thought into obedience, how can we not have control over our deeds? Most certainly, through the power of God, through the "mighty weapons" God gives us, we can also bring every action into obedience to Christ!

This means, of course, that *temptation is not sin*. No matter how horrid a temptation may be, as long as we bring it into obedience to Christ, and do not yield to it (it is a thought, after all), we have done nothing wrong. This is the clear teaching of Scripture. Matthew 4:1-11 tells us how Jesus was tempted, yet we can see that He never gave in. He resisted and He triumphed. Hebrews 4:15b tells us He "was in all points tempted like as we are, yet without sin." Being tempted is not sin; Christ was tempted, but He did not sin.

Many think they sin if an ungodly thought merely comes to mind. Friend, we often cannot control what comes into out thoughts. Psalm 139:2 tells us that God knows our thoughts afar off, but we don't. Because a thought can come to us without knowledge or will on our part, just having it enter our mind is not sin. *What we do with that thought*, through our knowledge and will, determines whether or not we sin. As we've already learned, if we, through the power of God, bring it into captivity to Christ (if we banish it rather than embrace it), there is no sin committed. After all, we are told that, if we resist the devil, he will flee from us (James 4:7). That lets us know that we *can* resist him and put him to flight—but he has to present himself to us first, and he always starts with a thought!

"How can anyone live in this wicked world and not sin?" How often this cry is heralded throughout Christendom today. The Apostle Paul, however, asked the exact opposite of this: "How shall we, that are dead to sin, live any longer therein" (Romans 6:2)? He was incredulous at the idea of Christians sinning. Certainly he had a vision of being saved that was different from that of most religious professors, and teachers, in our time. He believed that Jesus saved His people *from* their sins; therefore, Jesus' people were, and are, *dead to sin*!

Sin is a result of *giving in* to temptation. James told us this in James 1:14-15a:

14 But every man is tempted, when he is drawn away of his own lust, and enticed.

15 Then when lust hath conceived, it bringeth forth sin . . . .

Temptation is being drawn away by our fleshly desires. Satan urges us to follow those desires rather than following God's will. But no sin takes place until those lusts *conceive*. The *seed* of desire has to connect with the *sperm*, as it were, of choice. Again, only when lust conceives is its fruit—sin—brought forth. However, we do not have to give in to temptation. We do not have to allow lust, or desire, to *bear fruit*. First Corinthians 10:13 tells us that "There hath no temptation taken you but such as is common to man: but God is faithful, who will not suffer you to be tempted above that ye are able; but will with the temptation also make a way to escape, that ye may be able to bear it."

To say that God allows temptations to befall a Christian that he is not able to overcome is to say God is not faithful. But God *is* faithful. To do what? To *not suffer His people to be tempted above that they are able*; to make sure no temptation is too strong for them. To make a way, *with* the temptation, whereby they may *escape* it. Surely, if we escape temptation, we get away from it; we are not overcome by it. Through God's faithfulness to your soul, friend, you do not have to sin. Read that sentence again, and grasp hold on it! *God will not suffer His children to be tempted above what they are able to bear!* This is an unfailing promise, and it is one that you can safely rest your soul on.

The promises false Christianity is flooding the world with, on the other hand—that people can sin more or less and still be saved—are without a doubt going to cause souls to be lost who have hoped for acceptance into Heaven. Do not, for one minute longer, be taken in by these false hopes. They are not "dreams," they are *nightmares*.

For certain, the claim that we have to sin more or less every day is based in part on a misconception of what sin is. As we have seen in the preceding paragraphs, Christians do not sin where there is no knowledge, or understanding, of God's will. They do not sin where there is no conscious choice made by them to disobey a known command.

Sin is not committed by simply being tempted, nor by thoughts merely passing through one's mind. We couldn't bring thoughts into obedience to Christ, if they were not contrary to Him to begin with, so evil thoughts do come to mind. But, we can't do anything with our thoughts until they *become* thoughts. It's what we then do with them that matters. If we bring wrong thoughts into obedience to Christ, there is no sin involved. If, however, we

a) invite the thought by something we willingly look at or listen to, and/or
b) like the thought and dwell on it, enjoy and entertain it, and/or
c) act on it,

then it becomes sin. But many things that religious people think are sins, are not. Sadly, many sincere believers who truly repent of their sins, lose their victory simply because they're made to think they've sinned when they haven't, and, worse, that sinning day by day is a normal state of being for Christians. They fall into the belief that Christ saves *in* sin rather than *from* it and, therefore, are switched to "faith" in a Jesus that does not exist, and their souls are destroyed by false doctrine.

Let me digress, here, for a moment. Friend, if you have honestly confessed, and repented of, your sins, and placed faith in God's promise to save you, and have since been told that you're sinning because you've had temptations or because evil thoughts have passed through your mind, take heart. You have not sinned unless you understood God's will and went against it by choice. As long as you did not give in to the temptation, or as long as you banished the evil thought, you overcame by the power of God. You have the victory. You are a Bible Christian. Continue resisting Satan, continue bringing your thoughts into obedience, and you will continue to prosper spiritually.

Now, back to our study. Since sin only happens when we have knowledge and then choose to do wrong, we can begin to see how bringing every thought into obedience to Christ gives us victory over sin. This, of course, is not done in our own strength. It is by the power of God. Remember *Webster's* definition of *save* that I gave at the beginning of this chapter? It was from *Webster's New World Compact School and Office Dictionary*. However, I really like the definition given under "*Theol.*" in *Webster's New World* "uncompact" version, which says to save is "to exercise power to redeem from evil and sin."[3] God is the One, and the only One, Who has and can exercise this power. But He does have it, and He does exercise it for all who truly believe in the Jesus of the Bible. The teaching that Christians commit sin on an ongoing basis throughout their lives is not true. *Real* Christians don't!

This brings us back to our theme: Is your Jesus the Bible Jesus? If your believing has left you in a "sin-more-or-less" state, dear reader, you have either believed in a false Christ, or you have not believed, in biblical terms, at all. You have to believe that Jesus saves *His* people *from* their sins. This is what *the Scriptures* testify of Jesus, and believing anything else is placing faith in a "Jesus" that is not the Jesus of the Bible. Faith in such false Christs, my friend, has not, will not, and *cannot*, save you.

It boils down to a simple question—do you *want* to live above sin? Paul said, in 2 Corinthians 7:9-11:

9 Now I rejoice, not that ye were made sorry, but that ye sorrowed to repentance: for ye were made sorry after a godly manner . . . .

10 For godly sorrow worketh repentance to salvation not to be repented of: but the sorrow of the world worketh death.

11 For behold this selfsame thing, that ye sorrowed after a godly sort, what carefulness it wrought in you, yea, what clearing of yourselves, yea, what indignation, yea, what fear, yea, what vehement desire, yea, what zeal, yea, what revenge! In all things ye have approved yourselves to be clear in this matter.

Repentance is as necessary to being saved as is faith. "Just believe, and you're saved," as taught by nominal Christianity, is false, friend. While Acts 16:31 answers the question, "Sirs, what must I do to be saved?" with the command to believe, Acts 2:38 answers the same question ("Men and brethren, what shall we do?") with the command to repent. You see, true believing includes believing *all* that the Word of God says we must do. The Proverb writer tells us something we must do in Chapter 28, Verse 13. It says, "He that covereth his sins shall not prosper: but whoso confesseth and forsaketh them shall have mercy." No one will find mercy, no matter how much he "believes," unless he confesses and forsakes his sins!

What is repentance? What does it mean? According to *The* (Zondervan) *System Bible Study's* definition, "In its theological sense, this word denotes a sense of guilt, an apprehension of God's mercy, sorrow for sin, and a turning from sin to righteousness. The Greek word most commonly rendered 'repent' in the N.T. indicates a change of mind, and is equivalent to *conversion*."[4]

And Paul told us—we just read it, above—what repentance *does*. In the Corinthians it "wrought" carefulness, clearing of themselves, indignation, fear, vehement desire, zeal, and revenge. If you become godly sorry over your sins—required for true repentance—it will do the same for you. It will work a carefulness in you, and since repentance deals with sin, it is sin you will be careful about. The expression, "Be careful!" means to watch out in order to avoid something harmful or unpleasant, so being careful about sin is to watch out for and avoid it.

Repentance will work a clearing of yourself. You will begin to make your past wrongs right. (By the way, this clearing of yourself would be impossible if you just continued to do wrong from day to day.) Repentance will work an *indignation*—a righteous anger[5]—toward sin (*anger* means "hostile feelings."[6]) After all, sin tortured and killed our blessed Savior. Then, repentance works fear. With repentance unto salvation, we ought to lose a lot of fear, so what kind of fear does repentance work in us? The kind the Bible tells us we should have—a healthy, *godly* fear—a fear of failing God again. Next, repentance works a vehement desire. What for? Not for sin; since repentance is a turning from sin, it works a vehement desire to do what is right. It works zeal; again, since all of this is the result of turning your back on wrong, this zeal has to be for following God's will. And, finally, repentance works a holy revenge—instead of running after sin, you'll chase it away, with a purpose to "kill" it every time it rears its ugly head. Certainly, if repentance works all of this in a believer, that believer cannot just "sin more or less every day." If he did, he would be in constant conflict and misery. Reread those verses and think about it. The changed attitude would be in constant conflict with the unchanged behavior. This is *not* Bible salvation. Ironically, if what modern Christendom teaches were true, repentance would result in agony and depression, not peace, joy, abundant life, and glory!

Someone may say, "But the believer has no ability to change his overall behavior." That is true, of course, and it is why we have so much sin around us. Jeremiah 13:23 says, "Can the Ethiopian change his skin, or the leopard his spots? then may ye also do good, that are accustomed to do evil." Friend, what true Bible faith is all about is believing that "if I turn from sin to God with all my heart, *God will convert me.*" Not *you* will. *God* will. You cannot change your behavior, but God can, and when a soul is longing for this change and repents, and believes *biblically*, he will find this glorious deliverance. Remember, it is God Who exercises the power to save.

Ezekiel made conversion very clear in Ezekiel 36:26-27:

26 A new heart also will I give you, and a new spirit will I put within you: and I will take away the stony heart out of your flesh, and I will give you an heart of flesh.

27 And I will put my spirit within you, and cause you to walk in my statutes, and ye shall keep my judgments, and do them.

This is Bible salvation, the result of true faith in the true Savior. God takes out the old, hard, sinful heart and the old disobedient spirit. In their place we receive a new, pure, tender, heart, and a new, obedient, spirit. (That's the only kind God gives.) Then, to make the change complete, God gives us His very own Spirit. This is where the power to live holy comes from. With the new heart and new spirit, you want to live a holy life, and with God's Holy Spirit reigning within you, you can. Notice the source of all these changes: *I* will take away; *I* will give you; *I* will put within you; *I* will cause you. Only after *He* does all this, does what *we* will do come into the picture: with all this *supernatural* change, *we* shall keep His judgments and do them. He just causes us to.

Dear one, notice the last statement in 2 Corinthians 7:11, quoted earlier: "In all things ye have approved yourselves to be clear in this matter." Here Paul let us know for sure that we cannot be clear on this matter of repentance until and unless it produces these results in our lives. To go on with a nonchalant attitude and a sin-more-or-less experience only shows that we have not truly repented.

First Peter 1:22 says, "Seeing ye have purified your souls in obeying the truth through the Spirit . . . ." It is through the Holy Spirit that we are able to obey. Galatians 5:16 says, "This I say then, Walk in the Spirit, and ye shall not fulfil the lust of the flesh." Remember that lust is the thing that conceives to produce sin; lust conceiving and bringing forth is the same as lust being fulfilled. Those who walk in the Spirit do not fulfill their lusts. Their lusts do not conceive and bring forth sin. The bottom line: they do not sin! Paul was very emphatic; he said those who walk in the Spirit *shall not* fulfill their lusts, and since he instructed the Galatians and us to walk in the Spirit, we know it is something we can do, by God's power.

Again, friend, if you are not truly sorry for your sins, you cannot find forgiveness for them, no matter how earnestly you "believe." But if you are sorry, you will want victory over your sins, you will long for deliverance from them, and you will be glad to learn that you can have these. The reason some fight the thought of holy living is because they've been taught that it isn't possible, but if their hearts are honest they will be thrilled to find out that it is. Many others fight holiness, however, because they love their sins. They are glad to believe "they can't help it." They savor getting to live in sin, following and fulfilling their lusts, and still getting to go to Heaven. Can you see how this doctrine only enables sinfulness, rather than reproving it? It is nothing but a tool of Satan that makes sin "prettier," supposedly, while leaving souls, for whom Christ died, in its bondage. But such "Christianity" won't work. An old preacher once said that the trouble with the ways that "seem right," is that they come apart at the "seems." They really *aren't* right, and they will fail to produce the desired end. Let me repeat, and stress, that to believe in a "Jesus" that leaves you in your sins, is to believe in a false Jesus. The real Jesus "saves His people from their sins," just as the angel said He would. If you, dear reader, are a "believer" who loves your sins, I entreat you to cast aside your religious profession. Please don't reproach Christ's name by claiming His approval on, or even just acceptance of, your sinful life.

In Mark 10:25, Jesus astonished His disciples by stating that it was difficult for a rich man to enter into the Kingdom of God. They asked Him, "Who then can be saved" (verse 26)? The Greek word translated *saved* in this verse is *sozo*, the same as that translated *saved* in Acts 16:31, our leading text for this book (and so is that in Matthew 1:21, where the angel said Jesus would *save* His people *from* their sins). This is the *saved* that believing in the Lord Jesus Christ produces. What was Jesus' answer to His disciples' question? He said, "With men it is impossible, but not with God: for with God all things are possible" (verse 27). To those who cry, "That's impossible!" concerning living without sin in this world, I can only say, are you calling Jesus a liar? He said this *saved*—the saved that is *from sin*, the saved that believing on the (true) Lord Jesus Christ results in—is possible with God. Remember, it is God Who makes the transformation we read about in Ezekiel 36. The miracle is the work of God Himself. Our part of salvation is to repent and believe, and true believing embraces this miracle. True faith takes it in.

From God's Word, then, we can see what believing in the Bible Jesus produces: salvation from sin. It brings, to dwell within the believer, One Who is greater than he that is in the world. It brings grace that much more abounds than sin, wherever and however sin may abound. It gives weapons that enable the believer to bring every thought, and therefore every act, into obedience to Christ. It produces a carefulness and indignation concerning sin, and a vehement desire for righteousness. It takes out the wrong spirit and defiled heart, replacing them with new, tender, and submissive, ones. Then it brings the indwelling of God's own Holy Spirit to cause one to obey Him, enabling one to walk in the Spirit and not fulfill the lusts of the flesh. Again, this is the experience the Scriptures testify that Jesus would bring to us. We have searched the Scriptures, as Jesus instructed us to do, in order that we may *know*, and not just *think*, that we have eternal life. Do you have this Bible experience, dear one? If not, and you claim to be a believer, your faith has been placed in a "Jesus" that is not the Jesus of the Bible.

We have said a good deal about the contrast between being saved *from* sin and being saved *in* it, but there's another angle of this point that I want to mention. Many believe that Jesus saves *in* sin, but *from* its consequences. How convenient! How self serving! Those who relish this thought are like Cain. Remember how God warned Cain about sin (Genesis 4:6-7)? Well, Cain wasn't interested in being saved from wrongdoing, but he surely wanted to be spared from its consequences. However, Matthew 1:21 does not say Jesus will save His people from sin's *consequences*, here or hereafter. It says He will save them from sin itself. Dear one, please let me warn you, to the real saving of your soul: if your believing has come short of producing these results in you, you need to trade it in for the real thing!

CHAPTER THREE

Grace—What It Is and Is Not, Does and Does Not Do

Many, today, misunderstand what the grace of God is, and they certainly misunderstand what it does. Here is a list of the things the Bible says about grace:

- it came by Jesus Christ (John 1:17)
- its results can be seen (Acts 11:23)
- we believe through it (Acts 18:27)
- Jesus' Gospel is "the gospel of the grace of God" (Act 20:24)
- it justifies (Romans 3:24, Titus 3:7)
- it gives "standability" (Romans 5:2)
- it reigns (Romans 5:21)
- it abounds (Romans 5:20, 6:1; 2 Corinthians 9:8)
- it makes elect (Romans 11:5)
- it can be perceived (Galatians 2:9)
- it is, in respect to saving ability, opposed to works (Romans 11:6)
- it effectively makes us what we ought to be, and enables us to labor (1 Corinthians 15:10)
- it redounds to the glory of God (2 Corinthians 4:15)
- it is sufficient (2 Corinthians 12:9)
- it is accompanied by peace (Galatians 1:3, Ephesians 1:2, Philippians 1:2, Colossians 1:2, etc.)
- we are called into it, and by it (Galatians 1:6, 15)
- it can be frustrated (Galatians 2:21)
- we can fall from it (Galatians 5:4)
- it is rich (Ephesians 1:7, 2:7)

- it works with faith to save (Ephesians 2:8)
- it fits our gifts (Ephesians 4:7)
- it was ordained for us before the world began (2 Timothy 1:9)
- there is strength in it (2 Timothy 2:1)
- it brings salvation, and it teaches us (Titus 2:11-12)
- Christians can boldly ask for it (Hebrews 4:16)
- we can fail of it (Hebrews 12:15)
- by it we may serve God acceptably (Hebrews 12:28)
- our hearts can be established with it (Hebrews 13:9)
- God "giveth more" of it, and that unto the humble (James 4:6)
- we are instructed to be good stewards of it (1 Peter 4:10)
- it is "manifold" (1 Peter 4:10)
- we can grow in (not in*to*) it (2 Peter 3:18)
- lastly, and of great importance to our study, men turn it into lasciviousness (Jude 4).

One thing concerning this list is conspicuous by its absence. There is no Scripture stating, nor even hinting, that grace covers sin in a Christian's life! If you do not believe me, get a good concordance and look for one.

What, exactly, is grace? *Webster's* defines it under "*Theol.*" as "*a*) the unmerited love and favor of God toward man *b*) divine influence acting in man to make him pure and morally strong *c*) the condition of a person thus influenced *d*) a special virtue given to a person by God."[1] So, what grace actually is—and the Bible backs Webster up on all of this—is a divine action within us that makes us *pure*, and *morally strong*, because of special virtue given us by God, all of which is unmerited love and favor. But, again, there is nothing here that suggests that grace covers sin in Christians. One has to wonder what these "Christian" theologians base their notion on. It must be upon their own sinful experiences. Because the "grace" they've received hasn't wrought holiness in them, they think holiness isn't possible. But, friend, their "grace" is not a model for you to follow; it is one for you to shun. We have seen what true faith in the Bible Jesus produces, and it is not a life of sinning more or less from day to day.

Perhaps one of the best studies on grace is found in the Book of Romans. Let us examine what Paul said there about grace.

Grace Produces Obedience

The first mention of grace in the Book of Romans is found in Chapter 1, verse 5, where Paul said, "By whom [Christ, verse 4] we have received grace and apostleship, for obedience to the faith among all nations, for his name." Herein is the foundational truth that we receive grace by Jesus Christ, and this is confirmed in John 1:17, which says, "For the law was given by Moses, but grace and truth came by Jesus Christ." Without Christ, there is no grace. This lets us know that those who do not believe in Christ Jesus cannot receive of God's grace, and this applies too, of course, to those who believe in any "Jesus" besides the true Savior sent from God.

In this verse, we also learn what we receive grace for: obedience to the faith. We do not receive grace for a cloak for our "failures," our day-to-day sinning, but for *obedience*. We do not obtain it as a "license" to sin, but for *obedience*.

What do I mean by a "license" to sin? Well, where I come from, it is illegal to go deer hunting without a specific deer hunting license, which covers a limited period of time. If someone who does not have such a license goes deer hunting, that person can be fined, but if he obtains and adheres to the deer hunting license, he can go deer hunting without fear of any penalty. In like manner, many think Jesus, or His grace, gives people a "sin license." If they sin without Jesus, they will go to hell, but if they obtain that "sin license," or "grace," they can sin and still be saved. I say it kindly, but it must be said: this is nonsense! It is 100 percent contrary to the Word of God. To say that Christ, the blessed Lamb of God, Who came to take away the sin of the world (John 1:29), instead gives people a "license" to sin, is an insult to Him. It is blasphemy! He came to destroy the works of the devil, not to, through a "license," enable them (1 John 3:8). He does not make them "legal" for those who are under grace.

Remember the last Scripture in our list of Bible comments on grace? It is Jude 4, which reads, "For there are certain men crept in unawares, who were before of old ordained to this condemnation, ungodly men, turning the grace of our God into lasciviousness ['lust,'[2] that which conceives to bring forth sin], and denying the only Lord God, and our Lord Jesus Christ." Whew, that is one serious indictment! Did you get it? These were religious leaders who were "creepers in" and not ordained by God. These were men who actually perverted God's grace by using it to make room for disobedience rather than to bring power for obedience. *Pervert*, according to *Webster's*, is to "corrupt," "misuse," and "distort."[3] Certainly, teaching that God's grace, which is to save and keep us from sin, instead allows and defends sin in a Christian, is misusing and distorting, and therefore corrupting, the grace of God. If this is not a picture of Christendom as a whole, today, I don't know what it is. And look: these "men of God" were denying God, denying Christ, not representing Him. Sadly, but justly, Christ said that He will, in turn, deny them (Matthew 10:33)!

Disobedience. James 2:10 says, "For whosoever shall keep the whole law, and yet offend in one point, he is guilty of all." The state of "Christianity" in general is one of keeping some of God's commandments, but being unable to keep all of them. This will not pass Bible muster. If we break one commandment, we are as guilty before God as if we broke all of His commandments. If we break God's commandments, His Law, we are biblically "lawless." When religious leaders tell "believers" the grace of God "covers" their more-or-less-every-day breaking of God's Law, those leaders are, again let me stress, perverting the grace of God. It is turning God's grace into *lawlessness* to say Christians, being "covered" by grace, can break God's Law and remain Christians.

Grace Enables One to Stand

Next, Romans 5:2 says, "By whom also [our Lord Jesus Christ, verse 1] we have access by faith into this grace wherein we stand, and rejoice in hope of the glory of God." True faith in the Bible Jesus brings us into a grace where we stand. What does it mean, to stand? Well, standing is opposed to falling. If we stand, we do not fall; conversely, if we fall, we do not stand. Falling is used in the Scriptures to describe failing God. For example:

Romans 14:13 . . . but judge this rather, that no man put a stumblingblock or an occasion to fall in his brother's way.

1 Corinthians 10:12 Wherefore let him that thinketh he standeth take heed lest he fall.

Hebrews 4:11 Let us labour therefore to enter into that rest, lest any man fall after the same example of unbelief.

21

2 Peter 1:10 Wherefore the rather, brethren, give diligence to make your calling and election sure: for if ye do these things [verses 5-7], *ye shall never fall.*

2 Peter 3:17 Ye therefore, beloved, seeing ye know these things before, beware lest ye also, being led away with the error of the wicked, fall from your own stedfastness.

When Paul told the Romans that we have access, through Christ, into a grace wherein we can stand, he meant that grace would keep us from falling, or failing God. We can see that this is God's purpose for us in Jude's epistle. Verses 24-25 read:

24 Now unto him that is able to keep you from falling, and to present you faultless before the presence of his glory with exceeding joy,

25 To the only wise God our Savior, be glory and majesty, dominion and power, both now and ever. Amen.

Notice that Jude not only said God could keep us from falling, but that He could present us *faultless* before the presence of His glory. This does not mean He will make us faultless when we stand before Him someday. He will *present* us faultless. We'll already be faultless before we get there. We can be faultless, and able to stand that way, because, through grace, God keeps us from falling.

Grace Enables One to Reign

Another thing the Book of Romans shows us about grace is found in Romans 5:17. It says that " . . . they which receive abundance of grace and of the gift of righteousness shall reign in life by one, Jesus Christ." Did you notice that receiving grace and receiving God's righteousness go together? Those who receive the one receive the other. And those who receive these reign. They reign in life, *this* life. What does it mean, to reign? *Webster's* says *reign* means "to rule as a sovereign."[4] *Sovereign* means, "a monarch or ruler."[5] In Revelation 1:6, it says, "And hath made us kings and priests unto God." Whom is the Revelator talking about? Verse 5 says it is those God loves and has washed from their sins in the blood of Jesus. Those under the Blood are made priests so they can "come boldly unto the throne of grace" with no intercessor other than Jesus Himself (see Hebrews 4:16 and 1 Timothy 2:5), and they are made kings so they can "reign in life by Jesus Christ." Has your

Jesus enabled you to reign in this life, or are you still under the power of another (sin)?

The Bible speaks of sin and death reigning. We quoted from Romans 5:17 above, regarding those who receive grace and reign, but this verse also says that "by one man's offence death reigned." Since the wages of sin is death (Romans 6:23), death reigns over those who are in sin. Verse 14 talks about how "death reigned from Adam to Moses," and verse 21 says that "sin hath reigned unto death." Then Romans 6:12 lets us know *where* sin reigns. It says, "Let not sin therefore reign in your mortal body, that ye should obey it in the lusts thereof."

Sin and (spiritual) death reign over mankind. It reigns in men and women's lives. It has dominion over them. Hardly anyone argues this point. Nearly everybody agrees that sin has control over men and women. But we need to see that grace makes a difference for those who believe in the true Jesus. When saving grace is loosed in one's life, sin—and, therefore, its reign—come to an end in that life. We just quoted where the Bible says that we—believers—are *not to let sin reign in our mortal bodies*. We have mortal bodies in this world, not in the next. The power that sin exercises over our mortal bodies is broken when we really believe in the Jesus of the Bible.

As stated earlier, where sin abounds, grace doth much more abound. Because of grace, people who were ruled over by sin can be translated and can rule over it instead. Instead of being on the bottom, they are on the top. Instead of being reigned over, they reign. *Webster's* first definition for *translate* is, "to change from one place, position, or condition to another."[6] The Apostle Paul tells us what condition we are changed from and what condition we are changed to:

Colossians 1:12a Giving thanks unto the Father . . .

13 Who hath delivered us from the power of darkness, and hath translated us into the kingdom of his dear Son.

Praise God! Bible believers are no longer under the power of darkness, or sin. Its reign over us is broken. Instead, we are kings and priests ourselves. We reign in life. What over? Over what used to reign over us: sin and Satan. By the way, please notice that we are delivered from the power of darkness *and* into the Kingdom of Christ. Friend, there is no such thing as being in Christ's Kingdom while we are still under the power of sin. Sinning "Christians" are not saved.

Let me quote Romans 5.17 in its entirety: "For if by one man's offence death reigned by one; much more they which receive abundance of grace and of the gift of righteousness shall reign in life by one, Jesus Christ."

Jesus said, in John 8:34, "Verily, verily, I say unto you, Whosoever committeth sin is the servant of sin." And He confirmed this through Paul, in Romans 6:16, saying, "Know ye not, that to whom ye yield yourselves servants to obey, his servants ye are to whom ye obey; whether of sin unto death, or of obedience unto righteousness?" We yield to sin *or* to the obedience of God; Paul here banishes completely the thought that we, as Christians, can *do both*. And Jesus' words there in John are plain: if we sin, we are servants of sin. Now look at His words in Matthew 6:24: "No man can serve two masters." We simply cannot be servants to sin and servants to Jesus at the same time. To claim that we can be is to call Jesus a liar. I'd rather call these false prophets liars. Wouldn't you?

Paul said, in the verse quoted above, that we yield to sin or to obedience, so all disobedience is sin. And the consequences of our choice will bring us to death or righteousness, Paul said. Not to death or life, but to death or righteousness. Dear one, righteousness, the righteousness of God, lived within us by the Holy Spirit, *is* life, and without it, we are but dead in our sins.

Again, God made us creatures of choice; again, He said to Israel of old, "I call heaven and earth to record this day against you, that I have set before you life and death, blessing and cursing: therefore choose life, that both thou and thy seed may live" (Deuteronomy 30:19). Unfortunately, everyone who reaches the age of accountability chooses death (sin). Romans 3:23 says, "For all have sinned, and come short of the glory of God." When we choose to commit sin, we become the servants of sin, just as Jesus said. As Paul put it, to whom we yield ourselves servants, his servants we are. This is how sin comes to reign over us. So-called Christian leaders tell their people that they cannot fully get out from under this reign, that as long as they live, they will sin "more or less." This is so contrary to the Scriptures!

Yielding to sin brings very serious results. We get to make a choice, but once we make the choice to sin, we become servants to sin. Paul told Timothy to instruct those who had yielded to sin, peradventure God would give them repentance, "that they may recover themselves out of the snare of the devil, who are taken captive by him at his will" (2 Timothy 2:26). Exercising our will in choosing to sin, and thereby becoming slaves to sin, brings us under the power of Satan's will. This is a very dangerous condition, and it is the state that the world as a whole is in. It is the state grace finds us all in—but, praise God, grace does not leave us there. Grace does not "save us" and leave us sinning still. Grace does not merely cover our sins as we commit them. Through grace we can *recover* ourselves from sin's bondage through repentance and faith, and then we can reign, through grace, with consistent victory over all sin. Grace came through Jesus Christ, you recall, and it is how He saves His people from their sins (Ephesians 2:8).

At the dawn of the Gospel Day, when God was ready to send His Son, the Lamb of God, to take away the sin of the world, Zacharias, the father of John the Baptist, rejoiced that the long-promised deliverance had come. In Luke 1:68-70 and 74-75 he said:

68 Blessed be the Lord God of Israel; for he hath visited and redeemed his people,

69 And hath raised up an horn of salvation for us in the house of his servant David;

70 As he spake by the mouth of his holy prophets, which have been since the world began:

74 That he would grant unto us, that we being delivered out of the hand of our enemies might serve him without fear,

75 In holiness and righteousness before him, all the days of our life.

Did you catch it? Being delivered out of the hand of our enemies, we can serve God, in holiness, all the days of our life. This was the message of the prophets since the world began! Any "Jesus" who does not fulfill these prophecies is not the Jesus of the Bible, dear one.

Grace's Recipients Forbidden to Sin

Finally, Romans teaches us that God forbids sin in those who are under grace. Paul said, "What then? shall we sin, because we are not under the law, but under grace? God forbid" (Romans 6:15). Paul must have had to contend with people who had trouble accepting this truth, just as we do today. Why? Because twice in that 6th Chapter he emphasized that *God forbids* sin in believers who are under grace—once in verse 1 and again in verse 15. I would say that anything he felt, under the inspiration of the Holy Spirit, needed to be repeated within just a few verses is something we ought to "give the more earnest heed to" (Hebrews 2:1).

Here we have looked at some of what the Book of Romans sets forth concerning grace. It is absolutely not a cloak for Christians' day-to-day sinning. Just as surely, the rest of the New Testament confirms the message Romans gives us about grace. Let us look at some of these other texts.

Grace is Sufficient

In 2 Corinthians 12:9a Paul said, "And he [Christ] said unto me, My grace is sufficient for thee: for my strength is made perfect in weakness." Our weakness, whether individually or as a human race, is no excuse for sin in our lives, because God's grace is sufficient and His strength is only made perfect in our weakness, not hindered by it. No matter how sin may rage all around us, His grace is sufficient! There will always be enough of it, no matter what the demands on it are. And since it is *in our weakness* that His strength is perfected, claiming our weakness as an excuse for sinning is ridiculous. No matter how weak we may be, it is by His strength that we live as Christians, and *His strength only excels in our weakness.* The weaker we are, the stronger He is in our behalf! Our weakness has absolutely nothing to do with whether or not we can live holy lives. His perfected strength is able to keep us from falling!

Grace Teaches Holy Living

Do you know something? While people claim that God's grace shields them from sin's wages, although they still commit sin, God's grace actually teaches us to live holy lives! Have you ever read Titus 2:11-12? Has your minister ever preached from this text (and, if so, did he attempt to explain it away)? Let's read it:

11 For the grace of God that bringeth salvation hath appeared to all men,

12 Teaching us that, denying ungodliness and worldly lusts, we should live soberly, righteously, and godly, in this present world.

How can anything be more clear? Notice how the Scriptures tell us where and when we are to be holy. Romans 6:12 says sin is not to reign in our *mortal* bodies, and this verse in Titus says we're to be godly *in this present world.* The word *present*, as used here, is an adjective that modifies, or describes, the *world* being discussed, and it has two meanings. One relates to place and the other relates to time. With *place*, we have present, or "here," as opposed to absent, or "not here." With *time*, we have past, present, and future, or what used to be, what is right now, and what will be later. So, *present*, as Paul used it in his letter to Titus, means "here," and it means "now." Thus what grace teaches us is that we can, and must, have victory over sin right here, on this earth, and right now, in this life. God is holy; therefore, living a godly life is definitely living a holy life. God said, "Be ye holy, for I am holy" (Leviticus 11:44-45, 1 Peter 1:15-16).

By the way, when the psalmist wrote that "God is . . . a very present help in trouble" (Psalm 46:1), the same is true. When troubles befall us, if our hearts are honest and true toward God, He will be "right here, right now" to help us. This is His Word. He is a *present* help. We can count on it. Sometimes He removes the problem, sometimes He gives grace to endure it, but in any case, He will be *right here, right now.* Isn't that sweet? Praise God!

Grace Breaks Sin's Control

Notice that Colossians 1:13a says God "hath delivered us from the power of darkness." The power of darkness is the power of Satan (see Acts 26:18). Being delivered from the power of darkness and Satan means it no longer controls us. The Book of Romans, again, confirms this in Chapter 6, verse 14: "For sin shall not have dominion over you: for ye are not under the law, but under grace." *Sin does not have control over those who are under grace.* And sin does not have control over these *because* they are under grace. This is so indisputable! Read it again: "For sin shall not have dominion over you: *for* ye are . . . under grace." (Emphasis added.) Being delivered from the power of Satan does not leave us in a sin-you-must-and-sin-you-can't-help-it condition!

Notice what Acts 26:18, just referenced above, says. The Apostle Paul was giving his testimony to King Agrippa, and he quoted the Lord

Jesus' words when giving Paul his commission. Christ was sending him out to preach the Gospel to men and women "[t]o open their eyes, and to turn them from darkness to light, and from the power of Satan unto God, that they may receive forgiveness of sins, and inheritance among them which are sanctified by faith that is in me." Friend, we must be delivered from the power of Satan in order to receive forgiveness of our sins and an eternal inheritance. Away with the idea that we'll always be under the power of Satan, so we ask forgiveness every night.

Grace does and is a lot of things, but there are also some things it is not and does not do. It does not "cover" sin in believers; it delivers believers from sin. It does not give believers a "sin license"; it gives them a "sin release." It does not excuse their weaknesses; it provides perfected strength in their weaknesses. It does not leave them under sin's power, under its reign; it gives them power, and causes them to reign, over sin. It does not enable them to "do better"; it enables them to do righteousness. It is not struggling to, yet unable to, handle sin; it is sufficient to handle sin. Where sin abounds, grace doth *much more* abound. Dear reader, if your believing has not brought you this grace that is more abounding, sufficient, transforming, and delivering, I tell you kindly, but I must tell you, your believing has not saved you. Your Jesus is not the Jesus of the Bible.

CHAPTER FOUR

Paul's Testimony

Many times, when religious leaders want to defend sin in Christians, they call the Apostle Paul to the witness stand, as it were. Somewhat smugly, perhaps even gleefully, they quote his words from Romans 7:19-20:

19 For the good that I would I do not: but the evil which I would not, that I do.

20 Now if I do that I would not, it is no more I that do it, but sin that dwelleth in me.

And then, for emphasis, they add verse 23, "But I see another law in my members, warring against the law of my mind, and bringing me into captivity to the law of sin which is in my members."

This is conclusive proof, they claim, that Christians cannot help but sin more or less from day to day. After all, if *the Apostle Paul* couldn't help but sin, what chance do the rest of us have? Well, that very Apostle told us, in 2 Timothy 2:15, to "Study to shew thyself approved unto God, a workman that needeth not to be ashamed, rightly dividing the word of truth." When preachers and teachers quote Paul's words in Romans 7 as proof that he sinned as a Christian, they are certainly not rightly dividing the Scriptures. How's that? Well, they are completely ignoring what he said in Romans 6 and Romans 8. In these Chapters he positively and emphatically taught that Christians *do not sin*! And he was not contradicting himself. Paul was an intelligent man; too intelligent to say in Chapter 6 that God forbids Christians to sin, then testify in Chapter 7 that he, himself, did sin as a Christian, then proclaim in Chapter 8 that he was free from that law of sin and death he said he was in bondage to in Chapter 7, verse 23. And not only was he intelligent, but he was also inspired and directed to write these things by the Holy Spirit of God. Never would the Holy Ghost inspire confusion, and, especially, He would never inspire lies and deception!

What, then, is the explanation behind this seeming incongruity? Is this one of those places where the Bible contradicts itself? No! The Bible does not, ever, contradict itself. All the supposed contradictions are eliminated when the Scriptures are rightly divided. And the answer to this one is simple, really. Let me tell you a little story to illustrate what I mean: "A senior citizen that lives in my neighborhood buys a bicycle, and when she takes her first ride on it, it's really funny to watch. She can keep the thing upright, though it wobbles around quite a bit, but she can't seem to steer it. You can tell she is trying to ride along the sidewalk, but instead she veers across the yard. Sometimes, when the bike won't go where she wants it to go, she simply stops it in order to aim it back in the right direction.

"At first she thinks her problem is that she hasn't ridden for a long time, but she remembers that she rode a friend's bike just four or five years earlier, and did very well at it. Instead, she decides that she is having trouble steering the bicycle because she is leaning into the handlebar. She lowers the seat, raises the handlebar, and tries again. This time she does better, but she still finds her weight resting on that handlebar. Since the handlebar is as high as she can make it, and the seat as low, she figures there has to be another answer. Finally she thinks she has the mystery solved—with the kind of seats they put on bicycles these days, one can't really *sit*, so one's weight ends up being borne on one's arms. She decides she'll have to buy a 'decent' seat. Will that work? Time will tell."

Do you see my point? Do you see what Paul was doing in Romans 7? Or are you wondering, "What does some old woman's bike riding have to do with the Apostle Paul's being, or not being, a sinning Christian?" Okay, I'll explain: I told that little *past event* in present tense. You didn't even notice, did you? The reason you didn't, is because this is a common form of narration. For example, someone says, " . . . then this guy comes flying around the corner and bumps into this lady, and . . . ." We do not see any "guy" flying around any corner, or any lady being bumped into. It's just the narrator telling his story in present tense, and we understand because we do this all the time. That is all the Apostle Paul was doing. He was telling a past experience in present-tense narration.

You may ask, "How do you know that's true?" Look at his own words in Romans 7:5. He said, "For when we were in the flesh, the motions of sins, which were by the law, did work in our members to bring forth fruit unto death." When we *were* in the flesh (past tense), the motions of sins *did* work in our members (past tense). Here Paul spoke of sin working in his members, just as he did in verse 23, only here he told when it was: *when he was in the flesh*. That was not after he became a Christian! Read Romans 8:9. It says, "But ye are not in the flesh, but in the Spirit, if so be that the Spirit of God dwell in you. Now if any man have not the Spirit of Christ, he is none of his."

It is very easy to see that if we do not have the Spirit of Christ, we are not Christ's own, and if we do have the Spirit of Christ, *we are not in the flesh*. Surely no one would argue that Paul didn't possess the Holy Spirit when he wrote to the Roman Christians. Well, when he had the Spirit of God, he was not in the flesh, and all that he "testified" of in Chapter 7 happened while he was in the flesh. He makes this very obvious, I repeat, in verse 5. This completely does away with any supposed "contradiction" between Romans 7 and Romans 6 and 8. To make this clear, let's study on. Romans 6:1-2a tells us:

1 What shall we say then? Shall we continue in sin, that grace may abound?

2a God forbid.

In this text, Paul very plainly told us that Christians are forbidden, *by God*, to continue in sin after conversion. Another proof that this was not Paul's testimony of his life as a Christian is found in Romans 8:1-2. Here, he explicitly gave his "now," or Christian, testimony. What was it?

1 There is therefore now no condemnation to them which are in Christ Jesus, who walk not after the flesh, but after the Spirit.

2 For the law of the Spirit of life in Christ Jesus hath made me free from the law of sin and death.

"God," Paul said here, "has made me free from that law of sin I just told you I was under while in the flesh." At the time he wrote to the Romans, he *had been set free* from that bondage to sin! He was no longer under condemnation, as he described being under before conversion! His words here are emphatic, friend: "There is *no condemnation* to them which are in Christ Jesus." Why, Paul? Because Christ Jesus sets those who are His *free from that law of sin*. How much clearer can this be? Friend, there is no way anyone can rightly use Romans, Chapter Seven, as a cloak for sin in the lives of true believers. True believers have the same "now" experience as Paul had.

I will cover this more thoroughly in chapter 9, but I want to touch on it here. Modern theologians claim that the "law of sin" Paul said he was delivered from, in Romans 8:2, was the Law of Moses. While it is very true that Christ sets the entire human race free from the ceremonial Law of Moses, this was not—it was *not*—the law of sin Paul said he was in captivity to in Romans, Chapter Seven. The Word of God makes this absolutely and abundantly clear.

Certainly this false "interpretation" serves to support modern "Christianity's" infatuation with sin, for it hides the true promise of being delivered from sin's power. But it is totally unscriptural, as we shall now see. Paul said, "What shall we say then? is the law sin? God forbid" (Romans 7:7a). He was referring to the Mosaic Law in this verse (read the context), and he said it was *not sin*. The law of sin that worked in Paul's members was not the Law of Moses! Let's look further. Paul clearly describes what was working in him: "Now if I do that I would not, it is no more I that do it, but sin that dwelleth in me." That "law of sin" was the *power* of sin. Next, Paul makes it even clearer that his "law of sin" was distinct from Moses' Law. Let's read verses 21-23:

21 I find then a law, that, when I would do good, evil is present with me.

22 For I delight in the law of God after the inward man:

23 But I see another law in my members, warring against the law of my mind, and bringing me into captivity to the law of sin which is in my members.

He found a law that caused him to do wrong when he didn't want to. *The Law of Moses never caused anyone to break it.* He said he delighted in the Law of God in the inner man, but his problem was with the outer man. Then he distinctly said that the law that caused him to sin was *another law*! It was not—it was separate from—the Law of God that he delighted in, in his heart! The bottom line is that this idea is a false interpretation. The law of sin that worked in Paul to make him do wrong when he didn't want to was not the Law of Moses! When he went on to say, in Chapter Eight, that he had found deliverance from that law of sin, from that captivity to the power of sin, he was talking about the amazing power Christ's redemption Plan brings to us that frees us from sin, itself, right here and right now!

Paul's words in Romans 6:22 show that this experience of real deliverance from sin, itself, was what Paul was talking about: "But *now* being made free from sin, and become servants to God, ye have your fruit unto holiness, and the end everlasting life" (emphasis added). This is so explicitly clear, and, by the way, it is this deliverance from sin's power over us, and our subsequent life of holiness, that secures everlasting life. Sinning "Christians" have no such promise, dear one. And look at what Paul said in Romans 6:14: "For sin shall not have dominion over you: for ye are not under the law, but under grace." For sure, Paul's "testimony" in Chapter 7 referred to when he *was* under the law and *not* under grace. While today's nominal Christian leaders use "grace" as a cloak for sin in so-called Christians, Paul said grace wrought in a believer a life free from sin's dominion (not just its condemnation). I'll take Paul's word; after all, God included *his* teaching on it in the Holy Scriptures. That means his teaching was inspired by the Holy Ghost and is the *divine truth*, and final word, on the matter.

By the way, do you know what the word *nominal* means? *Webster's* says it comes from *nomen*, which is Latin for "a name," and means, "**1** of or like a name **2** in name only, not in fact."[1] Interesting, right? No wonder Christendom, today, is revealed by the Word to be Christianity *in name only*!

All right, at this time let us do a verse-by-verse examination of what Paul was teaching the Romans, starting with Chapter 5, verses 20-21:

20 Moreover the law entered, that the offence might abound. But where sin abounded, grace did much more abound:

21 That as sin hath reigned unto death, even so might grace reign through righteousness unto eternal life by Jesus Christ our Lord.

Romans 5:13 says, "But sin is not imputed when there is no law." The word *impute* is defined by *Webster's* as, "to attribute (esp. a fault or misconduct) to another."[2] So, Paul told us in verse 20 that the Law entered into the equation in order for sin to be laid to your and my accounts, since no one is guilty of breaking the law where no law exists. This does not mean that God just arbitrarily formulated a Law in order to *make* us sinners. God is righteous and holy *by His nature*, and sin is wrong and destructive *by its nature*. Right is right because it is right, and wrong is wrong because it is wrong. God didn't make things right or wrong, but He knew what was right and what was wrong. Therefore, because He is holy, His holiness required His children to be holy.

Under the Law Dispensation, however, men and women could not be made holy inwardly, because God had to show mankind that they needed a Savior before He provided one. So, as long as they kept the Law's ceremonies and lived as closely as they could, looking forward in faith to the promised Redeemer, they were accepted. Hebrews 9:15 tells us that Christ's blood atoned for them as well as those who live on this side of Calvary. What, then, does Romans 5:20 mean? Friend, it simply means that, since there *were* principles of right and wrong, God's teaching these to His people not only gave them a safe and sure guide for living, but also made them responsible for keeping those principles. When they violated these, they knew they had, and it was sin to them. Both knowledge and will were present. When they violated what they knew was right, they did wrong, and because of their knowledge, sin became exceeding sinful. All of this was necessary in preparing the way for the Savior.

Because "all have sinned" (verse 12), sin abounded under the Law. "For it is not possible that the blood of bulls and of goats should take away sins" (Hebrews 10:4). Then Paul gave us that wonderful news that where sin abounded, grace did much more abound, and that as sin hath reigned unto death, even so, now, might grace reign unto eternal life. Praise God! Jesus solved the dilemma!

Notice, friend, that Romans 5:20-21 does not say that grace reigns, or exercises its power, through continually covering the abounding sin we cannot get victory over. It says that more-abounding grace reigns *through righteousness*. Certainly it is Christ's righteousness, but it works in the truly saved. If we're not righteous, God's grace is not working in, or for, us. And grace reigns unto eternal life. There is no eternal life, I repeat, unless grace reigns through righteousness in us.

Let us look now at Romans 6:1:

What shall we say then? Shall we continue in sin, that grace may abound?

Since where sin abounded, grace did much more abound, this question naturally came up, and the Apostle answered it in 6:2:

God forbid. How shall we, that are dead to sin, live any longer therein?

"*God forbid.*" God *forbids* that "we"—Christians—continue in sin that grace may abound. Isn't this marvelously clear? Well, it is just as clear that nominal Christianity teaches the opposite. *They teach the opposite of what the Bible teaches*, friend! They insist that Christians can't help but continue in sin, but, because of this, grace abounds in them in order to cover their sins. May I repeat it? The Apostle Paul said *God forbids* such a thing. And *God forbids* such a teaching. It is false!

Dear reader, Paul asked a very important question in verse 2. Look at the contrast between what modern Christendom asks ("How can we live in this old sinful world and not commit sin?") and what Paul asked: *How shall we, that are dead to sin, live any longer therein?* In other words, "How can Christians continue to sin?" The answer is certain—they cannot. God forbids it. *They are dead to sin.* This brings us to verses 3 and 4, where Paul dealt further with the thought of being dead to sin:

3 Know ye not, that so many of us as were baptized into Jesus Christ were baptized into his death?

4 Therefore we are buried with him by baptism into death: that like as Christ was raised up from the dead by the glory of the Father, even so we also should walk in newness of life.

We who are baptized into Jesus, are baptized into His death. It's automatic, and it happens to *all* who get saved. But what does it mean? Well, *Webster's* says that the word *baptize* comes from the Greek word **baptizein** (*Webster's* doesn't give the pronunciation) and means "to immerse";[3] then it says that *immerse* means "to plunge, drop, or dip into . . . a liquid, esp. so as to cover completely."[4] So being baptized into Jesus Christ and His death is to be submerged, completely, in Him and His death. Paul went on, however, and said that Christian conversion is modeled after both Christ's death and His resurrection, and he enlarged on this in verse 5:

For if we have been planted together in the likeness of his death, we shall be also in the likeness of his resurrection.

Just as surely as we die with Christ, we shall be resurrected with Him. Conversion includes both dying to sin and being raised to a new life—which, of course, would have to be a life without sin, since we just died to sin. Paul plainly confirmed this fact in verses 6-11:

6 Knowing this, that our old man is crucified with him, that the body of sin might be destroyed, that henceforth we should not serve sin.

7 For he that is dead [in Christ] *is freed from sin.*

8 Now if we be dead with Christ, we believe that we shall also live with him:

9 Knowing that Christ being raised from the dead dieth no more; death hath no more dominion over him.

10 For in that he died, he died unto sin once: but in that he liveth, he liveth unto God.

11 Likewise reckon ye also yourselves to be dead indeed unto sin, but alive unto God through Jesus Christ our Lord.

Before you read further, dear one, please think about what you just read from God's holy Word. And read those words again, thoughtfully. Now, the Apostle was talking to those who had believed in Jesus and been saved. They were true Christians. He told them to reckon themselves to be dead indeed unto sin. Not just nominally dead, not just dead to the really vile stuff, but dead *indeed*. Untold millions of people think they have spiritual life through "believing in Jesus," but, friend, spiritual life only comes through *death to sin*. It is utterly impossible to have that life and still be sinning more or less from day to day. Let me remind you of what Paul said in verse 1 of Romans 6: *How shall we, that are dead to sin, live any longer therein?* The truly saved cannot and do not.

Next, Paul gave us some very pointed instructions. Indeed, they are actually New Testament commandments. Verses 12-13 say this:

12 Let not sin therefore reign in your mortal body, that ye should obey it in the lusts thereof.

13 Neither yield ye your members as instruments of unrighteousness unto sin: but yield yourselves unto God, as those that are alive from the dead, and your members as instruments of righteousness unto God.

Did you understand that? Paul said, "Do not yield to sin. Yield to God." We can't, from day to day, do both. Right while nominal Christian leaders tell people they can't help but yield to sin, God's Word says *not to*! Friend, who are you going to follow—these leaders or God?

In verses 14-15, Paul mentioned that true believers are no longer under the power of sin because they are no longer under the Law (where sin reigned) but under grace. I must say it again, dear one: being under grace does not allow sin in Christians, it gives them deliverance from it. So grace is not a cover for sin in believers, Paul said. Rather, he *repeated* that God forbids Christians to sin. Let's read it:

14 For sin shall not have dominion over you: for ye are not under the law, but under grace.

15 What then? shall we sin, because we are not under the law, but under grace? God forbid.

He said that *sin shall not have dominion over you: for ye are . . . under grace.* Paul certainly preached a different message from that which is prevalent in today's pulpits—"you can't help but be under some of the dominion of sin, but don't worry; you're a believer, you're under grace, so you're all right with God." Dear one, let me say it again: modern Christendom teaches the *very opposite* of what the Bible teaches.

In the next verse, Paul reiterated, very definitely, that we cannot live as Christians and commit sin at the same time:

16 Know ye not, that to whom ye yield yourselves servants to obey, his servants ye are to whom ye obey; whether of sin unto death, or of obedience unto righteousness?

We are one or the other. Paul, *writing to Christians*, put it in an "either/or" format. If *ye* yield yourselves in obedience to God, *ye* are God's servants, and the result is righteousness. (And, I might add, spiritual life.) *Or,* if *ye*—Christians—yield yourselves to sin, *ye* are sin's servants, and the result is spiritual death. There is just no way we can be, at the same time, servants of God and yet under the influence of sin. *We are "either/or"*; there is no room for being both. To believe one can be both is to be deceived by these false prophets and false "Jesuses."

You may wonder, "But sometimes I yield myself to God; while I am obedient, am I not righteous?"

No. You may, in some instances, be *doing* what is right, but to *be* right, or righteous, you must be as Christ is, and He is holy all the time. "Little children, let no man deceive you: he that doeth righteousness is righteous, even as he [Christ, verse 5] is righteous" (1 John 3:7). If you are not righteous as Christ is righteous—all the time, in everything you do—you are not biblically righteous at all. To put it another way, if you are unrighteous part of the time, you are not biblically righteous the rest of the time. This is not a "mixed" thing; you are one or the other. John had already stated, in verses 5-6:

5 And ye know that he was manifested to take away our sins; and in him is no sin.

6 Whosoever abideth in him sinneth not: whosoever sinneth hath not seen him, neither known him.

And then John added, in verse 10b, "Whosoever doeth not righteousness *is not of God.*" (Emphasis added.) So, whosoever abideth in Him sinneth not, and whosoever sinneth abideth not in Him. Whosoever doeth not righteousness, as Christ is righteous, is not of God. Friend, it's just that simple. Let us now look at Romans 6:17-18:

17 But God be thanked, that ye were the servants of sin, but ye have obeyed from the heart that form of doctrine which was delivered you.

18 Being then made free from sin, ye became the servants of righteousness.

Do you see? Only those who are made free from sin are righteous. Paul certainly told us, here, that we *can* be made free from sin, and that the Roman Christians had been. When did they become free from sin? When they obeyed from the heart the doctrine that had been preached to them. I tell you this with a heart of love, but modern Christendom is not preaching the true doctrine on this subject. Their "faith" is not the one that was once delivered unto the saints (Jude 3). As instructed, however, there are some who are still earnestly contending for that faith, and by God's grace I am one of them, sent to help *you* to be one of them. The Apostles did preach that faith, and when people obeyed it, they were made free from sin!

Verses 19-23 continue to make this obvious:

19 I speak after the manner of men because of the infirmity of your flesh: for as ye have [past tense] *yielded your members servants to uncleanness and to iniquity unto iniquity; even so now* [present tense] *yield your members servants to righteousness unto holiness.*

20 For when ye were the servants of sin, ye were free from righteousness.

[See, friend; if you can't help but sin now and then, you are sin's servant, and if you are a servant of sin, you are free from righteousness.]

21 What fruit had ye then in those things whereof ye are now ashamed? for the end of those things is death.

22 But now being made free from sin, and become servants to God, ye have your fruit unto holiness, and the end everlasting life [all present tense].

23 For the wages of sin is death; but the gift of God is eternal life through Jesus Christ our Lord.

Do you have the hope of eternal life, dear one? Are you thinking, "Well, yes, I'm a servant of God. Though I can't help but sin sometimes,

I'm not a *servant* of sin"? Are you resting your *soul* on that idea? Please don't! Verse 22 says we only have the "end" of everlasting life when we are made free from sin and bear the fruit of holiness. Oh, yes it does. Read it again: "Being *now* made free from sin" and having now "*become* servants to God," we now bear "fruit unto holiness" in our lives, which *ends* in everlasting life. Friend, do not be deceived by the persistent cry of false Christianity that "no one can live holy." Without holiness, we do not reap eternal life. We reap the wages of our sin, and that is death.

Before we look at Romans, Chapter 7, allow me to say again that this is not Paul's testimony of his experience with Jesus Christ, but of his life *in the flesh* and *under the Law*. Reading Chapters 6, 7, and 8, together, rather than lifting Chapter 7 out of its context, makes this abundantly clear. To interpret these three Chapters as the nominal Christian world interprets them is to accuse both Paul and God of insanity. Oh, yes it is. No sane person, under the inspiration of a sane God, could say that Christ made him dead to sin and alive unto holiness (in Chapter 6), then say that, even so, he was still held in bondage to the motions of sin and wretched under its condemnation (in Chapter 7), and *then* say that he was free from that *condemnation*, and from that *law of sin*, through Christ (in Chapter 8).

I know a lot of professed Christians give that kind of testimony today. They rejoice in the free pardon of their sins and the life of Christ within them. They say it's wonderful to know they're God's children and that they'll go to Heaven when they die. They declare how marvelous His grace is that covers all their sins—and then they get off the track and say, "even the ones I'm committing today."

This is a delusion, friend. This is not what Paul was saying. Read it with an open and honest heart. He clearly said real Christians are made free from sin and bear fruit unto holiness. Then read Romans 6:6 again. Now let's read Ephesians 4:22-24:

22 That ye put off concerning the former conversation the old man, which is corrupt according to the deceitful lusts;

23 And be renewed in the spirit of your mind;

24 And that ye put on the new man, which after God is created in righteousness and true holiness.

And, please, let's read Romans 8:8-9 again. We'll examine it in depth, later, but let's just look briefly at it now:

8 So then they that are in the flesh cannot please God.

9 But ye are not in the flesh, but in the Spirit, if so be that the Spirit of God dwell in you. Now if any man have not the Spirit of Christ, he is none of his.

Does your preacher herald the popular cry? What cry? That "we that are in this flesh cannot please God! The Bible says we can't, Paul said we can't, and I believe the Bible!" How many times have you heard these or similar words out of the mouth of nominal "Christianity"? Well, though they claim they are believing, and teaching, the Bible, they are in fact denying it. Again, they are lifting words out of their context to support the doctrines of men. Paul *did* say that those who are in the flesh cannot please God. He actually *said* that. But read the rest of what he said to those first-century believers: "but *ye are not in the flesh*; ye are in the Spirit." And he added that, if they did not have the Spirit, they were "none of His." If your pastor, or teacher, or youth leader, runs to this verse, just ask him to read the next verse too.

Now let us start our verse-by-verse study of Romans 7. Verses 1-3 tell us:

1 Know ye not, brethren, (for I speak to them that know the law,) how that the law hath dominion over a man as long as he liveth?

2 For the woman which hath an husband is bound by the law unto her husband so long as he liveth; but if the husband be dead, she is loosed from the law of her husband.

3 So then if, while her husband liveth, she be married to another man, she shall be called an adulteress: but if her husband be dead, she is free from that law; so that she is no adulteress, though she be married to another man.

Paul reminded "them that know the law" that a man's death frees his wife from the Law that binds her to her husband, and she is free to marry another man. Then he applied this truth, spiritually, to his readers, in verse 4:

Wherefore, my brethren, ye also are become dead to the law by the body of Christ; that ye should be married to another, even to him who is raised from the dead, that we should bring forth fruit unto God.

Through Christ's death, Paul said, we are freed from the Law, a Law that could not "take away sins" (Hebrews 10:4), and married to Christ, Who can. He went on, then, with verse 5:

For when we were in the flesh, the motions of sins, which were by the law, did work in our members to bring forth fruit unto death.

Here, I repeat, Paul distinctly told us when the "motions of sins" work in our members—not when we are in the Spirit, but *when we are in the flesh*. Remember, the Law entered that the offence might abound (Romans 5:20), or that sin might become sin. What Paul was saying is that the Law brought an awareness of sin—*our* sin—and that the motions of that sin worked in us while we were *in the flesh*. Those motions of sin worked by the Law because it is only when a law—any law—crosses our own will that rebellion surfaces. And every one of us "turned to our own way" and broke the Law of God at some point (Isaiah 53:6); so sin worked in us by the Law, because it was the Law we rebelled against. But by the death of Christ, we are freed from the Old Law that couldn't give life and, as he pointed out in 6:22, from the sin that the Law revealed in us. Our next verse, Romans 7:6, brings this out:

But now we are delivered from the law, that being dead wherein we were held; that we should serve in newness of spirit, and not in the oldness of the letter.

When in the flesh, men commit sin. The Law reveals that sin, but it cannot deliver from it. Christ came, and died, that we might be delivered from the Law and then given deliverance from sin through Him. The purpose of the Law, again, was to teach us of our need for such deliverance. Galatians 3:24-25 confirms this:

24 Wherefore the law was our schoolmaster to bring us unto Christ, that we might be justified by faith.

25 But after that faith is come, we are no longer under a schoolmaster.

The Law showed that mankind needed redemption so that, when the Lamb of God was offered, man would come to Christ to obtain it. Let us read on in Romans 7:

7 What shall we say then? Is the law sin? God forbid. Nay, I had not known sin, but by the law: for I had not known lust, except the law had said, Thou shalt not covet.

8 But sin, taking occasion by the commandment, wrought in me all manner of concupiscence. For without the law sin was dead.

9 For I was alive without the law once: but when the commandment came, sin revived, and I died.

10 And the commandment, which was ordained to life, I found to be unto death.

41

11 For sin, taking occasion by the commandment, deceived me, and by it slew me.

12 Wherefore the law is holy, and the commandment holy, and just, and good.

13 Was then that which is good made death unto me? God forbid. But sin, that it might appear sin, working death in me by that which is good; that sin by the commandment might become exceeding sinful.

Here we learn that the Law is not sin and the Law doesn't kill the soul, but it brought a *knowledge* of sin. Paul said he was alive without the Law once—while in the innocence of childhood, when he knew nothing about commandments—but when the Law came, when *understanding* of the Law came, sin revived, and he died. In other words, when he gained understanding of God's commandments, he did what Isaiah 53:6 says every one of us does—he went astray. How? *By turning to his own way.* That's what gets every one of us into trouble with God—wanting, and going, our own way. Sin finds its occasion to deceive and destroy us when we understand what God demands of us but we want, and go, our own way.

It wasn't the Law that brought spiritual death to Paul. It was sin that worked death *by* the commandment, because sin was (and still is) the breaking of the commandment. By the Law, then, sin became exceedingly sinful. Next, Paul described what that life in sin—while under the Law that brought knowledge of sin but could not deliver from it—was like:

14 For we know that the law is spiritual: but I am carnal, sold under sin. [Here, he brings this dilemma that all of us face into stark reality by switching to present-tense narration; *sin is an ever-present problem,* until we find deliverance through Jesus Christ.]

15 For that which I do I allow not: for what I would, that do I not; but what I hate, that do I.

16 If then I do that which I would not, I consent unto the law [of God] that it is good.

17 Now then it is no more I that do it, but sin that dwelleth in me.

18 For I know that in me (that is, in my flesh,) dwelleth no good thing: for to will is present with me; but how to perform that which is good I find not.

19 For the good that I would I do not: but the evil which I would not, that I do.

20 Now if I do that I would not, it is no more I that do it, but sin that dwelleth in me.

21 I find then a law, that, when I would do good, evil is present with me.

22 For I delight in the law of God after the inward man:

23 But I see another law in my members, warring against the law of my mind, and bringing me into captivity to the law of sin which is in my members.

24 O wretched man that I am! who shall deliver me from the body of this death?

Truly this is a sad picture, and many of us can relate to the inner turmoil that Paul here described, when we wanted to do right, but couldn't, and when we trembled under conviction, but had no power to change ourselves. Indeed there was a law—the law of sin—working in our members, and we were in captivity to it. But, thank God, the story doesn't end there! Paul asked who would deliver him from such a state, and then he gave the answer in the next verse, the last of Chapter 7. Verse 25a says:

I thank God through Jesus Christ our Lord.

"Who shall deliver me? Thank God, Jesus Christ shall!"

Yet, the rest of verse 25, Paul's summary of the lesson on the shortcomings of the Law, sets forth the "Christian creed" of almost all of modern Christendom. It says:

So then with the mind I myself serve the law of God; but with the flesh the law of sin.

That's the condition "Christianity" leaves the masses in today. How tragic! I'm glad that Paul didn't leave us there. He simply stated the condition the Law left him, and us, in. Not the Gospel, friend, but the Law. After digressing a moment to praise God for deliverance, Paul reverted back to, and wrapped up, his narrative on the condition he was in before he was delivered by Christ Jesus. But, yet again, he didn't leave it at that! Next, he elaborated on what Christ did for him—and for us—through the Gospel, in Romans 8:1-9:

1 There is therefore now no condemnation to them which are in Christ Jesus, who walk not after the flesh, but after the Spirit.

[Here, again, is Paul's "now" testimony. At the time he wrote to the Roman Christians, he had been delivered from living *in the flesh* and under *condemnation*.]

2 For the law of the Spirit of life in Christ Jesus hath made me free from the law of sin and death.

[He was "now" free from that law that worked in his members and made him do the things he didn't want to do. In 7:23 he called it the "law of sin," and "*now*" the Spirit of God had set him free from it.]

3 For what the law could not do, in that it was weak through the flesh, God sending his own Son in the likeness of sinful flesh, and for sin, condemned sin in the flesh:

[You see, it's not the Gospel, or Christianity, that is weak through our flesh; the Law, and life under the Law, were. But God sent His own Son to condemn sin in the flesh. Our flesh is still just as weak as theirs was under the Law, but, praise God, through Christ we have access to His divine power to save us, and to keep us, from sin.]

4 That the righteousness of the law might be fulfilled in us, who walk not after the flesh, but after the Spirit.

[This righteousness is not fulfilled *by* us, but *in* us. The Spirit of life in Christ Jesus fulfills it in us. It is not of our strength, but of God's unlimited power.]

5 For they that are after the flesh do mind the things of the flesh; but they that are after the Spirit the things of the Spirit.

6 For to be carnally minded is death; but to be spiritually minded is life and peace.

7 Because the carnal mind is enmity against God: for it is not subject to the law of God, neither indeed can be.

8 So then they that are in the flesh cannot please God.

[Here's what can't be subject to God—the carnal mind—but we are to be spiritually, and not carnally, minded.]

9 But ye are not in the flesh, but in the Spirit, if so be that the Spirit of God dwell in you. Now if any man have not the Spirit of Christ, he is none of his.

Praise God! Glory to His name! Hallelujah! What the Law could not do, God sent His Son to do. That *present, up-to-date,* testimony Paul had, can be yours, my friend. He said that he was *now* free from the condemnation that rested so heavily upon him while he was under the Law, and he was *now* free from that law of sin that had worked in his members to bring that condemnation. Let me stress again how he told us, in 7:5, that the condemnation state was while he was *in the flesh.* In 8:1, he gave his *present* experience—at the time of his writing—and he was no longer under condemnation because he was no longer in the flesh. Paul did not live, after he was saved, in a state of sinning more or less every day and under condemnation.

Notice again how he told us, in 8:7, that the carnal, or fleshly, mind is not subject to the Law of God, that it *cannot* be, and how he added in verse 8, "So then they that are in the flesh cannot please God." We touched on the fact that this Scripture is one that modern "Christianity" loves to lift out of context and claim as a foundation for their sin-you-must doctrine, but the "so then" refers back to what was said before: "the *carnal mind* is not subject to the Law of God." Do Christians have carnal, or fleshly, minds? Well, clearly, Christian babes can have a struggle with the flesh, but verse 9 sets this forth for mature believers: "But ye are not in the flesh, but in the Spirit, if so be that the Spirit of God dwell in you." Beyond a doubt, if you are a mature disciple, you are not *in the flesh*! All of Paul's sin and condemnation were while he was in the flesh, but right while he wrote to the Roman Christians, in the same letter where he spoke of the bondage of sin, he said he was delivered from the flesh—and its sin and condemnation—because the Spirit of God was "now" in him.

Someone may argue, "Well, Paul told the Corinthian church that *they* were yet carnal, but he also told them they were sanctified, enriched by Jesus, and came behind in no gift. If *carnal* means 'after the flesh,' how can you say Christians can't live after the flesh when the church in Corinth did?"

Friend, that is a good question, and I'm glad it has come up, because this can be confusing to a lot of people. I try to anticipate questions like this and give them biblically sound answers in order to avoid such confusion, so let's see if there's an answer to this one. We'll start by reading 1 Corinthians 1:2, 5, and 7, and then 3:1-4:

1:2 Unto the church of God which is at Corinth, to them that are sanctified in Christ Jesus, called to be saints, with all that in every place call upon the name of Jesus Christ our Lord, both theirs and ours:

5 That in every thing ye are enriched by him, in all utterance, and in all knowledge.

7 So that ye come behind in no gift; waiting for the coming of our Lord Jesus Christ.

3:1 And I, brethren, could not speak unto you as unto spiritual, but as unto carnal, even as unto babes in Christ.

2 I have fed you with milk, and not with meat: for hitherto ye were not able to bear it, neither yet now are ye able.

3 For ye are yet carnal: for whereas there is among you envying, and strife, and divisions, are ye not carnal, and walk as men?

4 For while one saith, I am of Paul; and another, I am of Apollos; are ye not carnal?

The Corinthian converts had, indeed, been given a great start. God had certainly done His part. They had been greatly enriched spiritually. The problem was that they were not rightly using God's rich gifts and *growing* in the things of God. The Greek word translated *carnal*, here, is **sarkikos** (sar-kee-kos') and means "pertaining to flesh, i.e. (by extens.) bodily, temporal, or (by impl.) animal, unregenerate."[5] *Carnal* in Romans 8:7 comes from the word **sarx**, meaning, "the body (as opposed to the soul [or spirit], or as the symbol of what is external . . .), or (by impl.) human nature (with its frailties [phys. or mor.] and passions), or (spec.) a human being . . . ."[6]

Basically, these two definitions are very similar, but notice a subtle difference. *Sarkikos* means, by implication, "animal, unregenerate." *Sarx*, by implication, means "human nature." So the carnality the Corinthians were enmeshed in was a level lower than that Paul warned the Romans about. Friend, the Corinthian Christians had fallen to a more dangerous "walk in the flesh" than that which the Roman believers were warned to avoid. How did this happen, and happen to a church so enriched by God? There is a simple reason, dear one. What Paul wrote to the Romans is true! Walking after the flesh—one's human tendencies—will lead to walking as one *unregenerate*. It will, indeed, bring death to the soul engaged therein. I repeat, the Corinthians' condition only proved that what Paul told the Romans is true: if you walk in the flesh, you will die. History tells us that, at the time Paul wrote these reproofs to the Corinthian church, their very survival was at stake. Their walking in the flesh *was* destroying their spiritual life.

Paul, by the way, was in no way *overlooking* that condition in the Corinthians. The main purpose of his epistle was to correct those problems. While he answered some concerns they had written to him about (1 Corinthians 7:1), his deeper burden was *his* concerns about them, and he strove to lead them to victory over their failures. Look at what the Corinthians' carnality was producing in their lives: clique-forming (1:10-13); envying, strife, and divisions (3:1-4); lack of proper response to gross immorality in their midst and being "puffed up" about this lack (5:1-7); going to heathen courts to settle differences among the brotherhood, instead of seeking remedies through spiritual brethren, or, even better, learning to follow Christ's example and suffer wrong rather than do wrong (6:1-8).

Additionally, they had allowed the sacred observance of the Lord's Supper to unravel into an exercise in gluttony, selfishness, and irreverance (11:17-30). Even their worship had developed serious flaws—it had become disorderly and full of confusion as they strove to exhibit their *spiritual gifts* (14:1-40). False doctrines were creeping in concerning the resurrection, both that of Christ and of the dead (15:1-8, 12-58). Their walking after the flesh was, indeed, destroying them.

The city of Corinth was a great center of commerce and very much in connection with the world around it. It also abounded with moral depravity. It is wonderful that Paul's preaching there was so well received, and this certainly shows the power of the Gospel unto salvation to everyone that believeth. We can read of Paul's going to Corinth in Acts 18, while on his second missionary journey. He spent "a good while" longer than eighteen months there, "teaching the word of God among them" (see verses 11 and 18). They certainly got off to a great start, and with Paul's giving them more than eighteen months of his time, he had every reason to expect them to continue growing in grace and spiritual might. But, instead, and in spite of how God had blessed and enriched them, *they were remaining as babes!* They were not making normal progress. They were too easily moved by their own fleshly tendencies.

Look, again, at what Paul said to them, in Chapter 3, verses 1-2:

1 And I, brethren, could not speak unto you as unto spiritual, but as unto carnal, even as unto babes in Christ.

2 I have fed you with milk, and not with meat: for hitherto ye were not able to bear it, neither yet now are ye able.

Paul could not write to the Corinthians as he wrote to the Romans. The Roman believers had progressed and matured in the Lord; the Corinthians had not. Because they had walked after the *sarkikos* flesh (the human nature), they had regressed to walking in the *sarx* flesh (as unregenerate men), and were *coming short* of Paul's, and God's, expectations for them. Indeed, if they didn't overcome quickly, they would *be* unregenerate once more. Their walking after the flesh would have destroyed them!

The Corinthian church's behavior is certainly not the norm, nor is it an example we should strive to copy. Rather, it is an example of what *not* to do! Just as walking in the flesh was destroying their spiritual life, doing so will work the same death in us, just as Paul said. I repeat that, unlike today's preachers, Paul was not overlooking Corinth's condition as a normal state for believers. Rather, he was urging them to get on top of their shortcomings, knowing that if they did not, they would lose their spiritual life. It was as true for them as it was for the Romans—and everyone else—that to be carnally minded is death. Again, the very reason Paul raised the issue was so he could correct it. This in no way translates into giving room among Christians, in general, for walking in the flesh. The *standard*, the *rule*, is just what the Apostle set forth in Romans 8:6-9. God gives all babes in Christ time to get established, and, so, works with their problems to bring them to maturity. But the normal process is that the babes do *steadily* and *rapidly* grow and mature, and in so doing, they become robust, strong, and consistently victorious, Christians. This normal process, I say again, was not happening in Corinth, and the lack of it was working destruction in them.

I feel weepy when I consider Paul's, and God's, love for these Corinthian converts. Although they were coming far short of spiritual growth and maturity, Paul did not just cast them away. He worked to strengthen their "pluses" as well as to move them above their "minuses." They did, in fact, have some strengths; God had given them a glorious launch, and although their survival was wavering, Paul labored to help them overcome. Remember (this is very important) that this was in the beginning of the Christian era, and although Christianity conquered paganism, it took some time. And it took time for those converts from paganism to learn everything that being saved included. Paul did not condone the Corinthians' slowness, nor the things they were doing after the flesh, but neither did he give up on them. He tenderly, as a father (1 Corinthians 4:15), saw beyond their faults and saw their needs. Patiently he worked to restore them, not willing that they should perish. This does not change the fact that, if they would not take correction and measure up, walking in the flesh would bring death to their souls. Paul desired to prevent this death, but he could not stop it if the people, themselves, did not take his, and God's, admonition. No wonder he warned the Romans of the dangers of walking in the flesh. The epistles to the Romans and to the Corinthians were written very close together, time wise; it may even have been the problems in Corinth that prompted Paul to write to the Romans as he did about the result of walking after the flesh.

I haven't studied the further history of the Corinthian congregation, yet, and I don't know whether they overcame or whether they died out. However, Paul did confirm repentance on their part, at one point, in 2 Corinthians 7:7-16.

Dear one, all of this only *confirms* what Paul told the Roman Christians. While God is willing to work with new, or weak, converts, to bring them to victory and maturity, the converts have to be willing, as well, to take reproof, and even rebuke, and *stop doing* whatever is causing them to come short. If they do not, they will die. *To be carnally minded is death,* and the Corinthian congregation only proved how true this is. Once more—and please lay hold on it—in no way is living in and after the flesh the normal, and acceptable, state for Christians! Christianity brings life, but walking in the flesh brings death. And, while some converts may struggle to measure up to the demands of the Gospel, the Gospel's demands never change, and that early ministry *preached* and *required* those exacting demands because God's grace was sufficient. It was "*overcome or else.*" Those who failed to make the grade simply fell away and were lost. How different it is in today's modern "Christian churches," where such fleshly living is an accepted part of one's *salvation*!

In addition to the verses we've already quoted from the book of Romans, Paul had much to say to the Gentile converts against being fleshly minded or walking in the flesh. Please read Romans 13:14, then see Galatians 5:13-21, Ephesians 2:3, Ephesians 4:22-24, Philippians 3:13-19, Colossians 2:11, and Colossians 3:5-10. It is clear that the Apostle Paul labored to get the Gentile converts, coming as they were out of pagan uncleanness, established in walking and living in the Spirit and that he made no room for walking in the flesh. Indeed, the first of these just-listed texts says, "But put ye on the Lord Jesus Christ, and make not provision for the flesh"!

Neither do God's true ministers, today, make room for walking after the flesh in the everyday lives of believers. Any time preachers allow it, condone it, and even teach that it's normal, those believers will die (and so will those preachers)! Friend, preachers are supposed to be condemning sin in the flesh, and condemning the walking after the flesh that leads to sin, but today's "preachers" are, instead, condemning those of us who earnestly contend for the faith once delivered to the saints (Jude 3)! Their Jesus, sadly, is not the Jesus of the Bible!

I consulted several sources for the above information about the conditions in Corinth at the time Paul wrote his First letter to them. I have shared these facts in a "general" sense rather than using direct quotations from any of these sources. It was a very beneficial study, and I encourage you, dear reader, to do a study of your own.

Having cleared up that question, let's read Romans 8:6-9 again:

6 For to be carnally minded is death; but to be spiritually minded is life and peace.

7 Because the carnal mind is enmity against God: for it is not subject to the law of God, neither indeed can be.

8 So then they that are in the flesh cannot please God.

9 But ye are not in the flesh, but in the Spirit, if so be that the Spirit of God dwell in you. Now if any man have not the Spirit of Christ, he is none of his.

Now I want to share with you something I ran across while studying for this book. There are some who believe that Paul's "testimony" in Chapter 7 and part of Chapter 8 refers, not to his own personal experience, but to the condition of the Jews in general, which, of course, *includes* him. They hold that these texts contrast the conscientious Jew's frustration and hopelessness under a Law that pointed out his dilemma under sin, but offered no cure—they contrast this, I repeat—to his coming to an understanding that Christ secured for him redemption and deliverance through the Gospel. Even though this teaches the same truth, it moves the narrative in Romans 7 from Paul, personally, to the Jews in general. In this scenario, then, the Jew passes from hopelessness to hope. He passes from sin and condemnation, under the Law, to justification and sanctification (being forgiven *and* delivered) through Jesus Christ. Indeed, he passes from being under the schoolmaster to being under the deliverance of the Messiah!

While this explanation seems to have some merit in light of Romans 7:1 and 5, and is worthy of further study, it still gives no place to the idea that any born-again believer remains under the power of sin after conversion. Although I use no man's commentary in this book to prove my points, arguing only from the Scriptures themselves, I do consult these study aids to learn a lot of things. It was in *Adam Clarke's Commentary* that I learned that some hold this belief concerning this text. You may find his comments on Romans 6 through 8 very interesting and informative.

Friend, if this study of Paul's testimony has found you short of a real experience with Jesus Christ, *do not despair.* The very reason God inspired me to write this book is so He can bring you light and understanding, so you can "make your calling and election sure" (2 Peter 1:10). God and I love you too much to allow you to go on being deceived by modern Christendom. There is a true Christianity, and it is God's desire that you enjoy it. In chapter seven of this book, we will look at many ways that modern Christendom is failing the souls of men and women today. Contrary to the thinking of the masses, it does not really represent the true Jesus Christ. But Jesus does have a people, and they are actually and definitely delivered from sin and Satan and living holy lives each and every day. You can be one of these. Finding this real deliverance is not hard. It simply takes

a) honest confession,
b) real repentance, and
c) faith—in the true Savior—that when you meet His conditions, He will actually save you from your sins.

Remember, not all "Christs" are the Savior sent to us from Heaven by the Lord God Almighty.

You may say, "Well, I did honestly confess, repent, and believe, but I am not living free from sin."

Well, let me reiterate some things I said earlier, to help you assess your situation. You may have been truly saved, but because you were taught holy living is impossible, you have allowed sin to creep in, thinking it was completely normal. Again, you may have been taught that things are sin which are not. Remember, temptation is not sin. Having ungodly thoughts is not sin, as long as you use those "mighty weapons" to bring "into captivity every thought to the obedience of Christ" (2 Corinthians 10:5). Friend, you can take this "to the bank": Paul was writing this to the church (1:1), and it wouldn't make sense to bring thoughts into captivity to the obedience of Christ if we, God's people, never had wrong thoughts that needed it. Satan loves to bring ungodly thoughts to Christians and then accuse them of being unsaved; he loves to convince nominal believers that such thoughts are sin, and that sinning is "business as usual" for Christians. Dear one, neither of these is true. When we banish ungodly thoughts as soon as we recognize them, we have not sinned.

Another reason you may have confessed and repented, yet didn't find this deliverance from sin is that your believing, itself, fell short. When you repented, did your faith take in deliverance unto holiness? True believing, in Bible terms, involves believing that Jesus can and will deliver you from sin and keep you from it day by day. One of the curses of modern "Christianity" is how they tell people they can't be delivered and kept from sin, thus robbing them of the faith which secures true salvation. "Believe on the Lord Jesus Christ, and thou shalt be saved" (Acts 16:31) is a promise many have trusted in and are basing their hope of eternal life on. But, friend, if you don't believe what the Gospel really teaches about Jesus, and if you don't believe in what Jesus truly came to do, your believing is in vain. It is not going to save you, leaving you without hope. Oh, how false Christianity is murdering souls!

"Salvation" that doesn't really *save* is as worthless as any and all other counterfeits. There is one immense difference, though: this counterfeit will bring eternal (that's everlasting, that's never-ending) woe to those who are taken in by it! To be saved, one must believe the truth about Jesus and what His death produces. Jesus was the Word incarnate, or in the flesh. To actually believe in Him, one must believe the entire Word of God. The Bible says He came to "save his people *from* their sins" (Matthew 1:21), and to be saved, you must believe this. To be saved, you must believe all that the Apostle Paul teaches in Romans 6 and Romans 8 about what Jesus does in the life of a true believer.

Someone may say, "But as long as I'm sincere, won't God accept me? I really am a sincere believer, doing all I know to do. That's surely enough."

Friend, I have to tell you that sincerity is not enough. There are idol worshipers (yes, they're still around) who are sincere. Many such worshipers have endured great suffering because they've been told their "god" requires it. That's very sincere, if you ask me. But the Bible tells us that there is none other name, given among men, except the

Name of Jesus, whereby we may find redemption (Acts 4:12), so their sincerity does not save them. Jesus told Nicodemus that except we're born again, we cannot enter God's Kingdom (John 3:3-7). No matter how sincere we may be, if we do not meet Bible conditions, we will be lost. Dear reader, I love you, and love does *not* compel me to aid in your deception; love compels me to tell you that sincerity alone will not save you. We can be sincerely wrong. That is why God charges *you and me* with the responsibility to "Search the scriptures; for in them ye think ye have eternal life: and *they are they which testify of me*" (John 5:39). (Emphasis added.)

It is also Christ's command to you and me to "Take heed that no man deceive" us (Matthew 24:4). This is our responsibility! How can we do this? John instructed us, "Beloved, believe not every spirit, but try the spirits whether they are of God: because many false prophets are gone out into the world" (1 John 4:1). The only sure and safe way to try the spirits is *by the Word of God.* That's exactly what we are doing in this study. Friend, everything else is subject to human error, but God makes no mistakes. And He promised, in John 7:17, that "If any man will *do* his will [the Father's, verse 16], he shall *know* of the doctrine, whether it be of God" or of man. (Emphasis added.) The key, then, to finding the truth, is in a full willingness to obey it, and then searching God's Word to learn of Him and to confirm, or disprove, the things we are taught. This is more than just looking to see if a quoted verse is in the Bible. It may, indeed, be there, but be *mis*quoted and/or misapplied. We will show, throughout this book, that many Scriptures are misrepresented and taken out of context to support some false doctrine or theory. In searching the Scriptures, we need to ask God to reveal to us what *He* intended when He inspired the sacred writers, and then study a given subject in a number of texts, and keep everything in its context. I have personally practiced this for most of my adult life. Even when I've had total confidence in the teacher or preacher, I've checked my Bible, and I've studied my Bible, to see if what he said is what *it* says. I haven't done this arrogantly, as if I know more than the preacher, but in a real quest for truth. Our ministers teach us to do this, and, as just shown, God teaches us to.

Now, back to the thought that God sent this book your way to help you see if your Christianity is genuine or not, and to help you get a true experience if you don't have one. It is not God's, or my, intention to merely steal away your confidence. It *is* His, and my, intention to make sure you have your confidence in the right thing. If your faith is centered on the true Gospel, and in the true Jesus, this book will only make it grow brighter. But if it is not, this book's sole purpose is to help you find true saving faith, and therefore, true salvation, and a true hope of Heaven.

I say, again, you can enjoy the real thing. That is God's desire. Jesus came to set up only one redemption Plan. It is a fallen "Christianity" that has complicated this thing and made it so hard for men and women to find the strait and narrow way. I know it sounds harsh and judgmental to say that modern Christendom has fallen short of leading souls to Christ, but, friend, this is simply the truth. You, yourself, know that its masses proclaim a sin-you-must "Christianity," and I trust you are beginning to see that this is not the Christianity the Bible Jesus came to bring to us.

The Apostle Paul definitely taught, and practiced, true deliverance from sin, true holy living. And God incorporated his writings on the subject into His holy and sacred Word. They are part of the Gospel. Modern ministers or churches that deny Christ's power to bring this experience are not true to the Gospel message. They are denying the faith once delivered to the saints. I know, *I know*, this is disturbing, but it is reality; it is the simple truth, and it is sent to set you free. Satan is out to destroy your soul!

Before I leave "Paul's testimony," I want to assure you that the 7th Chapter of Romans is not the only place in the Scriptures where you can find present-tense narration describing past events. The Gospel of Mark uses this technique often. Not so much in long portions of text, but it mixes present and past tenses in its narrative from time to time.

Precious soul, you don't have to be misled any longer. Put your faith in the holy and immutable Word of God alone. This—and only this—will bring you a genuine hope of being right with God here and accepted of Him in the end. May God help you to find all that He has in store for you, is my fervent prayer.

CHAPTER FIVE

"Trial and Error"

In today's "Christianity," people are instructed to continually carry on an exercise in futility. How's that, you wonder? Well, they are told, and no doubt you are too, that they should try to emulate Jesus Christ in their lives—yet they are also told that they absolutely cannot be holy, as He is. It is utterly futile to try to be something it's impossible to be. To instruct people to try to be like Jesus, and then tell them that they cannot be like Jesus, is ridiculous! It is also unbiblical. Nowhere in the divine Word does God instruct mankind to try to obey or serve Him. Old Testament and New, God's commands are very expressly "Thou shalts" and "Thou shalt nots." (This is not bad, friend; God's rules are for our good.) The Ten Commandments do not say, "Thou shalt try not to commit adultery," or "Thou shalt try not to covet." No. God always has demanded, and always will demand, perfect obedience. In every case where perfect obedience is not performed, judgment follows—with one exception. Under the Law of Moses, those who did their best to be obedient, yet failed, could bring sacrifices for atonement. It wasn't the lamb or bullock that atoned, but the offering of these *in faith in the promised Messiah*, whose blood could actually redeem from sin. When Jesus died on Calvary, remember, the sins of the Law Dispensation were covered for those sincere believers (Hebrews 9:15). But those who just had a disobedient spirit got judgment.

For those of us, however, who live under the New Testament Dispensation, the already-shed blood of Christ provides full deliverance from both the penalty and the power of sin. But when it comes to obedience, no one ever has gotten, or ever will get, "points" for coming close. Achan only took a little of the spoil at Jericho, but it brought severe punishment. Trying doesn't count. *Almost* doesn't count. Someone has said, and it is true, "Partial obedience is disobedience." The part left unobeyed renders the command *disobeyed.* King Saul was a "partial obeyer." Ordered by God to kill *all* of the Amalekites, he killed *most* of them—but this was not acceptable. (We will examine this in more detail later in this chapter.)

Do you suppose it is different today for those who are "under grace" than for Achan and Saul? Well, it is not. Everything God instructs us to do, He *requires* us to do. The Gospel did not bring in a weaker standard; it just brought power to obey. It did this by placing that Power right within every saved man and woman. Acts 1:8 says, in the words of Jesus Himself, "But ye shall receive power, after that the Holy Ghost is come upon you: and ye shall be witnesses unto me . . . ." Ezekiel 36:27 says, "And I will put my spirit within you, and *cause* you to walk in my statutes, and ye *shall* keep my judgments, and do them." (Emphasis added.) If your church doesn't bring you to an experience where you have this power, my friend, you are being cheated. Please allow me to say it again: your "Jesus" is not the Jesus of the Bible. When God tells us, today, to

- crucify self and die out to our will (Matthew 16:24, Romans 6:6)
- hate (or love less) our dearest family members (Luke 14:26-27)
- love our enemies (Matthew 5:44-46)
- leave vengeance up to Him (Hebrews 10:30, Matthew 5:38-39, Romans 12:17-18)
- not even commit murder or adultery *in our hearts* (Matthew 5:21-22 and 27-30)
- keep ourselves separate from the things of the world (James 4:4, 1 John 2:15-17)
- think on things that are pure (Philippians 4:8)
- bridle our tongues and not gossip or slander (James 1:26, 4:11a)
- do anything else He has commanded (John 14:15),

He knows full well that we can obey by His grace; dear one, disobedience brings death. Ezekiel 18:20 says, "The soul that sinneth, it shall die." Now it doesn't say that the *sinner* that sinneth shall die, while the Christian that sinneth shall still enjoy eternal life. (In fact, Ezekiel tells us the exact opposite, and we'll look at that in a minute.) This verse says the *soul* that sinneth shall die. Reading the context of this verse reveals that the subject being dealt with is a proverb. Verses 1-4 read:

1 The Word of the LORD came unto me saying,

2 What mean ye, that ye use this proverb concerning the land of Israel, saying, The fathers have eaten sour grapes, and the children's teeth are set on edge?

3 As I live, saith the Lord GOD, ye shall not have occasion any more to use this proverb in Israel.

4 Behold, all souls are mine; as the soul of the father, so also the soul of the son is mine: the soul that sinneth, it shall die.

Reading on, through verse 20, shows that the subject does not change. Let's read the entirety of that 20th verse. "The soul that sinneth, it shall die. The son shall not bear the iniquity of the father, neither shall the father bear the iniquity of the son: the righteousness of the righteous shall be upon him, and the wickedness of the wicked shall be upon him."

We can see, then, that God was telling Ezekiel that every man is responsible for his own conduct, and each man's conduct determines whether he lives or dies. Therefore, His words apply to *any* soul and *every* soul that meets the specified condition—the soul that *sinneth*. Since it applies to any soul, and every soul, that sins, then any soul, and every soul, that sins, dies. Sin brings death to *the soul* that commits it. The rest of the Bible absolutely substantiates this fact. As you read this book, you will see this if you have an honest heart.

We quoted Ezekiel 18:20, but look at what else Ezekiel said about sin bringing death in that Chapter: "But when the righteous turneth away from his righteousness, and committeth iniquity . . . shall he live? All his righteousness that he hath done shall not be mentioned: in his trespass that he hath trespassed, and in his sin that he hath sinned, in them shall he die" (verse 24). God wanted this fact so established that He had Ezekiel repeat it in Chapter 33, verse 12. He even says it *twice* in this single verse: "Therefore, thou son of man, say unto the children of thy people, The righteousness of the righteous shall not deliver him in the day of his transgression: as for the wickedness of the wicked, he shall not fall thereby in the day that he turneth from his wickedness; neither shall the righteous be able to live for his righteousness in the day that he sinneth." Dear reader, the soul that sinneth, it shall die; even the soul that had been righteous.

Ezekiel actually repeated this truth *three* times; do you not think God wanted it firmly fixed in our hearts and minds? Look at what he wrote in Chapter 3, verses 17-21:

17 Son of man, I have made thee a watchman unto the house of Israel: therefore hear the word at my mouth, and give them warning from me.

18 When I say unto the wicked, Thou shalt surely die; and thou givest him not warning, nor speakest to warn the wicked from his wicked way, to save his life; the same wicked man shall die in his iniquity; but his blood will I require at thine hand.

19 Yet if thou warn the wicked, and he turn not from his wickedness, nor from his wicked way, he shall die in his iniquity; but thou hast delivered thy soul.

20 Again, When a righteous man doth turn from his righteousness, and commit iniquity, and I lay a stumblingblock before him, he shall die: because thou hast not given him warning, he shall die in his sin, and his righteousness which he hath done shall not be remembered; but his blood will I require at thine hand.

21 Nevertheless if thou warn the righteous man, that the righteous sin not, and he doth not sin, he shall surely live, because he is warned; also thou hast delivered thy soul.

Please notice what God told Ezekiel here: when a righteous man commits sin, if the preacher has not warned him that his sin will bring death, it *will* bring death, but God will require that man's blood at the preacher's hand! This puts today's nominal ministry in terrible jeopardy, friend. They are, instead, telling believers that they can sin more or less from day to day and it will not bring death. "Oh," someone may argue, "that's talking about those who *turn from God* and go back to sin. It doesn't mean those who sin but still love God." Friend, what it says is that, in order to sin, the righteous has to *turn from* righteousness (verse 20). That *is* turning from God! There is no room in this text for one to be righteous and committing sin both. Read the next verse. It says that if the preacher warns the righteous not to sin, and the righteous *does not* sin, he will not reap death but life. Life rather than death is for the righteous one who heeds the preacher's warning and *doth not sin.* Again, woe to that preacher who does not give this warning!

I never cease to be amazed at how false prophets wrest the Scriptures. In these texts, in Ezekiel, God is answering Israel's charge against Him of being unfair. He defends His fairness with the fact that He judges sinners who turn from their sins to righteousness, and the righteous who turn from their righteousness to sin, on exactly the same terms. Yet nominal Christendom, today, claims that God is fair in treating repentant sinners one way and sinning "believers" another way. Why can't they grasp this simple truth? Ah, it's because the natural man cannot perceive spiritual things, and if they are still sinning, they are but natural men.

Again, someone may say, "Well, in the last chapter, you said that under the Old Testament, people *couldn't* keep God's commandments. How do you reconcile that with what you are saying now?" Well, dear one, it is true that those people could not obey God's commands in their everyday lives, although some performed great feats by God's direction and power. It is just as true, though, that God never, ever, told anyone under the Old Testament Dispensation to *try* to obey Him. *Trying* was not good enough then, and it is certainly not good enough now. There really isn't any contradiction here, because God's requirements were the same under the Law and under grace: perfect obedience. Failure to comply results in spiritual death. It always has and it always will. Remember, the Law was our *schoolmaster* to show us the need for salvation, and those who learned this lesson under the Law had a remedy through their sacrifices, as already mentioned, when offered in faith in the coming Savior. Again, in both Dispensations, God's demands were the same—obey or else—and in both Dispensations, He provided for disobedience to be forgiven *when His conditions were met.* But intentional disobedience brought death under the Law, and it brings death under grace. In any case, God has never accepted merely *trying* to obey. *All disobedience brings spiritual death.*

Since that is true, nowhere did Jesus ever tell anyone to try to keep His New Testament commandments. John 14:15 does not say, "If ye love me, try to keep my commandments." It says, *"Keep them."* Just as it was with Adam, in the day that we fail to keep God's commandments, *we* shall surely die (this all refers to spiritual death). But just as Satan told Eve "'thou shalt not surely die' if you break God's commandment," he is still propagating his lie to professed believers today: "'Thou shalt not surely die' if you sin a little, more or less, now and then." Let me emphasize it—*if you, as a believer, fail to keep any of God's commandments, you shall surely die.*

Neither did the apostles dish out this "trial and error gospel." First Corinthians 6:18 says, "Flee fornication." Second Corinthians 6:17 says, "Wherefore come out from among them [the unbelievers, the unrighteousness, the idolaters, etc., especially those who claimed to be God's people, verses 14-16], and be ye separate, saith the Lord, and touch not the unclean thing." Philippians 1:27 says, "Only let your conversation [conduct] be as it becometh the gospel of Christ," and 2:3 tells us, "Let nothing be done through strife or vain glory." Colossians 3:2 tells us, "Set your affections on things above, not on things on the earth." The Hebrew writer, in Hebrews 13:5, gave us two separate commands: "Let your conversation be without covetousness; and be content with such things as ye have." James said, in Chapter 1 and verse 21 of his epistle, "Wherefore lay apart all filthiness and superfluity of naughtiness." Peter said, in 1 Peter 3:1, "Likewise, ye wives, be in subjection to your own husbands." (Yes, this command is still binding, and it will be until the second coming of Christ, and Paul brought up the other side of it in Ephesians 5:28—husbands are commanded to love their wives as they do their own bodies. When the husband does that, the wife should have no trouble submitting to him. Paul was writing to Christians; saved wives do not have to obey unsaved husbands when they want them to do something against God or their consciences [Colossians 3:18, Acts 5:29].)

John told us, in 1 John 5:21, "Little children, keep yourselves from idols." James 4:11a says, "Speak not evil one of another, brethren." Peter wrote, "Use hospitality one to another without grudging" (1 Peter 4:9). None of these, nor any other, New Testament commands contain the words, "*try to* . . . ." Look at Ephesians 4:24; Paul told us that the "new man" is created, after God, in righteousness and true holiness, and we are *commanded* to put this new man on. Again, this is not something we accomplish in our own strength. This new man, or new life, is *created* in us by God. That's why 2 Corinthians 5:17 says, "Therefore if any man be in Christ, he is a new *creature* [emphasis added]." God *creates* this new *creature*. God does. But Paul tells us to "put it on." Again, this is doable. He did not say, "*Try* to put on the new man." He said to *do it*. And what about honesty? Are we supposed to *try* to be honest, but after all, everyone knows that there are times when a little white lie is best? Well, Romans 12:17b says, "Provide things honest in the sight of all men." See also 2 Corinthians 8:21. There are no exceptions, and there is no "try to."

Here is where *believing* in Christ comes in. You must believe that God can do this in you, through Christ. If you do not believe this, you do not really believe in Christ, because this is what Christ came to do. This is the essence of His mission. Remember, He said He came to seek and to save that which is lost, and this is what saving the lost is. This is what saving the lost does. This is what happens to all who are "in Christ." You must believe this or you cannot be saved. You must believe what *the Scriptures* testify of Jesus, or, no matter how much you think you have believed the Gospel, you are believing a falsehood, dear one. Believing in a "Jesus" who does not produce this in your life will be to believe in vain. Again I urge you to remember that the Gospel is *simple*. Don't let the devil complicate this for you. Every new *creature* in Christ Jesus is *created* in righteousness and *true holiness*.

Again proving that the early church did not spread a "trial and error gospel," James said, in Chapter 1 of his epistle, and verse 22, "But be ye doers of the word, and not hearers only, deceiving your own selves." Modern "Christianity" tells us that we can hear a lot of things from the Word of God that we can't actually do, yet we can be Christians. Nay, my friend. If you hear anything from God's Word that you do not obey, and think you are still a Christian, you are deceiving your own self. *I implore you to stop it!* James said, "Don't just hear it, *do* it!" And look at what he said in verse 27: "Pure religion and undefiled before God and the Father is this, To visit the fatherless and widows in their affliction, and to keep himself unspotted from the world."

Forgive my being repetitive, but, again, he did not say to *try* to keep yourself unspotted from the world. Are you unspotted from the world, or does the world have far too much influence over you? This same James said, "The friendship of the world is enmity with God" (James 4:4). More on this later, but are you caught up in this world's "pop culture" or its fads and fancies? Do you run after its entertainment and pleasures? Do you follow its trends? If so, and if you are on any other point a hearer but not a doer of the Word, I say it kindly, friend, but you do not have pure religion. Please, *don't* deceive yourself!

Dear precious soul, I know these truths can sound harsh, but I am honestly not after *you*. I am after the devil and his ministers who transform themselves into *angels of light* in order to deceive hearts.

Please be assured that my only goal is to see honest souls rescued from a counterfeit salvation and a counterfeit hope of eternal life. Again, I can think of nothing more tragic than slipping into hell when one expected Heaven. I am writing this book because *I do not want that to happen to you*!

Let's read 1 Peter 1:15-16:

15 But as he which hath called you is holy, so be ye holy in all manner of conversation;

16 Because it is written, Be ye holy; for I am holy.

Wow! When Peter read something out of God's Word, *that's* what he told people to do. He didn't say, "Oh, that's impossible!" He *believed* God's Word, and he *taught* it, rather than giving out his own ideas! Peter did not instruct us, as do modern preachers, "Now, *try* to live as close to holy as you can in this sinful world," which, of course, is not holy at all. Right while they're telling you to "try to," they'll tell you that you can't. Again, how utterly futile. Not Peter. He said, "*Be ye holy.*" And he added, "in all manner of conversation," or in everything you do. *Conversation*, here, is taken from the Greek word **anastrophe** (an-as-trof-ay'), which means "behavior,"[1] and *behavior* is defined by Websters as "conduct."[2] So God, through Peter, was telling us, here, to be holy in all manner of behavior or conduct.

The Apostle John said, "Love not the world, neither the things that are in the world" (1 John 2:15). He said, "He that saith he abideth in him [Christ] ought himself also so to walk, even as he [Christ] walked" (2:6). He said, "And every man that hath this hope in him [the hope of being like Christ when He comes, verse 2] purifieth himself, even as he [Christ] is pure" (3:3).

Christendom, today, says we can't be like Jesus until we get to Heaven. John said, however, that everyone who has a hope of being like Christ when He comes again, needs to be like Christ here and now, purified as Christ is pure, and that's pure! Someone may say, "Well, John said we are to purify *ourselves*. How can we do that?" Friend, Peter gives us the answer: "Seeing ye have purified your souls in obeying the truth through the Spirit . . ." (1 Peter 1:22). We purify ourselves when we obey God's command to repent and forsake sin, and then believe that Jesus saves us *from* sin. As we receive further understanding of God's truth, we continue to purify ourselves through obedience, by walking in the light as Christ reveals it to us. This is part of "the washing of water by the word" (Ephesians 5:26). And let me say, again, we do all this *through the Spirit*, not in and of ourselves.

John was the writer of the seven letters to the seven churches of Asia, recorded in Revelation, Chapters 2 and 3. Or, I should say, John was the secretary to whom Jesus dictated these letters (Revelation 2:1, 8, 12, 18; Revelation 3:1, 7, 14). Jesus said He had something against five of these seven congregations; Smyrna and Philadelphia were without fault. Jesus did not instruct those five to *try* to live by His precepts while He accepted their shortcomings due to their being "under grace." No! He demanded a change. Let's examine His rebukes.

In Chapter 2, verses 4-5, He addressed the church of Ephesus:

4 Nevertheless I have somewhat against thee, because thou hast left thy first love.

5 Remember therefore from whence thou art fallen, and repent, and do the first works; or else I will come unto thee quickly, and will remove thy candlestick [their being the church, Chapter 1:20] *out of his place, except thou repent.*

It was, "Repent and straighten up or I'm out of here."

To Pergamos He said, in verses 14-16:

14 But I have a few things against thee, because thou hast there them that hold the doctrine of Balaam, who taught Balac to cast a stumblingblock before the children of Israel, to eat things sacrificed unto idols, and to commit fornication.

15 So hast thou also them that hold the doctrine of the Nicolaitanes, which thing I hate.

16 Repent; or else I will come unto thee quickly, and will fight against them with the sword of my mouth.

As you can see, Jesus told them they were coming short and had to repent of, or turn from, those shortcomings. Fighting against them with the sword of His mouth meant with His holy Word (Ephesians 6:17). By this we know they were not *obeying* the Word. He did not overlook them because they were "believers," and His judgment would be swift.

In verses 20-23 He addressed Thyatira:

20 Notwithstanding I have a few things against thee, because thou sufferest that woman Jezebel, which calleth herself a prophetess, to teach and to seduce my servants to commit fornication, and to eat things sacrificed unto idols.

21 And I gave her space to repent of her fornication; and she repented not.

22 Behold, I will cast her into a bed, and them that commit adultery with her into great tribulation, except they repent of their deeds.

23 And I will kill her children with death; and all the churches shall know that I am he which searcheth the reins and hearts: and I will give unto every one of you according to your works.

It was, "Except they repent, I will cast them into great tribulation." And look at what Jesus said to these believers, those of the *church*: I will give unto every one of you according to your works. Friend, believers will be judged *by their works*, not by their *faith*.

Concerning Sardis, Chapter 3, verses 2b-3 state:

2b [F]or I have not found thy works perfect before God.

3 Remember therefore how thou hast received and heard, and hold fast, and repent. If therefore thou shalt not watch, I will come on thee as a thief, and thou shalt not know what hour I will come upon thee.

Here, Jesus said, "Repent; if you don't, I'm coming on you as a thief, unexpected and unprepared for."

Verses 15-20 told Laodicea this:

15 I know thy works, that thou art neither cold nor hot; I would thou wert cold or hot.

16 So then because thou art lukewarm, and neither cold nor hot, I will spue thee out of my mouth.

17 Because thou sayest, I am rich, and increased with goods, and have need of nothing; and knowest not that thou art wretched, and miserable, and poor, and blind, and naked:

18 I counsel thee to buy of me gold tried in the fire, that thou mayest be rich; and white raiment, that thou mayest be clothed, and that the shame of thy nakedness do not appear; and anoint thine eyes with eyesalve, that thou mayest see.

19 As many as I love, I rebuke and chasten: be zealous therefore, and repent.

20 Behold, I stand at the door, and knock: if any man hear my voice, and open the door, I will come in to him, and will sup with him, and he with me.

It was, "Because you're lukewarm, I'm spuing you out. I'll be on the *outside*. If you'll repent, however, and let me in, I'll come back."

These churches did not get by with falling short. *Even though Jesus commended them for the things they were doing right, their successes did not excuse their failures.* He rebuked them sharply and demanded that they measure up. It was "Repent or else." There is not one single instance where He told them to try harder, and, friend, you may be sure that Christ will not accept any person or church, today, that repeatedly falls short of His demand for complete obedience and holiness. He will give time for repentance, when we fall short, but if we don't repent and *forsake* the disobedience, He will spue *us* out; He will remove *our* candlestick.

As we have seen, nowhere did the writers of Scripture employ the term, "try." The reason is obvious: Christ did not die to give us a small dose of grace that would make us *better* people and keep us striving for an impossible goal of being like Him. He came to *save* us *from* our sins, to *cleanse* us *from* all unrighteousness, and to give us the privilege, not only of being like Him when He appears, but of being like Him right now. His grace will enable us to do just exactly that, rather than merely "cover" our failures.

Friend, can you see it? Can you see the difference between today's "Christian" ministers, who tell people to "try to be as close to Christlike as you can, although you cannot," and the *Bible*, which instructs us to *be* imitators of Christ? He is our example in all things, and an example is to be *followed*. Reading 1 Peter 2:21-22 makes this abundantly clear:

21 For even hereunto were ye called: because Christ also suffered for us, leaving us an example, that ye should follow his steps:

22 Who did no sin, neither was guile found in his mouth.

We are to follow His steps, Who did no sin. In Romans 13:14 Paul instructed, "But put ye on the Lord Jesus Christ." We are to "wear" Christ every day of our Christian lives. When anyone looks upon us, he should see Christ Jesus. Paul added, in the rest of that verse, "and make not provision for the flesh, to fulfill the lusts thereof." If it were true that we're so under the influence of this wicked world that we cannot help but sin more or less every day, Paul's words would be ridiculous. But right here, in this present world, we are to make no room for the flesh's lusts. Remember, it is lust that conceives to produce sin. If we are to make *no* room for the flesh's lusts, they can hardly conceive within us and result in sin in our lives. Friend, this is not mere opinion. It is not some "creed." This is God's own holy Word telling us *to make no provision for the flesh, to fulfill its lusts!*

"Put ye on the Lord Jesus Christ," Paul said, and he told the Galatians (Chapter 3, verse 27) the same thing: "For as many of you as have been baptized into Christ have put on Christ." Remember what we learned, in chapter four of this book, about being baptized into Christ? Surely no one can successfully argue that being baptized into a spiritual union with Christ describes anything but being saved, regenerated, born again; so Paul was telling us that all who have been saved *have clothed themselves* with Christ.

Paul said essentially the same thing, again, in his letter to the Ephesians, but he put it into different words, stronger words. Chapter 4, verses 11-13 read:

11 And he gave some, apostles; and some, prophets; and some, evangelists; and some, pastors and teachers;

12 For the perfecting of the saints, for the work of the ministry, for the edifying of the body of Christ:

13 Till we all come in the unity of the faith, and of the knowledge of the Son of God, unto a perfect man, unto the measure of the stature of the fulness of Christ.

What do these verses teach us? I'm not going to say, "They teach us that we must be perfect," for the Greek words used in these verses for *perfecting* (**katartismos**, kat-ar-tis-mos') and *perfect* (**teleios**, tel'-i-os) mean "*complete furnishing,*"[3] and "*complete*" or "*completeness,*"[4] respectively, according to *Strong's Greek Dictionary*. There are those who would argue that *complete* does not mean "free from sin." So, instead, I will call your attention to a portion of verse 13, which says, "Till we all come . . . unto the measure of the stature of the fulness of Christ." Clearly, God *gave His ministry* to bring us to *all* that Christ is. Just as clearly, any ministry that does not bring people to this experience *is not God's ministry*. Hear John's words, again, as he backs Paul up: "And every man that hath this hope in him purifieth himself, even as he is pure" (1 John 3:3). We are to be as pure as Christ is. If you are not as pure as Jesus Christ is, you have no real hope of spending eternity with Him. We can, and must, measure up to all that Jesus is. If you still feel this is impossible, my dear reader, remember Jesus' words, quoted earlier. The disciples asked Him, "Who then can be saved?" and He replied, "With men it is impossible, but not with God: for with God all things are possible" (Mark 10:26-27). When your preacher, or teacher, or youth leader, tells you "that's impossible," just give him Jesus' words; just say, "Yes, with men it is, but not with God!"

I will add this, however. I didn't quote the entire definition for *perfect* above. When you read the whole thing, it does allude to holy living. Let's look: "*complete* (in various applications of labor, growth, mental and moral character, etc.)." Certainly, being complete in moral character would mean living a life without reproach, wouldn't you say?

I love prophecy. Let's look at some prophecy that shows that we can be as pure as Christ is. First, Isaiah 1:18 says, "Come now, and let us reason together, saith the LORD: though your sins be as scarlet, they shall be as white as snow; though they be red like crimson, they shall be as wool." Then, in Revelation 1:14, we get to share John's vision of Christ as He was when the Gospel Day, or Gospel Dispensation, was launched. Let's look: "His head and his hairs were white like wool, as white as snow." Jesus is pictured, here, as having hair like wool, as white as snow. Revelation is a symbolic book (more on symbols later), and this "white as snow" hair symbolizes Christ's purity. Jesus' purity was "like wool, as white as snow," and Isaiah said we would be made "as wool" and "as white as snow." *As Jesus is, so are we in this world!* And that's not just my idea. The Apostle John used those very words in 1 John 4:17: "Herein is our love made perfect, that we may have boldness in the day of judgment: because as he is, so are we in this world."

God's very nature is holiness. I doubt if anyone who seriously thinks about being a Christian would argue against that. But, just in case, let us look at some Scriptures that bear it out:

Psalm 145:17 The LORD is righteous in all his ways, and holy in all his works.

Exodus 15:11 Who is like unto thee, O LORD, among the gods? who is like thee, glorious in holiness, fearful in praises, doing wonders?

Psalm 99:9 Exalt the LORD our God, and worship at his holy hill; for the LORD our God is holy.

Psalm 92:15 To shew that the LORD is upright: he is my rock, and there is no unrighteousness in him.

Romans 9:14 What shall we say then? Is there unrighteousness with God? God forbid.

These verses do not imply that God just does holy things; they say He *is* holy. That is His nature. Now look with me at 2 Peter 1:3-4:

3 According as his divine power hath given unto us all things that pertain unto life and godliness, through the knowledge of him that hath called us to glory and virtue:

4 Whereby are given unto us exceeding great and precious promises: that by these ye might be partakers of the divine nature, having escaped the corruption that is in the world through lust.

This is so *clear*. If we partake of God's divine nature, we partake of His holiness. This is borne out by what the verse goes on to say: that those who partake of God's nature *have escaped the corruption that is in the world through lust*. Yes, the world is corrupt. Yes, its corruption is all around us. We are surrounded by it. Corruption is in this world through lust that conceives to bring forth sin, but again Romans 6:12 says, "Let not sin therefore reign in your mortal body, that ye should obey it in the lusts thereof." Surely, if we are not obeying the lusts of our mortal bodies, we are not sinning, and just as surely, we do not *have* to obey the lusts of our mortal bodies. Let me point out again that this is talking about our *mortal* bodies, while we are still *in the world*, and Peter said that *we have escaped* the world's corruption. I ask you, how much clearer can this be? This is the experience of all true believers in the Bible Jesus! Dear one, do *you* have it?

Look at *how* we escape the world's corruption: "According as his divine power hath given unto us all things that pertain unto life and godliness, through the knowledge of him that hath called us to glory and virtue." *His divine power* gives to us all things that pertain to living godly. Verse 10 adds that if we follow Peter's directions, given in verses 5-8, *we shall never fall!* Away with this evil doctrine that defies the perfectly clear principles of God's holy Word! When these unholy professors of religion cry that this world is so corrupt that no one can live in it without sinning, they are calling God a liar. No, friend. What *they* are saying is the lie.

In 1 Corinthians 6:20 Paul said, "For ye are bought with a price: therefore glorify God in your body, and in your spirit, which are God's." Modern "Christianity" readily agrees that we are to glorify God in our spirits, but Paul said to glorify Him in our bodies *and* our spirits. And Paul went even further in 1 Corinthians 10:31, which says, "Whether therefore ye eat, or drink, or whatsoever ye do, do all to the glory of God." How, may I ask, can we glorify God by disregarding His Word? Paul, who made this statement, also said, in Romans 3:23, "For all have sinned, and come short of the glory of God." Sin, friend, comes short of glorifying God, and we are to do all we do to His glory. Everything the Bible says about sin tells us it is against God and God is against it. I challenge you to find a Scripture that does not show this about sin. Sin shackles and destroys every soul that comes to the age of understanding. And breaking its power cost the precious blood of Jesus. There is no way sinning is compatible with glorifying God. Since we can do *everything we do* to the glory of God, and are commanded to do exactly that, it is certain that we are able to live lives of complete victory over sin and Satan through our Lord Jesus Christ.

Do you, or does your preacher, cry, "We do glorify God by sinning, once we are under grace, because our sinning makes His grace abound, shows His great love, and exalts His precious blood"? Friend, that is a false concept of God's grace, of His love, and of the merits of His blood. His grace gives power to live without sin; His blood cleanses the *deepest* stain and *all* stains; and His love provided all of this for mankind. It is that true redemption from sin and a subsequent holy life that glorify God. If you will read this entire book in honesty and readiness to receive what the Bible truly teaches, you will see that this is true.

Let's take these words of Peter apart, so we can really lay hold of what is in them:

"According as his divine power"—this has nothing to do with our strength, or lack of it. This salvation, *Bible* salvation, is entirely by and through God's divine and unlimited power, friend.

"hath given unto us"—we do not earn it, and we do not deserve it. It is *grace*, unmerited favor.

"all things that pertain unto life and godliness"—we are given absolutely everything we need for living the saved life, a godly life. Not one thing is lacking.

"through the knowledge of him"—all we need, for living righteous, holy lives, is to *know Him*. But we cannot know Him and *not* have godliness.

"that hath called us to glory and virtue"—it is God Who calls us to this experience; we cannot attain to it in ourselves.

"*Whereby are given unto us*"—again, this experience is given to us, not produced by us.

"*exceeding great and precious promises*"—complete deliverance from sin's power, as well as its penalty, is indeed great and precious. Look at how weak and ineffective modern Christendom's promises are, in comparison. All it offers is release from the eternal *results* of our sins, while we are still bound by, and ever struggling against, those sins! And it is altogether a self-centered offer, friend, catering to man's flesh and not to God's glory. It shows no regard whatsoever for the Savior Who bore God's wrath against sin, so we wouldn't have to. The Hebrew writer talked about crucifying Christ *afresh* (Hebrews 6:6), and that is what "believers" do by continually sinning! Finally, by these vain promises of false Christianity, we are only "delivered" to revel in our own way and our own lusts, yet cannot be punished for them. What nonsense! There is no way! That is not what God provided, through His Son. Thank God, His great promises *exceed* Christendom's flesh-centered "benefits"!

"*that by these ye might be partakers of the divine nature*"—here is the truth about what God's precious promises bring to us. The world may be altogether corrupt, it is true, but we walk on a plane above the world; we are partakers of the divine! We have His nature, not the unregenerate nature of this world; therefore, we aren't subject to sin's power!

"*having escaped the corruption that is in the world through lust*"—there you have it. We *have* escaped this world's corruption. Not just the results, or the penalty, of the world's corruption, friend, but the corruption itself, that comes through the lusts of the flesh. These are undeniable, and irrefutable, biblical facts, and no matter how much modern "Christianity" howls against them, they are forever settled in Heaven (Psalm 119:89)!

Do you know someone who is on a sports team? A son or daughter, a brother or sister—or maybe you play, yourself. What would you think if the coach sent the team out to play, saying, "Now, guys, *try* to win"? You'd probably think, "Well, coach, they won't, with that mentality." And that's true. Coaches tell their players very emphatically, "Go out there and *win!*" They do not allow a mentality of defeat, or even one of "trying." If that mind set gets among the players, the coach goes right after it. Why? Because *trying* does not produce *winning*. And, worse, what if the coach said, "Go out there and try to win, team, but you know, of course, that you can't." Wow! Everyone would want that coach fired. Yet pastors all over our world, today, tell their flocks to *try* to obey God, all the while insisting that they really can't do it consistently. Once more, let me say it: *what an exercise in futility!* What a bunch of losers such "coaches" are. The sad thing is that they are producing losers on their "teams" as well—people who will lose their souls for eternity!

Romans 12:21 tells us, "Be not overcome of evil, but overcome evil with good." Again, this is very simple and very clear. But notice how modern Christendom perverts this verse. They twist it to say, "You can't help but be overcome of evil sometimes. It's so powerful and so everywhere. Try to overcome it all you can, but as long as your good outweighs the wrong you do, you're still overcoming evil with good." Friend, did you read that in this verse? Paul did *not* say that. He did not allow for "sometimes" in either part of this equation. Paul said "Be not overcome of evil," period, and "but overcome evil with good," period. If you, as a believer, are overcome by evil *at any time*, you are not *overcoming it* at that time; therefore, you are breaking this New Testament commandment. Conversely, if you fail to overcome evil with good *at any time*, you are being *overcome by evil* at that time; therefore, you are not obeying this unmistakable precept of God. These are eternal *principles*, dear one, that govern the Kingdom of God. We cannot violate them at will and be a part of that Kingdom. No matter how horrid, ugly, and wicked, this world around us is, we *don't* have to be overcome by it. Instead, we can overcome.

Saying it's all right to be overcome sometimes, as long as we, ourselves, overcome sometimes, is another example of how the religious world sets its "wisdom" up against God's and makes God's Word of none effect through their traditions. And you cannot deny that this is what the masses in Christendom are saying. This brings you, dear one, to a crossroads. You must choose to believe either the Word of God or the cry of modern, so-called Christian leaders. And whom you choose to believe will determine your soul's eternal destiny. Partial obedience is disobedience!

Second Peter 2:19 says, "While they promise them liberty, they themselves are the servants of corruption: for of whom a man is overcome, of the same is he brought in bondage." Peter is specifically speaking here, with this *they*, of false teachers (see verse 1). False teachers promise "believers" liberty, all the while being, themselves, in bondage. If you were a slave, would you put much stake in the words of another slave who told you how easy it is to escape? If he knew that secret, why hadn't he already followed it? Well, please don't take the word of today's false teachers who promise *you* liberty while, all the time, they are themselves in bondage.

Let's look closely at their promise: they say you can have liberty from the *consequences* of sin, all the while insisting that no one can steadfastly overcome sin itself. They say Christians cannot help but be overcome by the sin that is all around them. How they have fallen from the simple message of the first Christians! Paul said not to be overcome of evil, while today's ministers say no one can help but be. Paul said for us to overcome evil with good, but modern Christendom says evil is too dominant; we cannot consistently overcome it. Peter said, however, that everyone, leader and layperson alike, that is overcome of evil, is brought into bondage to it. Sadly, that is the state of "Christianity" as a whole, in our day. This modern ministry doesn't call it bondage. Hey, they call it *normal!* They call these "believers" *delivered!* My friend, bondage to sin, having to be overcome by it, *is not* what Jesus Christ came to this world to bring. He shows the deliverance He brings in His conversation with the Jews in John 8:31-36:

31 Then said Jesus to those Jews which believed on him, If ye continue in my word, then are ye my disciples indeed;

32 And ye shall know the truth, and the truth shall make you free.

33 [This offended the Jews, and] *They answered him, We be Abraham's seed, and were never in bondage to any man: how sayest thou, Ye shall be made free?* [How blind they were! Right then, they were in bondage to the Roman Empire.]

34 Jesus answered them, Verily, verily, I say unto you, Whosoever committeth sin is the servant of sin.

35 And the servant abideth not in the house for ever: but the Son abideth ever.

36 If the son therefore shall make you free, ye shall be free indeed.

Here Jesus very plainly stated that whosoever commits sin is the servant of sin, just as Peter said, "Of whom a man is overcome, of the same is he brought in bondage." Both Jesus and Peter declared that those who are overcome by sin, those who commit sin, become sin's servants (just as Paul declared, remember, in Romans 6:16).

I repeat, bondage is not what Jesus came to bring. His own words, just quoted, make this crystal clear: "If the son therefore shall make you free, ye shall be free indeed." Free from what? Well, the Jews said, "What do you mean, free? We're no one's servants." The Lord replied, "Whoever commits sin is sin's servant." He was speaking specifically about sin here. He was speaking about being servants to sin and being set free from that servitude. And He was quite clear about how we are set free—through Him: if I set you free, you shall be *free indeed!* When religious leaders promise people liberty from the consequences of sin but not from sin, itself, they are false prophets, friend. They are not preaching the Gospel of the Bible Jesus. They are not furthering God's cause, but Satan's. Paul, Peter, and the Lord Jesus, Himself, all bore the same witness on overcoming sin or being overcome by it. Again, it's either/or, but not both. I don't know about you, but I will take their doctrine above that of today's sin-enslaved preachers and teachers. God's Word doesn't merely *advise* us to overcome evil, rather than being overcome by it; it *commands* us to. Nowhere does it say to just *try* to.

Partial Obedience is Disobedience

I promised you a deeper look into King Saul's partial obedience, as recorded in 1 Samuel, Chapter 15. In that Chapter, we see that God, through the prophet Samuel, told Saul to go and destroy the Amalekites. God was very specific about what He meant by "destroy them." Let's read verses 2-3:

2 Thus saith the LORD of hosts, I remember that which Amalek did to Israel, how he laid wait for him in the way, when he came up from Egypt.

3 Now go and smite Amalek, and utterly destroy all that they have, and spare them not; but slay both man and woman, infant and suckling, ox and sheep, camel and ass.

That is specific, is it not? But what did Saul do? Did he obey? Verse 13 tells us that the prophet came to Saul after the battle, and Saul said, "Blessed be thou of the LORD: I have performed the commandment of the LORD." Surely the king wouldn't lie to the prophet who anointed him, would he? Well, Samuel thought so. He answered, "What meaneth then this bleating of the sheep in mine ears, and the lowing of the oxen which I hear" (verse 14)?

Saul then began to make excuse. It was the people's fault; the people wanted to save the "best" of the livestock. And it was for the worship of God, after all. Friend, this isn't really so much different from so-called Christians today: "Well, yes, we fail to do *all* that God says to do, but it's because sin is so prevalent and human nature is so weak; after all, we obey God *most* of the time."

Look at the parallel between today's "Christians" and Saul. *"Everything that was vile and refuse, that they destroyed utterly"* (verse 9). In other words, he killed the "worst" and kept the "best." Today people destroy the "worst" sins but freely commit the "best" (lesser) ones. They stop committing the really bad stuff, but say they can't overcome the "lesser evils." But, just as God commanded Saul to destroy *all* the spoil, so He commands us to destroy all sin in our lives, through His power.

Saul claimed his action was justified because he intended to sacrifice the animals to the Lord God, but Samuel vetoed that when he told Saul the sacrifice of those animals would not be accepted. Why? Because of disobedience. God did not want the animals sacrificed to Him. He wanted them killed. And God gave no room for Saul to reason with His command and decide if it was really "necessary." Today, so-called Christian leaders "amend" God's laws here and there, in the name of "enlightenment," or "progress," or "tolerance," or "necessity," or "relevance," but it still won't work. God knows that the best way for us to grow and prosper is through His perfect will. After all, He knows everything, and He has already, and long ago, made His Word perfect for every situation and every era of time. It is really presumptuous, friend, for mere men to think they can improve on God's Plan. A preacher's job is not to filter God's message through the screen of "opinion"; it is his job to simply *preach* what God says in His Word. That is his whole duty!

Today's "Christians," like Saul, believe they can disobey a little here and a little there and still bring acceptable worship to God. But the Bible tells us differently. Samuel asked Saul, "Hath the LORD as great delight in burnt offerings and sacrifices, as in obeying the voice of the LORD? Behold, to obey is better than sacrifice, and to hearken than the fat of rams" (verse 22). In other words, obedience is more important than so-called "worship" and "service" without it. Indeed, worship without obedience is an insult to, and rejected by, God!

"*What?*! *Are you saying God is not accepting my weekly worship, and my doing service in the church, unless I'm perfectly obedient?*! Well, I'm repeating that, friend, but it is God's Word that says it. Isaiah 1:11-15 emphasizes this:

11 To what purpose is the multitude of your sacrifices unto me? saith the LORD: I am full of the burnt offerings of rams, and the fat of fed beasts; and I delight not in the blood of bullocks, or of lambs, or of he goats.

12 When ye come to appear before me, who hath required this at your hand, to tread my courts?

13 Bring no more vain oblations [their sacrifices were vain]*; incense is an abomination unto me; the new moons and the sabbaths, the calling of assemblies, I cannot away with; it is iniquity, even the solemn meeting.*

14 Your new moons and your appointed feasts my soul hateth: they are a trouble unto me; I am weary to bear them.

15 And when ye spread forth your hands, I will hide mine eyes from you: yea, when ye make many prayers, I will not hear: your hands are full of blood.

Even under the Old Testament, there was a sharp difference between willful, nonchalant, disobedience (that, by choice, disregarded God's will) and unintended disobedience due to lack of inner power to obey, which was covered by the animal sacrifices offered *in faith*. In Isaiah's day, Israel as a whole was living in willful disobedience to God, yet they were going right on with their sacrifices and offerings, their feasts and assemblies. God said He *hated* such worship and would *not* accept such sacrifices! Christendom, today, is full and running over with worship that God hates, because it is offered by disobedient hearts. This is what makes modern, so-called "Christianity" such a stench in God's nostrils. And they are not saving souls; they are destroying them.

When Saul told the prophet, after he disobeyed, that he just meant to do service to God with the animals he spared, Samuel sternly rebuked such nonsense. First of all, it is highly questionable that sacrifice was his sole reason for sparing the best of the animals. But, all the same, Samuel let him know very quickly that such worship is sacrilege. He added, in verse 23, "For rebellion is as the sin of witchcraft, and stubbornness is as iniquity and idolatry. Because thou hast rejected the word of the

LORD, he hath also rejected thee from being king." Saul reaped what he sowed. He rejected God's Word, and God rejected him.

People may go to church regularly, they may participate in the services, they may even hold offices in the church, but if they are not living according to all God has revealed to them as His will, God will not accept it. If they are only partially obeying what they know is right, their worship is just as vain as Saul's and old Israel's was. You see, we are now living under the Gospel, which Paul said is the *power of God unto salvation* (Romans 1:16). Today Christians *can* obey everything God has commanded. But, because people are taught that they have to sin now and then, millions of professed Christians do so without much alarm—if any. Since sinning is business as usual for "Christians," indifference sets in, and these poor souls go along in yet another exercise in futility. How sad—for mankind and for God!

Every year, at Lenten season, priests, preachers, and teachers, instruct their people to give up something for Christ. These people believe that if they sacrifice some favorite thing, or "give up" a bad habit, for the duration of Lent, they will be honoring God and earning His favor. They feel they've really done something if they can hold out without smoking or drinking, etc., for the entire time. Friend, the texts I have just studied with you show how foolish this is. If you do not obey God's will all year long, your Lenten "sacrifice" will not even be accepted, let alone, blessed. *Remember that obedience is better than sacrifice, and without obedience, sacrifice is unacceptable and vain.*

Verses 23 and 26 are where Samuel said that Saul's failure to *fully* obey God's command amounted to *rejecting* the Word of the Lord, and it resulted in God's *rejecting Saul*. But look a little deeper, friend; this matter is very serious: Saul's "partial" disobedience was not partial rejection of God's Word. Samuel said, "Thou hast rejected the word of the LORD." When we disobey any part of God's Word, we are rejecting it, and when we reject any part of it, we actually reject all of it. Friend, *we do*! You may say, "Well, *I'm* not rejecting all of it. I only failed in one little area . . ." That is what Saul thought. He only spared a *little*; he destroyed *almost all*; and he very clearly said, "I've kept the commandment of the Lord." But the prophet expressed what *God* thought about the matter, and God's judgments are true and righteous altogether (Psalm 19:9). God said Saul's partial obedience was disobedience, and his rejection of that one command was rejection of the whole Word of God. Dear reader, this is *God's judgment* on partial obedience! When your preacher tells you that you are accepted of God even though you disobey sometimes, the devil, through him, is lying to you! Your partial obedience will result in *your* being rejected by God. God is a "package deal," not a "pick and choose" one. It's all or nothing! His power, His grace, provides for perfect obedience.

Remember what it says in James 2:10: "For whosoever shall keep the whole law, and yet offend in one point, he is guilty of all." Please, I implore you, *think* about those words. If you obey *lots* of things in God's Word, yet fail to obey *all* of it, you may as well not obey anything, as far as being accepted of God is concerned. Friend, these *words of God* strike a death blow to the idea that Christians can get by with sinning more or less from day to day.

One parting thought needs to be mentioned before we move on. In 1 Samuel 15:23, Samuel called Saul's partial obedience *rebellion*. Verse 9 says he and the people "would not utterly destroy" everything. It wasn't that they could not obey; they *would* not do it. Friend, the same is certainly true in this Gospel Dispensation. It is not that we cannot obey everything God wants us to do. We have piled Scripture upon Scripture proving that we can. Many who would love to are told they cannot, but many more love their sins and are *tickled* to have Christendom tell them they can get by on partial obedience. But partial obedience is still disobedience, and it is rebellion in God's sight. Take this away with you: with his "almost all" obedience, Saul would have been considered a welcome member and a valuable asset in most modern "churches"—but God would have no part of him. Please understand that if you are like Saul, though you may be regarded as a wonderful Christian, God will have no part of you, as well.

To those of you who really desire to serve God, yet are left in your sins because of "doctrines of devils" (1 Timothy 4:1), to you who are actually kept from finding Bible deliverance—or robbed of it, if you did reach through the deception and find it, I reach out in yearning and heartfelt compassion with the truth. It is my sincere hope that I can help you find true deliverance!

CHAPTER SIX

Where Did the Devil Come From?

Isaiah 14:12 How art thou fallen from heaven, O Lucifer, son of the morning! How are thou cut down to the ground, which didst weaken the nations!

13 For thou hast said in thine heart, I will ascend into heaven, I will exalt my throne above the stars of God: I will sit also upon the mount of the congregation, in the sides of the north:

14 I will ascend above the heights of the clouds; I will be like the most High.

15 Yet thou shalt be brought down to hell, to the sides of the pit.

To many, this is the ultimate description of where the devil came from. He was an angel in Heaven. Some even claim he was Heaven's choir director, though I have never found one Scripture to back that up in over a half-century of Bible study. But, anyway, he got the big head and began to exalt himself, and it got so bad that he conspired to form an army and tried to take Heaven over. God's side won, however, and Lucifer was cast out of Heaven.

Probably this is what you believe, friend, for almost all of Christendom teaches it—but nothing could be further from the truth. The devil never was in Heaven. *Wait!* Please don't close the book. I assure you that I can prove what I just said by the pure Word of God. Hear me out, I pray you. After all, truth can stand investigation. It's only falsehood that runs from the light. If the teaching about the devil having been an angel is true, it can't hurt it to examine it by the Word of God, and believe me, that is what I am going to use to examine it. I won't be quoting what "so-and-so" says or what "so-and-so" believes; I will be using the Bible—what God, *Himself,* says.

To get understanding on this matter, it is first necessary to consider that there are at least three heavens mentioned in the Bible. As we look at these, I want to say that I am not trying to set forth their *order* here—which is first, second, etc.—but simply their existence. The first heaven we'll look at is mentioned in the following verses (among others):

Ecclesiastes 5:2 Be not rash with thy mouth, and let not thine heart be hasty to utter any thing before God: for God is in heaven, and thou upon earth: therefore let thy words be few.

Lamentations 3:49 Mine eye trickleth down, and ceaseth not, without any intermission,

50 Till the LORD look down, and behold from heaven.

Daniel 2:28 But there is a God in heaven that revealeth secrets.

1 Peter 1:3 Blessed be the God and Father of our Lord Jesus Christ, which . . . hath begotten us again . . .

4 To an inheritance incorruptible, and undefiled, and that fadeth not away, reserved in heaven for you.

1 Peter 3:22 Who is gone into heaven, and is on the right hand of God; angels and authorities and powers being made subject unto him.

This Heaven is the eternal Heaven where God dwells—the one we all hope to inhabit someday. The second heaven we'll consider is mentioned in the first verse of the Bible, Genesis 1:1: "In the beginning God created the heaven and the earth." Now look at verses 14-18 and verse 20:

14 And God said, Let there be lights in the firmament of the heaven to divide the day from the night; and let them be for signs, and for seasons, and for days, and years:

15 And let them be for lights in the firmament of the heaven to give light upon the earth: and it was so.

16 And God made two great lights; the greater light to rule the day, and the lesser light to rule the night: he made the stars also.

17 And God set them in the firmament of the heaven to give light upon the earth,

18 And to rule over the day and over the night, and to divide the light from the darkness: and God saw that it was good.

20 And God said, Let the waters bring forth abundantly the moving creature that hath life, and fowl that may fly above the earth in the open firmament of heaven.

This heaven is mentioned in many other Scriptures as well. Here are a few more:

Isaiah 13:10 For the stars of heaven and the constellations thereof shall not give their light.

Ezekiel 32:8 All the bright lights of heaven will I make dark over thee.

Joshua 10:13b So the sun stood still in the midst of heaven, and hasted not to go down about a whole day.

So, we see that this heaven is the firmamental heaven where the sun, moon, and stars, reside, and where the fowls of the air soar. What, then, is the other heaven mentioned in the Word of God? Paul told us about it in Ephesians 2:4-6:

4 But God, who is rich in mercy, for his great love wherewith he loved us,

5 Even when we were dead in sins, hath quickened us together with Christ, (by grace ye are saved;)

6 And hath raised us up together, and made us sit together in heavenly places in Christ Jesus.

Paul used the same expression in Ephesians 1:3: "Blessed be the God and Father of our Lord Jesus Christ, who hath blessed us with all spiritual blessings in heavenly places in Christ." This is a *spiritual* heaven, a place where spiritual blessings are enjoyed, Paul said. One songwriter penned that wherever Jesus is, it is Heaven there. The Greek word translated *heavenly* in these verses is ***epouranios*** (ep-oo-ran'-ee-os), which means "*above* the sky:—celestial."[1] Even though "above the sky" (above the firmamental heaven) would seem to describe God's dwelling place, Paul definitely used it, here, to refer to the experience we find when we are raised up together with Christ through salvation. Notice that Paul used this expression in *past tense*: "And *hath* [or has] raised us up," so he was not referring to the next world. On the other hand, if you think this spiritual heaven is not, in fact, a real heaven, look at Ephesians 1:20: "Which he wrought in Christ, when he raised him from the dead, and set him at his own right hand in the heavenly places." This verse is certainly talking about the Heaven where God dwells, but Paul used the same Greek word—*epouranios*—to describe both.[2] It's not just an expression. This blissful state salvation puts one into is a real heaven.

Jesus said in Matthew 24:24, "For there shall arise false Christs, and false prophets, and shall shew great signs and wonders; insomuch that, if it were possible, they shall deceive the very elect."

What does this tell us? It lets us know that while Christ and His ministry are bringing men and women into this wonderful heavenly experience with God, there are also those who try to mislead people and give them a *counterfeit* bliss. And it indicates that all but the very elect will fall prey to these pretenders. Because of this, we also find a spiritual heaven that is not the one Christ lifts us to. Some people who think they have been lifted up to heavenly places in Christ are, in fact, deceived, and dwell in a false heaven with a false Christ. It is, indeed, a spiritual realm, but it is not of God's Spirit. Do not be surprised that this false "heaven" exists. Most people recognize that there are two sides to the spiritual realm. For example, a person can be filled with the Spirit of God, or, alas, filled with demons, as was Legion (Mark 5:2-9). While true Christians worship the Lord Almighty, many in the world today worship devils. Witches, Satanists, and so on, do so openly, but many who are called Christians do so unawares. Friend, the evil side of the spiritual realm is very real, but thank God, we are safe from it as long as we walk close to Him.

In dealing with this spiritual realm, the Bible refers to both the holy, godly side and the demonic side by such terms as *heaven, heavenly, high places*, etc. Ephesians 6:12 mentions the demonic side: "For we wrestle not against flesh and blood, but against principalities, against powers, against the rulers of the darkness of this world, against spiritual wickedness in high places." These words can indeed make one shudder, but thank God, Paul tells us in this same text that we can "stand against the wiles of the devil" (verse 11), "withstand" (verse 13), and "quench all the fiery darts of the wicked" (verse 16), by putting on the whole armor of God (verse 13).

These words of Paul clearly set before us that there is a highly exalted, spiritual, yet evil, realm, and that the children of God are engaged in battle with it. The Book of Revelation refers to both sides of this realm, I repeat, as "heaven." We sometimes call it an "ecclesiastical heaven" because of how it encompasses the entire realm of religion, both true and false, where something, or someone, takes an exalted position in the hearts and minds of men and is worshipped. So, in summary, we can see that (1) God lifts His followers up to *heavenly places* in Christ Jesus, and (2) rulers of darkness ensnare souls in spiritual wickedness in *high places*. We'll be examining this ecclesiastical heaven throughout this chapter.

We will also find, in this chapter, that the Bible uses the term *heaven* to refer to anyone who exalts himself above God. And that is exactly what people do when they fight God's truth and elevate their own position or theory above His. More on this later, but this ecclesiastical heaven is the one John watched a war being fought in and the devil being thrown out of, symbolically, in the 12th Chapter of Revelation. This was done by the power of the pure Gospel of Christ.

Understanding these three heavens enables us to correctly interpret the Scriptures that are wrongly used to support Satan's having been an angel in God's abode. Let's go back, now, and see what was actually being taught in Isaiah 14:12: "How art thou fallen from heaven, O Lucifer, son of the morning!" Who is Lucifer? Does *Lucifer* mean "devil," or anything devil-like? If you would ask the average child, growing up in a nominal Christian home, what *Lucifer* means, no doubt he would say, "The devil." But, no, *Lucifer* means "day star." It means something bright and beautiful and splendid. "Well," someone may say, "that describes what the devil was before he got thrown out of Heaven?" Again, no. The devil was never an angel and never in *that* Heaven. Look once again at what Isaiah 14:13-14 says of Lucifer:

13 For thou hast said in thine heart, I will ascend into heaven, I will exalt my throne above the stars of God . . .

14 I will ascend above the heights of the clouds; I will be like the most High.

Even if this did refer to God's own Heaven, Lucifer distinctly said, in exalting himself, that he would *ascend into* heaven. That would mean he was not there at the time he exalted himself. Please allow me to say that again: he was not inside of God's Heaven when he exalted himself; his boast was that he would *ascend into* it. But, friend, no one—man, angel, or devil—can ascend into the Heaven of God's abode through pride and arrogance. God would not have needed to "kick Lucifer out"; He would never have allowed him in!

What, then, was Isaiah talking about? Read again what Lucifer said: "I will ascend into heaven, I will exalt my throne above the stars of God." These are the words of someone who got puffed up in himself, to be sure, but it wasn't Satan. If it does not refer to Satan, then whom does it refer to? We can find out by reading the context. Read the 4th verse; there God told Isaiah that, after He delivered Israel from Babylonian captivity (verse 3), Israel would "take up this proverb against *the king of Babylon.*" What Isaiah was saying in "this proverb" is referring to the Babylonian king, Nebuchadnezzar. Remember what verse 13 says: "I will exalt *my throne* [emphasis added]." No angel ever had a throne to exalt. Angels are "ministering spirits, sent forth to minister for them who shall be heirs of salvation" (Hebrews 1:14). What does *minister* mean? "To serve . . . to give help (to)."³ Servants do not have thrones; kings do. King Nebuchadnezzar had a throne. Someone may say that Lucifer meant the throne of God which he would hopefully gain when he defeated Him. No, friend. This Lucifer said he would *exalt* his throne, not that he would *have* a throne *after* he exalted himself. What the Bible *simply* says is *so* important!

We will read about Nebuchadnezzar's self-exaltation, and how God brought him down, in the book of Daniel, but before we leave Isaiah 14, let's consider verses 16 and 17, which say this of Lucifer:

16 They that see thee shall narrowly look upon thee, and consider thee, saying, Is this the man that made the earth to tremble, that did shake kingdoms;

17 That made the world as a wilderness, and destroyed the cities thereof; that opened not the house of his prisoners?

Is this *the man?* Satan is not now, nor was he ever, a man. The same is true for the heavenly angels. Furthermore, what kingdoms *on earth* did "Lucifer" shake? What cities *of the world* did he destroy? Satan was a devil when he approached Eve in the Garden of Eden, and there were no kingdoms or cities on the earth at that time. Nebuchadnezzar, however, ruled the mighty Babylonian Empire, which had conquered several cities and kingdoms. *He* had prisoners; the Israelites were his prisoners. But what prisoners would a celestial angel have? Are any prisoners kept in God's Heaven?

In a few minutes we'll study *the man* Nebuchadnezzar, but let us first consider Israel's *taking up this proverb against the king of Babylon.* In order to correctly interpret Scripture, I repeat, we must keep it in its context. All of the 13th Chapter of Isaiah, and verses 1-28 of the 14th Chapter, concern Babylon. Chapter 13:1 reads, "The burden of Babylon, which Isaiah the son of Amoz did see." Then, in verse 19, we find, "And Babylon, the glory of kingdoms, the beauty of the Chaldees' excellency, shall be as when God overthrew Sodom and Gomorrah." Hmm. That sounds a lot like what happened to Lucifer, right? Right! Chapter 14, verse 4, as we already noted, says, "That thou shalt take up this proverb against the king of Babylon." Verse 22 of the 14th Chapter says, "For I will rise up against them, saith the LORD of hosts, and cut off from Babylon the name, and remnant, and son, and nephew, saith the LORD." Then, in verse 28, the prophet wrapped up his vision for Babylon with these words: "In the year that king Ahaz died was this burden."

Notice how this prophecy against Babylon (13:1 through 14:28) started and ended with reference to "the [or this] burden." Beyond dispute, this entire text deals with Babylon, which conquered Jerusalem and carried God's people into captivity. This was a prophecy sent to comfort God's people by letting them know that the mighty Babylonian Empire would be overthrown and they would be able to go back to their homeland. In 13:17, God said, "Behold, I will stir up the Medes against them." History will tell you that it was the Medes that conquered Babylon. Verse 12 of Chapter 14 refers to the king of Babylon, not Satan, just as verse 4 states. And please notice that "Lucifer's fall from heaven" was described at least two other times, but in different words, in this prophecy. We already read of them above, in Isaiah 13:19 and in Isaiah 14:22. I won't quote them again, here, but go back and reread them. All right, now let us study Nebuchadnezzar, and you will see what Isaiah was talking about.

In the 3rd Chapter of Daniel, we read where Nebuchadnezzar built an image, an idol, and demanded that everyone bow down and worship it. But three Israelite captives, Shadrach, Meshach, and Abednego, refused to bow and worship, and they got thrown into a fiery furnace. Most of you know the story. King Nebuchadnezzar watched in fury until he saw that there were four men in the fire. That startled him. And that old, heathen king had enough perception to see that One of them wasn't a man after all. He said, "the form of the fourth is like the Son of God" (verse 25). Now look at verses 28-29:

28 Then Nebuchadnezzar spake, and said, Blessed be the God of Shadrach, Meshach, and Abednego, who hath sent his angel, and delivered his servants that trusted in him, and have changed the king's word, and yielded their bodies that they might not serve nor worship any god, except their own God.

29 Therefore I make a decree, That every people, nation, and language, which speak any thing amiss against the God of Shadrach, Meshach, and

Abednego, shall be cut in pieces, and their houses shall be made a dunghill: because there is no other God that can deliver after this sort.

Nebuchadnezzar got a picture of Who and What God was through the faithfulness of His servants. It's too bad, but the story doesn't end there. In Chapter 4 we read about Nebuchadnezzar having a dream, and how God gave Daniel the interpretation of the dream for him. Daniel said, "My lord, the dream be to them that hate thee, and the interpretation thereof to thine enemies" (verse 19c). Why? Well, Nebuchadnezzar was about to "fall from heaven."

In his dream, Nebuchadnezzar saw a great tree. Verse 11 of Chapter 4 says, "The tree grew, and was strong, and the height thereof reached unto heaven, and the sight thereof to the end of all the earth." Did you notice that the tree's height reached *unto heaven*, where Lucifer said he would exalt himself to? *Heaven*, in both these texts, is taken from Hebrew words—*shamayim* (shaw-mah'-yim) in Isaiah 14, and *shamayin* (shaw-mah'-yin) in Daniel 4—which both mean, "to *be lofty; the sky* (as *aloft* . . . perh[aps] alluding to the visible arch in which the clouds move, as well as to the higher ether where the celestial bodies revolve)."[4] Friend, the heaven Nebuchadnezzar's tree reached to was not God's eternal abode, and neither was the one Lucifer fell from!

Daniel went on to tell how the tree provided nurture for bird and beast: "In it was meat for all" (4:12). What interpretation did God, through Daniel, give Nebuchadnezzar for his dream? Verses 20-22 tell us:

20 The tree that thou sawest, which grew, and was strong, whose height reached unto the heaven, and the sight thereof to all the earth;

21 Whose leaves were fair, and the fruit thereof much, and in it was meat for all; under which the beasts of the field dwelt, and upon whose branches the fowls of the heaven had their habitation:

22 It is thou, O king, that art grown and become strong: for thy greatness is grown, and reacheth unto heaven [emphasis added], *and thy dominion to the end of the earth* [all of these "heavens" are taken from that same Hebrew word].

Daniel said, "Thy greatness is grown, and *reacheth unto heaven.*" This great tree was Nebuchadnezzar, but this rosy picture suddenly ended. Let's look at more of this dream, in verses 13-15:

13 . . . a watcher and an holy one came down from heaven;

14 He cried aloud, and said thus, Hew down the tree, and cut off his branches, shake off his leaves, and scatter his fruit . . .

15 Nevertheless leave the stump of his roots in the earth . . . .

Hew down the tree. Whew! That sounds bad. How did Daniel interpret that? Verses 23-26 tell us:

23 And whereas the king saw a watcher and an holy one coming down from heaven, and saying, Hew the tree down, and destroy it; yet leave the stump of the roots thereof in the earth . . . and let it be wet with the dew of heaven, and let his portion be with the beasts of the field, till seven times pass over him;

24 This is the interpretation, O king, and this is the decree of the most High, which is come upon my lord the king:

25 That they shall drive thee from men, and thy dwelling shall be with the beasts of the field, and they shall make thee to eat grass as oxen, and they shall wet thee with the dew of heaven, and seven times shall pass over thee, till thou know that the most High ruleth in the kingdom of men, and giveth it to whomsoever he will.

26 And whereas they commanded to leave the stump of the tree roots; thy kingdom shall be sure unto thee, after that thou shalt have known that the heavens do rule.

In the next verse Daniel gave Nebuchadnezzar some advice:

27 Wherefore, O king, let my counsel be acceptable unto thee, and break off thy sins by righteousness, and thine iniquities by shewing mercy to the poor; if it may be a lengthening of thy tranquility.

Get the picture here. Nebuchadnezzar was portrayed as a great tree that reached *unto heaven* but got hewn down to the ground, whose leaves and fruit were stripped away. All of his royal glory crumbled at his feet. He became as one of the beasts of the field. King Nebuchadnezzar actually lost his mind and roamed about as a wild beast, naked, and eating grass like a cow. What humiliation! Why? Because he exalted himself, and he failed to take Daniel's counsel. Look at verses 28-30:

28 All this came upon the king Nebuchadnezzar.

29 At the end of twelve months [a year had passed since Daniel urged him to 'break off his sins by righteousness'] *he walked in the palace of the kingdom of Babylon.*

30 The king spake, and said, Is not this great Babylon, that I have built for the house of the kingdom by the might of my power, and for the honour of my majesty?

What is this? After being given the dream by God as a warning, and after being counseled by Daniel to do right, King Nebuchadnezzar still exalted himself, boasting of what *he* had built by *his* might and for *his* glory.

31 While the word was in the king's mouth, there fell a voice from heaven, saying, O king Nebuchadnezzar, to thee it is spoken; The kingdom is departed from thee.

32 And they shall drive thee from men, and thy dwelling shall be with the beasts of the field: they shall make thee to eat grass as oxen, and seven times shall pass over thee, until thou know that the most High ruleth in the kingdom of men, and giveth it to whomsoever he will.

33 The same hour was the thing fulfilled upon Nebuchadnezzar: and he was driven from men, and did eat grass as oxen, and his body was wet with the dew of heaven, till his hairs were grown like eagles' feathers, and his nails like birds' claws.

"How art thou fallen from heaven, O Lucifer!" Again, at least twice, the Book of Daniel tells us that Nebuchadnezzar was pictured as being exalted to the heaven—the same heaven Lucifer fell from. I repeat, God told Isaiah that Israel would take up that "Lucifer" parable against *the king of Babylon.* Nebuchadnezzar was called "Lucifer" figuratively, simply because he considered himself to be as the day star, or the sun. He thought he was the brightest thing around.

Jesus said in Matthew 23:12, "And whosoever shall exalt himself shall be abased; and he that shall humble himself shall be exalted." To this Nebuchadnezzar agreed. God had mercy on the king, and restored his mind and his reign. And after God humbled him, thank God, he humbled himself. Verses 34-37 read:

34 And at the end of the days I Nebuchadnezzar lifted up mine eyes unto heaven, and mine understanding returned unto me, and I blessed the most High, and I praised and honoured him that liveth for ever, whose dominion is an everlasting dominion, and his kingdom is from generation to generation:

35 And all the inhabitants of the earth are reputed as nothing: and he doeth according to his will in the army of heaven, and among the inhabitants of the earth: and none can stay his hand, or say unto him, What doest thou?

36 At the same time my reason returned unto me; and for the glory of my kingdom, mine honour and brightness returned unto me; and my counsellors and my lords sought unto me; and I was established in my kingdom, and excellent majesty was added unto me.

37 Now I Nebuchadnezzar praise and extol and honour the King of heaven, all whose works are truth, and his ways judgment: and those that walk in pride he is able to abase.

Nebuchadnezzar admitted that he had been lifted up in pride, and that God had brought him down. That is all Isaiah 14:12, and its context, is portraying to us. Remember, Isaiah said his burden in Chapter 13 and most of 14 was concerning Babylon, and God told Isaiah that *this proverb* would be taken up against the *king of Babylon* in Isaiah 14:4.

By the way, Isaiah 14:12 is the only place "Lucifer" is mentioned in the entirety of the Bible. If you check any exhaustive concordance—one that has every word of the Bible in it—you will find this to be true. While Satan is spoken of many, many times in the Scriptures, Old Testament and New, not once was he ever referred to as Lucifer. He is called the wicked one, Beelzebub, the prince of this world, the Accuser, the devil, the prince of devils, the serpent, the tempter, the ruler of darkness, the god of this world, and the Adversary, among other things, but nowhere, at any time, was he called Lucifer. Jesus never called him Lucifer. The apostles and other N. T. writers never called him Lucifer. The Old Testament writers never called him Lucifer. Isn't it strange that, if Lucifer were the devil, no Bible writer ever called him by that name, not even once? The only ones who have called Satan by that name are ones who have made up Christendom *since* the days of the Apostles. God has revealed, however, that there is a great deal within and surrounding that verse to prove "Lucifer" *does not* refer to the devil. Friend, that's the simple reason no Bible writer ever called Satan that.

Someone may say, "Well, that's not the only place where the Bible says the devil fell from heaven." That is certainly true, but, like this text, the others do not teach that the literal devil was in, and then kicked out of, the literal Heaven where God dwells. They refer to that ecclesiastical heaven. Let's examine them too.

Luke 10:18 says, "And he said unto them, I beheld Satan as lightning fall from heaven." *Ah*, you may be thinking, *here Jesus, Himself, said Satan fell from Heaven, and that He saw it happen*! Yes, that's true. You are absolutely right. And this time, the reference is, indeed, to the devil. But it's not referring to the Heaven of God's abode. Again, to use this verse to support this false doctrine is to lift it entirely out of its setting and isolate it. We need to find out what Jesus was talking about, here, so let's do that.

First, however, let me say this: I have heard some preachers say that Jesus was talking, here, about lightning falling from heaven, not the devil. These preachers oppose the teaching that Satan was once an angel in God's Heaven, the same as I do. They, too, were trying to disprove that teaching. However, in all due respect to them, I don't believe their rendering of this verse is correct. I believe Jesus was, in fact, saying He saw Satan fall from heaven. If the verse were talking about lightning falling, it would have said, "as lightning *falls*," not, "as lightning *fall*." On the other hand, saying, "I beheld Satan *fall*" would have been, and was, grammatically correct.

The original Greek doesn't shed any light on this matter; it isn't any clearer about whether Jesus was referring to Satan or lightning. But let's read this text as if Jesus *had* been referring to lightning: "I beheld Satan as lightning *falls* from heaven."

Hmm, wait. That is an incomplete sentence. "As lightning falls from heaven" merely tells *how* Satan did whatever he did, but *what did he do*? Don't say "fall," because, according to my friends' interpretation, that is what the lightning did, not Satan. Let me say it again. While telling what the lightning did, there is nothing to describe what Jesus beheld Satan doing! So, as much as I respect those who say Jesus meant the lightning fell and not Satan, I cannot agree with them on this. While trying, honestly, to refute the false idea that the devil was once an angel in Heaven, they are inadvertently misinterpreting the Scriptures themselves. *When left in its context*, this Scripture does not teach that Satan was cast out of God's abode.

Rendering Jesus' statement in correct, and up-to-date, grammatical terms, on the other hand, would make it read, "I beheld Satan, as lightning, fall from heaven." This is exactly what Jesus did say, minus the commas. This sentence is complete and it makes sense. And, I repeat, it is grammatically correct. It is also what Jesus meant to say. But while Jesus here referred to the actual devil, and while He, in fact, referred to the devil's fall, he did not refer to His Father's heavenly abode in the term *heaven*.

Saying that Jesus was referring to lightning, rather than Satan, falling, is actually stretching the Scripture to make it support our doctrine. We should never try to mold the Word of God around our beliefs; we should align our beliefs with what the Word of God says. We do not, ever, have to stretch the Scriptures to support truth. Admitting that our Lord was, indeed, saying that He saw Satan fall from heaven, here, does not hurt truth at all. Why? Because when left in its context, we have plenty of support for the truth here, without stretching Scripture. Let's look at that context, then, and see what the subject in this whole exchange was.

Luke 10:1 says, "After these things the Lord appointed other seventy also, and sent them two and two before his face into every city and place, whither he himself would come." Then verse 17 tells us, "And the seventy returned again with joy, saying, Lord, even the devils are subject unto us through thy name." It was *then* that Jesus said, if you will allow me to paraphrase it, "I know, boys. I saw that old devil fall, as fast as lightning." When did Jesus see him fall? When the seventy disciples had mastery over him and cast him out of men and women's lives. When he lost his exalted position in the hearts of those people. The context shows that Jesus was *replying* to the disciples' ecstatic statement that the devils were subject to them. The reference is conspicuously to *that* fall of Satan, his fall from his control over people's lives—through Jesus' name. If you don't believe me, look at verses 18-20 together. Immediately after Jesus said He beheld Satan fall, He makes it clear that He was talking about His having given the seventy disciples the power to *cast Satan out of people*:

18 And he said unto them, I beheld Satan as lightning fall from heaven.

19 Behold, I give unto you power to tread on serpents and scorpions, and over all the power of the enemy . . . .

20 Notwithstanding in this rejoice not, that the spirits are subject unto you; *but rather rejoice, because your names are written in heaven.* (Emphasis added.)

Dear one, for Jesus to have referred to anything but Satan's fall from men and women's hearts, when that is what the disciples were telling him about, would have been entirely off subject. It would have been like putting the proverbial square peg into a round hole. For further emphasis, however, let's picture this incident according to "the devil in heaven" theory:

The disciples come running up to Jesus and exclaim, "Jesus, guess what? *Guess what?*! We were able to cast devils out through your name. They *obeyed* us! It was *marvelous!*"

Jesus says, "Well, *I* saw Satan cast out of *Heaven* once."

"Yes, but . . . we, we, uh . . . ."

The disciples' ecstatic joy takes a nosedive. It's as if Jesus is dismissing their victory, as if he is "stealing their thunder."

Not so, friend! Jesus was validating their triumph. He was telling them that He saw them prevail over Satan when they cast him out of men and women. He was *sharing* the joy and the fruits of their labor. After all, He had commissioned and sent them to do it. They were workers together with Him.

(By the way, I gave that little narrative in present tense: "The disciples *come* [not *came*]." "Jesus *says* [not *said*]." "The disciples' joy *takes* [not *took*]." Jesus "*is dismissing* [not *dismissed*]." I doubt that you even noticed; that's how common a practice it is.)

Did you catch something else in Jesus' words, there in Luke 10:19? It is vital that you do. What is it? Jesus told His disciples, "I give you power over all the power of the enemy." Dear one, think about these words. No matter how the sin-defenders in "Christianity" yell about how powerful sin and Satan are, and how we simply cannot overcome these all the time in everything, Jesus refuted such teaching with these few simple words. May I stress them again? Jesus gave His disciples power over all—that's *all*—the power of the enemy. And this power is still ours today. The commission to take the Gospel "into all the world" is still ongoing. And when we have power over *all* of Satan's power, friend, we have victory over sin all the time in everything we do. To say otherwise is to infer that Jesus lied to His disciples.

In case someone tries to argue that this promise was only for the original disciples, or only for the early days of the church, but not for us or our time, look again at John 17:15 & 20:

15 I pray not that thou shouldest take them out of the world, but that thou shouldest keep them from the evil.

20 Neither pray I for these alone, but for them also which shall believe on me through their word.

That's you and me, friend. Anyone who believes on Jesus today believes through the words of those original church leaders. Their words comprise the holy Scriptures of the New Testament!

"Well," you may say, "Jude and Peter talked about angels that *sinned* and *kept not their first estate*. It sounds as if they believed in fallen angels. So, if we're supposed to believe through their words, shouldn't we take their word for this as well?" Friend, they did, in fact, talk about angels that sinned and fell, and, certainly, we must believe their accounts, but let me say again that we cannot just lift Scriptures out of their settings to build doctrines on. Let us study what Peter and Jude were discussing. That will clear things up. But let me forewarn you: they were not teaching that the literal devil was in God's literal Heaven. They were not saying these "angels" that sinned had been in God's heavenly abode. Let's look and see.

Second Peter 2:4 says, "For if God spared not the angels that sinned, but cast them down to hell, and delivered them into chains of darkness, to be reserved unto judgment . . . ."

And Jude 6 says, "And the angels which kept not their first estate, but left their own habitation, he hath reserved in everlasting chains under darkness unto the judgment of the great day."

If we go back to that 10th Chapter of Luke, where Jesus sent those seventy disciples out, in verses 10-12 we will read:

10 But into whatsoever city ye enter, and they receive you not, go your ways out into the streets of the same, and say,

11 Even the very dust of your city, which cleaveth on us, we do wipe off against you: notwithstanding be ye sure of this, that the kingdom of God is come nigh unto you.

12 But I say unto you, that it shall be more tolerable in that day for Sodom, than for that city.

Then Jesus turned, as it were, and spoke, Himself, to some cities that had already not received Him; verses 13-15 read:

13 Woe unto thee, Chorazin! woe unto thee, Bethsaida! For if the mighty works had been done in Tyre and Sidon, which have been done in you, they had a great while ago repented, sitting in sackcloth and ashes.

14 But it shall be more tolerable for Tyre and Sidon at the judgment, than for you.

15 And thou, Capernaum, which art exalted to heaven, shalt be thrust down to hell [emphasis added].

In verse 15, Jesus used almost the same words that Peter used—cast, and thrust, down to hell—and He even said Capernaum *was exalted to heaven*. Read it again. It sounds a lot like what supposedly happened to

Peter's fallen angels. But Christ was certainly not talking about the city of Capernaum being thrown out of God's Heaven. His use of the word *heaven*, here, described people who were, for one thing, exalted in pride (as was Nebuchadnezzar), and for another, highly favored by God with great opportunity that they rejected. Their rejection cast them out of God's favor. Likewise, Peter and Jude were referring to *preachers* who had sinned and been cast out of God's favor.

You may argue, "Well, Isaiah may not have *said* Lucifer was the devil, but Peter and Jude *did* say 'angels that sinned.' Why can't you just accept this and not try to say they meant something else?" Friend, that is a very valid question, and you have every right to ask it. You will find that I do not get offended when challenged by honest questions. After all, I am myself a seeker after truth.

The best way I can answer this question is to let Peter and Jude explain it, themselves. You see, they tell us exactly what they were talking about. So, as I said, let's see what they were, in fact, discussing in these texts. Jude started out by saying that when he took up a pen to write his epistle, he had a real burden to urge them to earnestly contend for that faith which was once delivered to the saints (verse 3). Then, in verses 4-6, he told them why:

4 For there are certain men crept in unawares . . . ungodly men, turning the grace of our God into lasciviousness, and denying the only Lord God, and our Lord Jesus Christ.

5 I will therefore put you in remembrance, though ye once knew this, how that the Lord, having saved the people out of the land of Egypt, afterward destroyed them that believed not.

6 And the angels which kept not their first estate, but left their own habitation, he hath reserved in everlasting chains under darkness unto the judgment of the great day.

The subject, here, is "certain men [who] crept in unawares, ungodly men [who were] turning the grace of God into lasciviousness." Jude was reminding the saints of how that, although God delivered Israel out of Egypt, He later destroyed many of them because of unbelief. He then said that, *just so*, the fallen angels would be destroyed. What fallen angels? The ones he mentioned in Verse 4, fallen preachers. Read all the way through Jude's epistle and you will see that he never changed subjects. Therefore, to understand this truth, let's look at verses 11-13 and 16-18:

93

11 Woe unto them! For they have gone in the way of Cain, and ran greedily after the error of Balaam for reward, and perished in the gainsaying of Core.

12 These are spots in your feasts of charity, when they feast with you . . . clouds they are without water, carried about of winds; trees whose fruit withereth . . .

13 Raging waves of the sea . . . wandering stars . . . .

16 These are murmurers, complainers, walking after their own lusts . . . .

17 But, beloved, remember ye the words which were spoken before of the apostles of our Lord Jesus Christ;

18 How that they told you there should be mockers in the last time, who should walk after their own ungodly lusts.

I repeat, friend, all the way through his letter, Jude was speaking of the same thing; his core subject never changed: certain men who had crept in unawares and were turning the grace of God into wantonness. All of Jude's graphic descriptions were of these men, including the one where he said, "And the angels which kept not their first estate . . . he hath reserved . . . unto the judgment." Jude's burden was to keep the saints from being seduced by these men.

More on "angels" referring to preachers shortly, but now let's look at Peter's words: "For if God spared not the angels that sinned, but cast them down to hell, and delivered them into chains of darkness, to be reserved unto judgment;" . . . (2 Peter 2:4). What was Peter discussing in this text? We can find out in verses 1-3, leading right up to the verse above:

1 But there were false prophets also among the people, even as there shall be false teachers among you, who privily shall bring in damnable heresies, even denying the Lord that bought them, and bring upon themselves swift destruction.

2 And many shall follow their pernicious ways; by reason of whom the way of truth shall be evil spoken of.

3 And through covetousness shall they with feigned words make merchandise of you: whose judgment now of a long time lingereth not, and their damnation slumbereth not.

Next, in verses 4 through 9, Peter says, "if God spared not the angels that sinned . . . and spared not the old world—*but saved Noah* . . . and turned Sodom and Gomorrha into ashes—*but delivered Lot* . . . the

94

Lord knows how to deliver the godly, and to reserve the unjust unto the day of judgment." God has shown, Peter assured the saints, that He knows how to deliver His people, and punish the wicked, by the way He has done both in the past. In verse 10, he continues with his main subject, false teachers, and describes both them and the "reward of unrighteousness" they will receive (verse 13), throughout the rest of the Chapter.

In both of these texts, the writers were dealing with *apostates*, or fallen preachers, who were beginning to creep in, and their burden was to warn the saints to beware, lest they be moved from their own steadfastness. The term *angels* often refers to preachers in the Scriptures, as well as to celestial beings, so "fallen preachers" and "fallen angels" can refer to the exact same persons. To see that this is true, turn with me to Revelation 21:9-10:

9 And there came unto me one of the seven angels which had the seven vials full of the seven last plagues, and talked with me, saying, Come hither, I will shew thee the bride, the Lamb's wife.

10 And he carried me away in the spirit to a great and high mountain, and shewed me that great city, the holy Jerusalem, descending out of heaven from God.

John then described the city, but remember the vial angel carried him there and showed it to him. When Chapter 22:1 says, "And he shewed me . . . ." John was still speaking of this vial angel. Then, in 22:8-9, he said this:

8 And I John saw these things, and heard them. And when I had heard and seen, I fell down to worship before the feet of the angel which shewed me these things.

9 Then saith he to me, See thou do it not: for I am thy fellowservant, and of thy brethren the prophets, and of them which keep the sayings of this book: worship God.

This angel was not a celestial being. He was someone who *kept the Word of God*, he was one of John's *brethren*, a *prophet*, or a *preacher*. Angels of the celestial sort are messengers of God, and so are preachers. The Revelation is simply using an *angel*—one type of messenger—to portray a *preacher*—another type of messenger. Let's look at some more proof in Revelation 1:19-20 and 2:1:

1:19 Write the things which thou hast seen, and the things which are, and the things which shall be hereafter;

20 The mystery of the seven stars which thou sawest in my right hand, and the seven golden candlesticks. The seven stars are the angels of the seven churches: and the seven candlesticks which thou sawest are the seven churches.

2:1 Unto the angel of the church of Ephesus write . . . .

Jesus addressed the other six letters that He dictated to John, in Chapters 2 and 3, in the same way. What was He talking about when He told John to write to the angels of the seven churches? Read the seven letters. He was clearly addressing the conditions of each congregation to its *pastor*. Here, again, angels were symbols of preachers. Don't be surprised that Jesus was using symbolic language. He reveals, Himself, that He was speaking in symbols when He said that stars were angels and candlesticks were churches. I promised you a closer look at this matter of symbols in the book of Revelation, so let's look at Chapter 1 and verse 1, where John said that God *signified* the Revelation to him. What does that mean? The original Greek word for *signified* is **semaino** (say-mah'-ee-no), which means "to *indicate*"[5] according to *Strong's Greek Dictionary*. *Webster's* agrees, defining *signify* as "**1** to be an indication of; mean," then adding "**2** to make known, as by a sign, words, etc."[6] And it says a *sign* means "**1** something that indicates a fact, quality, etc.; token . . . **3** a mark or symbol having a specific meaning."[7] *Token*, then, is defined as "a sign, indication, symbol, etc."[8] So, to paraphrase John, God gave the Revelation to him in *symbols that indicate something else*.

There are keys to correctly interpreting the Revelation, and we'll look further into them in a later chapter, but one key is that every symbol therein is answered right within the Scriptures themselves. You don't need to go outside of the Bible to find what the symbols mean, and, in fact, you will only get off the track by trying to explain the Revelation by "outside" sources or events. So then, using only these Bible texts, let's see just what is meant by *angels*. *Strong's* says the original Greek word for *angel* in all of Revelation is **aggelos** (ang'-el-os), which means "(to *bring tidings*); a *messenger*; esp. an '*angel*'; by impl. a *pastor*."[9] So, an angel is a messenger, and the word, *by implication*, means a *pastor*. Remember that the Bible was not written in English. Since the original word's meaning indicated both an angel and a pastor, though *pastor* was implied, these Apostles' reference to *angels* may have been nothing more than the translators' choice of words. Either one was technically accurate.

If you will study 2 Peter, Chapter 2, and the book of Jude, side by side, verse by verse, you will find many similarities, and it will become clear that these writers were very concerned about, and very indignant with, false teachers who were, and would be, slipping in among the people of God and leading them astray. But, if you are still not sure I'm interpreting things correctly, consider this as well: if these angels spoken of by Peter and Jude had been celestial angels, why were they being reserved unto judgment? No Scripture that talks about the Judgment suggests that celestial angels—or devils, for that matter—are going to be judged. Such texts all refer to being judged according to "the deeds done in our bodies;" celestial angels and devils do not have bodies. They are spirits (Hebrews 1:7 and 14). Scriptural evidence denies any thought that either angels or devils will stand at God's Judgment Bar.

Let's look at some of the other things these brethren said about their "fallen angels." Jude said, "These are spots in your feasts of charity, when they feast with you" (verse 12). Certainly no renegade angels of the celestial sort ever feasted with the saints of Jude's day. In verse 13, Jude calls them wandering stars. Jesus already told us that stars represent angels, or preachers, so we see that these were *wandering* preachers, or apostates. Verse 16 says, "These are murmurers, complainers, walking after their own lusts; and their mouth speaketh great swelling words, having men's persons in admiration because of advantage." What does this reveal? That these were men, not heavenly angels. Celestial angels do not have lusts to walk after; lusts are a trait of the flesh. Furthermore, what advantage can men possibly give angels, that would cause them to "admire," or speak great, swelling words about, men?

Next, look at Verse 8, which reads, "Likewise also these filthy dreamers defile the flesh, despise dominion, and speak evil of dignities." He is still speaking of the same people, friend. Follow verse by verse and you will see that. So, then, how can angels defile the flesh, when they do not partake of flesh and blood? And, Verse 10 says, "But these speak evil of those things which they know not: but what they know naturally, as brute beasts, in those things they corrupt themselves." *What they know naturally, as brute beasts*—again, this is not referring to celestial angels, but men. The Apostle Paul said, in 1 Corinthians 15:32, that he had fought with beasts at Ephesus over the resurrection of the dead. He was not talking about four-legged beasts, but about two-legged beasts—men. Four-legged beasts know nothing about resurrections. Finally, in Verse 15, Jude described them as ungodly sinners.

Let us now look at Peter's descriptions of these "angels." In 2 Peter 2:1-3, Peter clearly was talking about false teachers. Verses 4 through 9 then refer to the past dealings of God in delivering the righteous while punishing the wicked, to encourage the saints. Verse 10 reverts back to the description of the "angels that sinned," or apostates, Peter's main topic. This continues to the end of the Chapter. What are some of the things Peter said about them?

Verse 11 says, "Whereas angels, which are greater in power and might, bring not railing accusation against them before the Lord." This time "angels" refers, in fact, to celestial ones, because they were "greater in power and might." In Psalm 8:4-5a, David asked God a question, and gave a description, about man:

Psalm 8:4 What is man, that thou art mindful of him?

5 For thou hast made him a little lower than the angels . . . .

Again, since man is a little lower than celestial angels, these who were greater in power and might had to be celestial angels. The "them" that the celestial angels would not accuse, then, had to be men. And those men were the same persons that Peter called "angels that sinned." Throughout that 2nd Chapter of 2 Peter, the Apostle was talking about apostates, or ministers who had abandoned the faith and were endangering the saints.

Let us examine Verses 14-15 and 18-20, still dealing with the "angels that sinned" (Verse 4), and the "false teachers among you" (Verse 1), and you will see that these are one and the same:

14 Having eyes full of adultery, and that cannot cease from sin; beguiling unstable souls: an heart they have exercised with covetous practices; cursed children:

15 Which have forsaken the right way, and are gone astray . . .

[These were beguiling unstable souls, after forsaking the right way. They were apostate preachers, friend.]

18 For when they speak great swelling words of vanity, they allure through the lusts of the flesh, through much wantonness, those that were clean escaped from them who live in error.

19 While they promise them liberty, they themselves are the servants of corruption: for of whom a man is overcome, of the same is he brought in bondage.

[Here, Peter said that these fallen angels were, themselves, enslaved, while promising their followers liberty, and he gives the reason: "for of whom *a man* is overcome . . ." These were *men*, dear one!]

20 For if after they have escaped the pollutions of the world through the knowledge of the Lord and Savior Jesus Christ, they are again entangled therein, and overcome, the latter end is worse with them than the beginning.

These "angels that sinned," my friend, had been saved. They had known Jesus. They had escaped the pollutions of the world. But they were again entangled therein. They had become servants of corruption, and they were beguiling unstable souls. The conclusion? *They were apostate preachers.* Peter's, and Jude's, whole burden in these texts was to warn the people of God about them so they would not be among the beguiled.

It is clear, then, from Peter's and Jude's own words, in the very texts that speak of fallen angels, that they were not referring to celestial angels at all. Again, dear one, lifting Scriptures out of their contexts is a dangerous way to build beliefs and doctrines.

By the way, before we move on from these words of Jude and Peter, think about the term *first estate* that Jude used in verse 6. In John 8:44, it says, "Ye are of your father the devil, and the lusts of your father ye will do. He was a murderer from the beginning, and abode not in the truth, because there is no truth in him. When he speaketh a lie, he speaketh of his own: for he is a liar, and the father of it."

Once I heard a preacher use this text as proof that the devil was never in Heaven. He emphasized that the devil was a murderer *from the beginning.* The young man he was talking to came back with the argument that this didn't really mean from Satan's actual beginning. He quoted Revelation 13:8, where it talks about "the Lamb slain from the foundation of the world," and said that, just as Jesus wasn't literally slain when the world was founded, Satan wasn't literally a devil in the beginning. He claimed that Jesus' words about Satan's "beginning" were equivalent with those about the slain Lamb.

It is true that Jesus wasn't literally slain from the beginning of time. He wasn't slain until thousands of years after time began. But *prophetically* speaking, He was slain from the beginning because His death was in God's Plan of Redemption before man was created, and everything that transpired throughout all those years—in the Law, in the Prophets, and even in the days of the patriarchs—foreshadowed in types and figures the coming, death, burial, and resurrection of Jesus Christ.

This young man argued, I repeat, that Jesus' statement about Satan's being a murderer from the beginning was equally prophetic, foretelling that "Lucifer" would someday become a murderous devil. It didn't mean he was *literally* one from the start. This sounds like a reasonable argument. It seems to raise serious doubts about what Jesus meant when He said Satan was always a murderer. Is there an answer, a biblically sound answer, to the young man's argument? Yes, friend, there is. It is, permit me to say, very simple, really. Were it true that the devil had been an angel in Heaven, he had to have been cast out *before* he approached Eve in the Garden of Eden. Adam and Eve were the first people on earth, and they had not had any children at that point. Why would God *prophesy* that Satan *would* be cast out of Heaven when he already had been? There was nothing to *prophesy*. It would have been a *past event* to the very first people. Prophecy *foretells* some event and gives mankind a promise or a warning about that event. Prophecy is needed to *prepare* people for the event to come. In other words, prophecy has practical applications for those who receive it. It details what God is going to do, and how mankind should prepare for, or respond to, it. There could have been no preparation on man's part for Satan's fall, since it had already happened before mankind first encountered him.

The Lamb of God, slain from the foundation of the world, on the other hand, was *foretold* in the prophesies of God for *centuries*, because it had not happened before man was created. It was a *coming* event, and God gave men and women definite promises and warnings about that event through those prophesies. They were to *prepare* people for the coming Messiah. It is ludicrous to claim that Jesus' words about Satan in John 8:44 were prophetic like the words about the Lamb in Revelation 13:8. These texts cannot be compared as having similar applications. In reality, Jesus' statement about Satan was *historic*. It told those Jews, and us, exactly *when* Satan was first a murderer, which was, again, before Adam and Eve met him. My friend, since this statement about Satan was not a prophetic statement, it must be taken for what it was—a simple truth—and that simple truth is that Satan was a murderer *from the beginning*. He never was an angel in Heaven.

Jesus went on to say something else about the devil that proves conclusively that he has always been a devil: "When he speaketh a lie, he speaketh of his own: for he is a liar, and the father of it" (John 8:44c). A *father* is an "originator, founder, or inventor"[10] according to *Webster's*, and it says *originate* means "to bring into being; esp., to invent; to begin; start."[11] So, Satan brought lies into being; lies originated, or began, with him. This being true, there would have been no one to lie to Lucifer, while he was an angel, and tell him he could take Heaven over. That *would* have been a lie, of course; when he tried it, God kicked him out. Plainly, there was no one to tempt Satan in Heaven, for all temptations involve a lie.

Before he supposedly became the devil, there was no tempter. When there's no tempter, there can be no temptation! Furthermore, we have already learned that temptation comes from the lusts, or desires, of the flesh. Angels and devils do not have flesh, so, again, not only must we wonder who could have tempted Lucifer, but *how* could he have been tempted without flesh? We must conclude, then, that Satan was never in Heaven, that from the time he existed, in any form, he was a devil.

But wait. There's more. When Jesus gave His disciples the model prayer in Matthew, the 6th Chapter, He said in verse 10, "Thy will be done in earth, as it is in heaven." These words, too, would have been meaningless, even ludicrous, if God's will was not always done in Heaven. If the occupants of Heaven can rise up against God, and secure a following of others who do so, how could these words of Jesus make sense? Jesus said that we can, and should, pray that God's will be done in earth, as it is done in Heaven. Why would He want us to pray this way if God's will can be disobeyed in Heaven? Surely our Lord never intended that this prayer might result in our exalting ourselves and trying to take over anything that belongs to God!

Furthermore, there is a comma in Jesus' statement—"Thy will be done in earth, as it is done in heaven." Jesus was not telling the disciples to say, "Thy will be done in earth just the same way it's done in Heaven." No; that comma separates two independent clauses, and the second clause says that God's will *is* done in Heaven. No one in Heaven ever did, or ever will, rise up against it. And since Jesus instructed us to pray that God's will be done just as perfectly in our "earth," and also said that, if we ask, we'll receive, He certainly must have meant that doing God's will perfectly in earth is possible.

All over Christendom, people recite this "Lord's Prayer," asking for God's will to be done in earth, as it is in Heaven. Many church services include it as a part of their collective "worship." Yet they do not believe in what they are praying for. They say, "Thy will be done" with one breath, as it were, and "Everyone disobeys sometimes," with the next.

Someone may say, "Well, what about Revelation, the 12th Chapter? There it tells of how there was war in Heaven until God prevailed over the dragon (called the devil and Satan) and cast him out." Yes, it actually says that. It actually says there was a war, and that God's army and "Satan's" army fought each other. It really seems that there was quite a struggle, and it really seems to upset all I've been saying. But, friend, it doesn't, when properly interpreted. The 12th Chapter of Revelation is not talking about the literal devil or God's habitation. I know that is upsetting, but will you study it with me? I'm only trying to help you see the truth. Please allow me that opportunity. It's for you I'm doing this.

Revelation 12:1 And there appeared a great wonder in heaven; a woman clothed with the sun, and the moon under her feet, and upon her head a crown of twelve stars:

2 And she being with child cried, travailing in birth, and pained to be delivered.

3 And there appeared another wonder in heaven; and behold a great red dragon, having seven heads and ten horns, and seven crowns upon his heads.

4 And his tail drew the third part of the stars of heaven, and did cast them to the earth: and the dragon stood before the woman which was ready to be delivered, for to devour her child as soon as it was born.

5 And she brought forth a man child, who was to rule all nations with a rod of iron: and her child was caught up unto God, and to his throne.

6 And the woman fled into the wilderness, where she hath a place prepared of God, that they should feed her there a thousand two hundred and threescore days.

7 And there was war in heaven: Michael and his angels fought against the dragon; and the dragon fought and his angels,

8 And prevailed not; neither was their place found any more in heaven.

9 And the great dragon was cast out, that old serpent, called the Devil, and Satan, which deceiveth the whole world: he was cast out into the earth, and his angels were cast out with him.

10 And I heard a loud voice saying in heaven, Now is come salvation, and strength, and the kingdom of our God, and the power of his Christ: for the accuser of our brethren is cast down, which accused them before our God day and night.

Here is a list of reasons why this is not referring to the literal devil being cast out of God's Heavenly abode:

1) The woman that appeared in the same heaven the dragon was in was pregnant and ready to deliver her child. In Matthew 22:23-30, the Sadducees tempted Jesus by asking Him about seven brothers who had married the same woman, one after the other, as each died. They wanted to know which husband she would have in eternity. Jesus replied, in verse 30, "In the resurrection they neither marry, nor are given in marriage, but are *as the angels of God in heaven* [emphasis added]." And Paul let us know that, when we enter eternity, "this mortal must put on immortality" (1 Corinthians 15:53-54). Both being "as the angels of God in heaven," and "putting on immortality" when we die, show us that no *mortal* conditions exist in the eternal realm. Yet this woman of Revelation 12 was pregnant. Since marriage, and childbearing, do not happen in the Heaven of God's abode, this is definitely symbolic language.

2) In addition, we find this woman clothed with the sun and wearing a crown of twelve stars upon her head. We all know this cannot be literal. No one could be clothed with the sun and live through it. Nor could anyone wear a crown of stars, unless he had one marvelously big head. "Oh," you may say, "this sun and these stars are figurative language." Exactly! But if these items the woman was clothed in are not literal, but symbolic, then it follows that the woman wearing them is also symbolic, and *then* it follows that the rest of this scene is symbolic as well. This is not a picture of literal happenings in the Heaven where God dwells. Rather, these are symbols of activity in that *ecclesiastical heaven*, showing the Church (the woman) and one of her battles in the Gospel Day. The sun represents the New Testament; the moon, the Old Testament; and the stars—twelve of them—typify the twelve Apostles who pioneered the precious Gospel Era. Remember how Jesus said, in Revelation 1:20, that stars were symbols of the "angels," or pastors,

of the seven churches? Throughout Revelation, stars are used as symbols of ministers.

3) If this is speaking of the literal devil, how did he ever stir up a conspiracy against God, winning other angels to himself, until he had an army capable of taking on God's army? God knows all things. He knows the end from the beginning. If He could look ahead, before He ever created the world, and know, and make plans for, all the future, are you telling me He wouldn't have known a rebellion was "secretly" taking place? We read where Jesus knew the thoughts of men while here on earth, so how could God not have known the thoughts of "Lucifer" while he was getting the big head and growing dangerous? Can you picture God doing nothing about such a thing and just allowing it to build and build until it became a full-scale war? God would have nipped it in the bud! He never would have allowed "Lucifer" to ruin so many other angels.

4) Again, who tempted "Lucifer" to rise up like that? Who suggested such a foolish idea to him? Don't say he tempted himself, becoming, as it were, a devil all along. *In the beginning, before he fell, he was an angel, after all* (supposedly). His first temptation had to have come while he was still pure; at the beginning of temptation, there is no sin yet. *Who tempted him?* I repeat, besides Satan, himself, there is no record, or even a suggestion, of any other tempting power.

Not only that, but angels do not have a free will of choice. Humans do. Without a free will, a free moral agency, no one can sin; no one can make a choice to change from good to evil. There is absolutely no possibility that any angel in Heaven could have chosen to rebel.

5) Verse 10 says " . . . *the accuser of our brethren . . . which accused them before our God day and night*" is cast down. This accuser *accused* (past tense) the brethren *before* he was cast out. If this scene were depicting the literal devil's being cast out of God's literal Heaven, who were the "brethren" he had been accusing? John called them "our brethren," so this is not talking about the other angels in Heaven; nowhere in the Bible does it say that humans are brothers to the angels. The Bible *does* say we were made a little lower than the angels, however (Psalm 8:5), so we're not on the same level they're on. We're not of the same nature as they are. We have

human natures; they do not. We have a free will of choice; they do not. Every time the word *brethren* is used in the Bible, with but one exception, it is talking about humans' relationships to humans. That one exception is that Jesus made us *His* brethren through salvation (Hebrews 2:10-12); so there *is* a spiritual brotherhood, but angels do not partake of salvation (1Peter 1:12) and therefore are not in this spiritual brotherhood with us.

Another thing, whenever humans saw angels, they were afraid, saying they had seen God. That does not mean angels are gods, but they *were* the Almighty's ambassadors, they were of a higher realm, and they were tremendously awesome to behold. What it does mean, as well, is that men and angels are radically different beings.

This verse also says "Satan" accused the brethren day and night. Dear friend, is there any night in Heaven? In all of my fifty-plus years of Bible study, I haven't found anything that indicates there is. The truth is, this is a symbolic picture of the early Church and her battle with paganism; particularly, at that time, it was with the pagan Roman Empire, the dragon of Revelation. Follow early church history, and read *Foxe's Book of Martyrs*, and you will learn with what horror and brutality this dragon fought against the Church. Indeed, this dragon, the pagan Roman Empire, was an accuser of the brethren. Both natural and man-made disasters were blamed on the Christians, as excuses to torture and murder them. By the end of the third century, there had been fully nine waves of persecution brought upon the Church by various Roman Emperors.

6) Next, verse 11 says, "And they overcame him by the blood of the Lamb, and by the word of their testimony; and they loved not their lives unto the death." Who overcame him? Michael and his angels prevailed against the dragon and his angels when this wayward bunch was kicked out of heaven; but if these were celestial angels, how did they overcome him by the blood of the Lamb? Jesus' blood was given for humanity's sins, not angels' wars. Then it says "by the word of their testimony." The term *testimony* in the Greek is *marturia* (mar-too-ree'-ah), which *Strong's* says means "*evidence given (judicially or gen.):—record, report, testimony, witness.*"[12] What testimony, what witness, did they overcome the dragon with? Did

105

Michael and his angels testify against "Lucifer" in Heaven's Court? Was that what convicted him? But, wait. God wouldn't have needed any witnesses; He, Himself, would have known all about this "crime." Besides, verses 6 and 7 say that they overcame him in battle, and he was cast out. There is no mention of a trial. So I ask, also, how did the "good" angels prevail over Satan by *their testimony?*

Friend, remember, we found in point #2, above, that this whole scene is symbolic. What we see here, in Michael and his angels, is a portrayal of how Christ and His early ministry cast down this enemy, paganism, from its high religious pinnacle in the hearts and lives of the masses of that day.

7) Next it says those who overcame the dragon loved not their lives unto death. Someone may say, "Yes, Michael and his angels were so brave, so valiant! They were willing to defend God with their lives!" My precious friend, *angels cannot die.* What death were they not afraid of?

Again, this is clearly a figurative picture. As Christ's Church faced the foe of paganism, in the first days of the Gospel Dispensation, the saints overcame that dragon by Christ's blood, for they were redeemed by it from his influence and control. Millions were brought out of pagan worship to salvation. Then, they overcame by the word of their testimony, their witness. What was that? They had been commissioned to go forth to the whole world as *witnesses* to Christ and what He had come to earth to do. So they went out, *testifying* against paganism and it's ungodliness, and when they did this, they "turned the world upside down." Truly they loved not their lives unto the death, because many gave their lives up in loving service to their Master. Let me repeat, Michael and his angels represent Christ and the ministry of the early Church of the living God. The Apostles led the charge, and all of them but John, as well as a multitude of others, died as martyrs. They were slain for their faith. But in dying with victory, rather than giving in, *they overcame Satan!* This is what Revelation 12 shows us.

I could go on, but let's look at just one more:

106

8) Verses 9-10 tell us, "the great dragon was cast out," and a loud voice in Heaven cried, "Now is come salvation, and strength, and the kingdom of our God, and the power of his Christ." Here we supposedly have a rebel angel being routed and banished, cast to the earth to wreak havoc among men, and someone shouts that salvation is come! How could Lucifer's fall be credited with bringing salvation? How could it have produced the Kingdom of God?

Someone may say, "This just means salvation, or God's Kingdom and Christ's power, came *because* Lucifer fell. Before he became the devil, no one needed to be saved." I'll agree that this may seem logical at first, but it has a couple of problems. The text does not say his being cast out brought a *need* for salvation. It says that when he was cast out, someone shouted, "*Now is come* salvation." That means salvation is "come *now*" when the dragon was cast out. You don't think that's what it says? Read it again. The same is true concerning the Kingdom of God and the power of Christ; they were *now come* when that dragon was cast out. In reality, it was *because* salvation and the Kingdom *had* come, that the dragon *got* cast out.

Dear friend, when John the Baptist, and Christ Himself, first started proclaiming the Gospel message, they said, "Repent, for the kingdom is *at hand.*" (See Matthew 3:1-2 and 4:17.) Now, according to those who teach that Satan was once an angel in Heaven, we have someone shouting that the Kingdom came when he was cast out, before he ever approached Eve. Yet John and Jesus said, thousands of years later, that it was *about to come.* And, don't be confused about the Kingdom of God and the Kingdom of Heaven. They are both the same Kingdom. Matthew 4:17 tells us, "From that time Jesus began to preach, and to say, Repent: for the kingdom of heaven is at hand." Then, in Mark 1:15, we read, "And saying [Jesus talking, verse 14], The time is fulfilled, and the kingdom of God is at hand: repent ye, and believe the gospel." Compare also Matthew 5:3 and Luke 6:20.

This shout makes perfect sense, however, when properly interpreted. As I said earlier, there are some keys to understanding the Revelation. Some more of these keys are as follows:

1) One must be a child of God to receive the truths taught there. Revelation 1:1 says this Book is "The Revelation of Jesus Christ,

which God gave unto him, to shew unto his servants . . . ." You could say that God had this Book penned in "code," and only His servants receive the code key. Without that key, it is impossible to unlock the Book, but with it, the Book is not a mystery; it's a *revelation*!

2) The book of Revelation is written in series. You cannot read it from the first to the last as a continuing narrative. There are seven series in all, which, for the most part, start at the beginning of the Gospel Day, in A.D. 33, (remember, this is a revelation of *Jesus Christ*) and run to the end of time. The seven letters, given in Revelation 2 and 3, are the first series. The seven seals (Revelation 5:1-11:19) are another, the second. The seven trumpets form a series within a series, the third (Chapters 8:2-10:11). Chapter 11, still within the seals series, is a series in itself, the fourth. Chapters 12-19 make up the fifth series, showing the great apostasy and how God brought His people back to full light. Chapter 20 is a series in itself, the sixth. Chapters 21 and 22 make up the seventh, and last, series, with marvelous descriptions of the glorious Church of God. It is impossible to understand the Revelation without taking these series into account.

Why is Revelation written in series? Because God wanted to give His servants a clear understanding of Christ's body, the Church, and of her enemies and triumphs throughout the Gospel Day as she carried out the commission Jesus gave her. The Church has many characteristics and many enemies, or I might say her enemy has many faces. Therefore, God has given us many "pictures" (series) of her and her triumphs as relate to these different characteristics and enemies. Understanding these series opens up a glorious panorama of our invincible Lord and His Kingdom. It's a victorious Kingdom, friend, and its members live victoriously over sin!

3) What the Book of Revelation portrays is not a series of literal happenings. We have already covered that its language is symbolic, but John also let us know that "I saw the horses in the vision" (Revelation 9:17). The horses weren't literal horses standing nearby. They were seen *in a vision*. John called it "*the* vision." The whole picture John relates to us in the Book of Revelation was a

vision—the horses, the beasts, the angels, the elders, the bottomless pit, the candlesticks, and on and on and on. These were all symbolic pictures, not literal happenings.

4) It only covers time from Christ's first advent until His second. Again, it covers the Church, as the body and Bride of Christ, and her triumphs over her various enemies. It deals, thus, with this time world; when Jesus comes again, the Church's conflicts will be over. Getting these basic facts straight eliminates massive confusion about what the Book of Revelation actually teaches.

Let us go on with our study. Since this 12th Chapter of Revelation is the beginning of the fifth series, it commences in A.D. 33, and it reveals one side of the first enemy that the Church, or the Woman clothed with the sun, faced. Let me repeat, that enemy was unbelief and pagan darkness, embodied in the Roman Empire that ruled the world in the days of Jesus and the Apostles. This is what the dragon represents. Its seven heads depict the seven different heads of government under the Roman Empire, and its ten horns represent the ten minor kingdoms that the Empire was made up of. Verse 9 says the dragon was *called* the devil and Satan. It is referred to as the devil and Satan symbolically, as it was a tool he used, a force through which he moved, to attack the Church. Remember that Jesus also referred to Peter once as Satan (Matthew 16:23). The word *Satan* is taken from the same Greek word in both of these Scripture passages, **Satanas** (sat-an-as'). That Greek word, meaning *"the accuser,* i.e. the *devil"*[13] is derived from a Hebrew word (**satan;** saw-tawn') that means "an *opponent:* espec . . . *Satan,"* and "adversary."[14] Although *Strong's* says the Hebrew term refers *especially* to Satan, it does not say it *always* refers to him. It also applies to any *opponent.* Again, we know this from Jesus' calling Peter by this term. And this dragon was no more the literal devil than Peter was. This dragon's being "cast out of Heaven" is portraying the way the pristine Church, through the mighty power of the Gospel, brought down the influence of paganism throughout the then-known world; so much so, I repeat, that some termed it as the apostles *turning the world upside down* (See Acts 17:6). It was a grand-scale triumph, a change-the-course-of-history event, that the early Church was used by God to bring about.

It is not possible to cover these facts in detail in this book, as our focus is on believing in the true Bible Jesus, but the reader will find much to help him in understanding these truths by going to this web site: http://gospeltrumpeter.com/revelation/index.html.

With the correct interpretation, we can see how that cry in Revelation 12:10 makes perfect sense. As the Gospel of salvation broke down paganism and unbelief, salvation truly came to millions, Jew and Gentile alike. No wonder the cry rang out, "Now is come salvation, and strength, and the kingdom of our God, and the power of his Christ: for the accuser of our brethren is cast down!"

You may ask, "Where, then, *did* the devil come from?" Well, hold onto your seat. Are you ready for this? Are you *sure*? Okay, here goes . . . . God created the devil. "*What*?!" you may say. "*No way!*" But it's true. God created the devil. You may wonder, "Whatever for?" Well, friend, in order for God to give man a free will, so that he could choose whom he would serve, there had to be *more than one choice* he could make. Of what good is a free will when there is only one thing to choose? God created evil so man could *choose between* good and evil. Does the Bible back this up? It certainly does. Read Isaiah 45:5-7:

5 I am the LORD, and there is none else, there is no God beside me: I girded thee, though thou hast not known me:

6 That they may know from the rising of the sun, and from the west, that there is none beside me. I am the LORD, and there is none else.

7 I form the light, and create darkness: I make peace, and create evil: I the LORD do all these things.

In Deuteronomy 30:15, God spoke through Moses, saying, "See, I have set before thee this day life and good, and death and evil." God set these before mankind. Why? Read verse 19: "I call heaven and earth to record this day against you, that I have set before you life and death, blessing and cursing: therefore choose . . . ." He set evil, as well as good, before us so we can *choose*. I repeat, without evil, there could be no choice. For God to give us a free will of choice, He had to provide us with some things to choose between.

The Hebrew word translated *evil* in both these texts is **ra** (rah), and *Strong's Hebrew Dictionary* says it means, among a host of similar things, "bad or evil," and, most important, "wicked one."[15] God created *ra* (evil), and Satan is referred to as "the wicked one"; see Matthew

13:19, 38, 1 John 2:13-14, 1 John 3:12, and 1 John 5:18. See also 2 Thessalonians 2:8.

Colossians 1:16 says, "For by him [by Christ, verse 14] were all things created, that are in heaven, and that are in earth, visible and invisible, whether they be thrones, or dominions, or principalities, or powers: all things were created by him, and for him."

In Ephesians 6:12, Paul told us we wrestle "against principalities, against powers, against the rulers of the darkness of this world, against spiritual wickedness in high places." In this text, "principalities and powers" distinctly refer to forces of Satan, for they are what we, as Christians, wrestle against. While it is true that the term, *principalities and powers*, doesn't always refer to evil forces (see Ephesians 3:10 and Titus 3:1), as a general expression it certainly *includes* the devil and his agents, and we are told that God created the "principalities and powers."

What does all of this mean to you and me? Well, some people think Satan is an independent power *almost* as great as God, and who sometimes gives God a real struggle. They say that God, as great as He is, can't enable His redeemed "new creatures" to overcome Satan all the time. Not so, my friend! The devil is not some runaway power out here that God can barely control. He only has the power that God gave him. If you doubt this, look at Job 1:6-12 and 2:1-7:

Job 1:6 Now there was a day when the sons of God came to present themselves before the LORD, and Satan came also among them.

7 And the LORD said unto Satan, Whence comest thou? Then Satan answered the LORD, and said, From going to and fro in the earth, and from walking up and down in it.

8 And the LORD said unto Satan, Hast thou considered my servant Job, that there is none like him in the earth, a perfect and an upright man, one that feareth God, and escheweth evil?

9 Then Satan answered the LORD, and said, Doth Job fear God for nought?

10 Hast not thou made an hedge about him, and about his house, and about all that he hath on every side? thou hast blessed the work of his hands, and his substance is increased in the land.

11 But put forth thine hand now, and touch all that he hath, and he will curse thee to thy face.

12 And the LORD said unto Satan, Behold, all that he hath is in thy power; only upon himself put not forth thine hand. So Satan went forth from the presence of the LORD.

Job 2:1 Again there was a day when the sons of God came to present themselves before the LORD, and Satan came also among them to present himself before the LORD.

2 And the LORD said unto Satan, From whence comest thou? And Satan answered the LORD, and said, From going to and fro in the earth, and from walking up and down in it.

3 And the LORD said unto Satan, Hast thou considered my servant Job, that there is none like him in the earth, a perfect and an upright man, one that feareth God, and escheweth evil? and still he holdeth fast his integrity, although thou movedst me against him, to destroy him without cause.

4 And Satan answered the LORD, and said, Skin for skin, yea, all that a man hath will he give for his life.

5 But put forth thine hand now, and touch his bone and his flesh, and he will curse thee to thy face.

6 And the LORD said unto Satan, Behold, he is in thine hand; but save his life.

7 So went Satan forth from the presence of the LORD, and smote Job . . . .

Satan couldn't do a thing to, or with, Job until he got permission from God. He is totally subject to God and His Word. The only power he can have regarding us, initially, is just what he manifested with Eve—the power to provide another option to choose between, and deceptive persuasion that entices us, through our flesh, to make the wrong choice. He only gains more power over us when we *give* it to him. It is in our *yielding* to his suggestions that he becomes our master (Romans 6:16). And this is true after we are saved, as well. But when we are delivered from sin, by the mighty power of God, Satan no longer *rules* us. *We do not have to do what he says; we are not under his power!*

God, however, will give Satan some "rope" from time to time to try our faith, our will, and our commitment, as happened in Job's case. It is in these times of trial that we're to grow stronger and deeper in Christ. Although Job's test was a severe one, God brought him out of it shining yet brighter than before, and into a richer life. And, friend, when we see Satan as the created being that he is, when we see that he basically serves to provide mankind with choices, and to test the Christian's commitment and faith, we come to understand that we can choose *not* to be under his power, by God's grace. Christians can choose *not* to follow his suggestions. I repeat, the Bible tells us it is only when we yield to him that he becomes our master; once born again, however, we do not have to yield to him. By the power of God, we can refuse to. Certainly everyone does yield to Satan when one first comes to the age of accountability. The Bible says, "All have sinned." But, praise God, when we come in old-time repentance, and get washed in the blood of the Lamb, God imparts to us His Spirit. Through the power of His Spirit, we can say no to the devil. We can, in every choice between good and evil, yield to God and righteousness. Again, the 6th Chapter of Romans makes this clear.

You need to see Satan as a defeated foe. This, of course, does not mean that you should take the devil lightly (read 1 Corinthians 10:12). He is ever trying to persuade us, to deceive us. And we can only stand against him by the power of God. That is so important that I want to say it again. *We can only stand against him by the power of God!* Whenever we begin to lean to our own resources, our own strength, our own wisdom, we are in danger of falling under his power again. But we don't *have* to. James 4:6 says, "But he [God, verse 4] giveth more grace." No matter how big a bluster the devil puts on, God gives His children *more grace*. God's grace is bigger than Satan's bluster. We can *resist* the devil, Peter said. "Whom [Satan, verse 8] resist steadfast in the faith" (1 Peter 5:9). And James agrees, saying, "Submit yourselves therefore to God. Resist the devil, and he will flee from you" (James 4:7).

Did you get that, friend? Christians *can* resist the devil until he flees from us, by God's "more grace." There's no such thing as "we can't help but yield sometimes." We may yield, yes, but it's not because we're unable to help it. The Scriptures are so *opposite* to what modern Christendom teaches. Finally, "The Lord knoweth how to deliver the godly out of temptations" (2 Peter 2:9). We do not have to live under Satan's power as Christians. God may allow him to test us, but He will *never* allow him to overcome us. That would have to be *our* choice—not an *inevitability*, mind you, but a *choice*. Friend, I say it kindly, with love, but I *must* say it: any "Jesus" that leaves you under Satan's power, in any way or to any degree, is not the Jesus of the Bible, and any church that does so is not the Church of the Bible.

CHAPTER SEVEN

How Nominal Christianity Has Failed

Modern, nominal, "Christianity" is a failure. The primary reason for this is, simply, that it is not Christianity at all. In the preceding chapters of this book, we have seen over and over how it flies directly in the face of what the Word of God really teaches. And the rest of this book will show the same thing. Today's "Christianity" is a counterfeit. It is Satan's *pet project* for deceiving the souls of mankind. Haven't you ever wondered why there are so many scandals, so many frauds, so many despicable actions, taking place on a consistent basis throughout the realms of modern Christendom? Have you never wondered why history has been stained with "Christian" wars? Remember, the Apostles warned that *apostasy* was coming. *Webster's* says that *apostasy* means, "an abandoning of what one has believed in, as a faith, cause, etc."[1] That's why Jude pleaded with the saints of his day to *earnestly contend for the faith once delivered to the saints.* God was showing His leaders that there was going to be a wholesale abandoning of the original faith.

Certainly not everyone abandoned the Faith, but more did than did not. That is why those who still hold to that original, biblical, Plan and worldview are so few, yet today. That is why the masses of "Christian churches" do not teach the Bible accurately and faithfully. That is why they lean so much toward excusing sin in the lives of believers, rather than showing believers the way out of sin.

In spite of all of its efforts to supposedly redeem mankind, modern "Christianity's" own followers are a million miles from what Christians ought to be. There are fewer and fewer American "Christians," especially among the young, who still believe in absolute moral truth. You can find a lot about this on the Barna Research website (www.barna.org). Search for the March, 2009, report entitled, "Barna Survey

Examines Changes in Worldview Among Christians over the Past 13 Years." For example, that study shows that only 19 percent of "*born again* Christians" hold a biblical worldview, which means such things as believing the Bible is accurate in the principles it teaches, believing that God is the all-powerful, all-knowing Creator of everything, believing that Jesus was sinless while He lived in this world, and believing that Satan is an actual person.

I find this alarming, friend! With all the "churches" we have in America, and with all their radio and TV broadcasts, magazines, books, outreach programs, evangelistic campaigns, Internet sites, camps and retreats, and countless numbers of regular services, only *19 percent* of those who are supposedly born again believe in what constitutes a biblical worldview!!! The Word of God is very clear on these basic points about God, about itself, and about Satan. These things, indeed, form a *biblical* viewpoint; without them, it's impossible to be saved, for *not* believing the Word of God certainly does not bring salvation. The holy Word says, "Without faith it is *impossible* to please God" (Hebrews 11:6a; emphasis added). These basic principles are *essentials* of Christian faith. That 81 percent of "born-again Christians" do not believe in them, my dear reader, certainly reveals that modern "Christianity" has failed and failed miserably.

Can *born-again* believers *really* not believe the Bible principles are true and accurate? Can they *actually* not believe that God is all-powerful and created everything? Can they *truly* not believe that Christ was sinless while on earth? If the so-called real Christians (those who are born again) don't believe the Bible's testimony about God and itself, how can the world ever be expected to? *What,* pray tell, are these "Christians" going to win the world to? When 81 percent don't believe, all they can win people to is *unbelief!*

Stop, here, and think on these statements for a few minutes.

Now, look at Jesus words in Mark 16:15-16:

15 Go ye into all the world, and preach the gospel to every creature.

16 He that believeth [!] *and is baptized shall be saved; but he that believeth not* [!] *shall be damned.*

Those who believe not *shall be damned!* Believe what? *The Gospel.* The Bible is so crystal clear, friend. How can "preachers" who don't even believe the Gospel, preach it with a power that inspires others to believe? The simple answer is, they cannot; and, in fact, the overwhelming majority of their "converts" are not saved by faith; they are damned by unbelief. A "Christianity" where 81 percent of its elite followers do not believe Christianity's most basic teachings, is simply futile, useless, and impotent. It is absolutely *not qualified* to represent Christ in the world. In fact, dear one, such "Christianity" *does not* represent Christ in the world. It is corrupt and it is destructive, and it is nothing short of an abomination in God's eyes.

You may ask, "Is it really necessary to believe and follow *everything* in the Bible? Don't we all have our own interpretations of what it says and what it means?"

Friend, while it's true that people have their own ideas about what the Bible teaches, we are not to just be content to follow our own ideas (Isaiah 55:7a, Proverbs 3:5). We are to *seek* (Isaiah 34:16), to *hunger* and *thirst*, after understanding (Matthew 5:6, Proverbs 2:1-6). These are our responsibilities and duties. God commands it. He provides the miracle; we must provide our own due diligence, and without this effort on our part, God's part will not be done. He does not reward laziness (Hebrews 6:11-12). By the way, I ask you to do your duty in looking up and reading the Bible references I give you. If I quote every Scripture I use, this book will be much, much, too long, and they are necessary for understanding these truths.

All right—"Is it really necessary to know, to believe, and to follow, everything in the Bible?" Dear one, none of us will ever, in this world, know everything in the Bible. Our minds are finite, while the Word of God is infinite: "The secret things belong unto the LORD our God: but those things which are revealed belong unto us and to our children for ever, that we may do all the words of this law" (Deuteronomy 29:29). Again, however, it is our job to seek for knowledge and understanding. Where do we seek? At the throne of God, in earnest—and honest—prayer, for He, and He alone, is The Teacher (John 14:26, John 16:13). All we human teachers can do is set His truth before you. You must search it out.

It is, however, *absolutely necessary* to believe and obey everything He reveals to us. Not one word of Scripture is "take it or leave it." Certainly, some of it has been fulfilled. The era of time for which it was intended has passed. Yet there are wonderful lessons found within even these passages, and their *principles* still hold true today. For example, Moses taught that Israel was not to plow with different species of animals, wear mixed garments (Deuteronomy 22:10-11), or eat *unclean* things (Leviticus 11:1-23), and these ceremonial edicts have since been nailed to Christ's cross (Colossians 2:14) and are not required under grace, because Christ fulfilled them (Matthew 5:17). *The principle of separation*, however, between clean and unclean, is as valid today as it was in Moses' time. Under the Law, inward purity was not possible, so "clean" and "unclean" were outward, ceremonial things. Under the Gospel, however, they are inward. The principles of God are eternal, however, and they flow throughout the Scriptures. We are obligated to live by them.

Matthew 4:4 Man shall . . . live . . . by every word that proceedeth out of the mouth of God.

Hebrews 2:1 Therefore we ought to give the more earnest heed to the things which we have heard, lest at any time we should let them slip.

2 For if the word spoken by angels was stedfast, and every transgression and disobedience received a just recompence of reward;

3 How shall we escape, if we neglect so great salvation; which at the first began to be spoken by the Lord, and was confirmed unto us by them that heard him.

Jesus said we must live by *every* word of God. The Hebrew writer followed with the fact that God's Word is *steadfast*, and to neglect any of it will bring a just recompense. How, then, can truly born-again believers be unsure about the accuracy of what it teaches? Bible principles can never be "take-it-or-leave-it" fare if we live or die by *every word* of it! Leave out one word of what God has shown you, and you will die! Friend, listen to what the Bible says for itself:

Deuteronomy 32:4 He is the Rock, his work is perfect: for all his ways are judgment: a God of truth and without iniquity, just and right is he.

Psalm 33:4 For the word of the LORD is right; and all his works are done in truth.

Psalm 111:7 The works of his hands are verity [truth] *and judgment; all his commandments are sure.*

8 They stand fast for ever and ever, and are done in truth and uprightness.

Isaiah 25:1 O LORD, thou art my God; I will exalt thee, I will praise thy name; for thou hast done wonderful things; thy counsels of old are faithfulness and truth.

John 14:6 Jesus saith unto him, I am the way, the truth, and the life: no man cometh unto the Father, but by me.
John 16:13 Howbeit when he, the Spirit of truth, is come, he will guide you into all truth: for he shall not speak of himself; but whatsoever he shall hear, that shall he speak: and he will shew you things to come.
John 17:17 Sanctify them through thy truth: thy word is truth.
Psalm 19:9 . . . the judgments of the LORD are true and righteous altogether.

I still can't get over it! Only 19 percent of those who claim to be born again believe this. Clearly, God's Word is *truth*. All of it. And we must live by all of it. Yet only nineteen out of every one hundred so-called *born-again* believers actually believe it is accurate in what it teaches. *Talk about a failed "Christianity"*! Alas! Modern Christendom only aids and abets such flagrant unbelief. One way we can know this is by how many biblical principles modern ministers say are "no longer necessary."

If only 19 percent of the "born-again" really believe, where does this leave everyone else? Well, it gets worse: the statistic for American adults, in general, is *only 9 percent*! If only 9 percent, or 19 percent, of our military troops held an "American" perspective, would you want them defending you? I wouldn't. Wouldn't *you* say that modern "Christianity" has failed, when only 9 percent of the public believes its message? Oh, wait. Remember, *they* don't even believe their message. In fact, if only 19 percent of "Christians" believe the Bible, then Christianity, in the nominal sense, doesn't even have a message. No wonder our nation, and our world, are in such a mess.

Without moral absolutes to give a firm basis for our faith, how can we even know what to believe? Friend, God does not leave us in the dark! Jesus said, "I am the light of the world: he that followeth me shall not walk in darkness, but shall have the light of life" (John 8:12). Since Christ is *the light* in this world, the Bible is, as well, for Jesus was the Word made flesh (John 1:14).

Certainly, we can't share what we believe with others when we don't know, ourselves, what to believe in. And, worse, if moral truths are relative, rather than absolute, how to apply "truth" to any given situation must be figured out on a case-by-case and person-by-person basis. But if this were all that was necessary for determining the right way to go, God would not have given the instructions for living that

118

He provided us. But God *has not* just left us to our own reasonings. The truth is that He tells us *not* to go by these! Proverbs 3:5 says, "Trust in the LORD with all thine heart; *and lean not unto thine own understanding.*" (Emphasis added.) But wait; there's more. Verse 6 says, "In all thy ways acknowledge him, and he shall direct thy paths." We are not to try to figure out our own paths—we are to acknowledge that He knows the right way and follow the paths *He* directs us in. How do we do that? Through His holy Word—and for sure, we must believe it in order to follow it.

Such "situational ethics" as are presented today are not ethics at all; they're no more than individual opinions and preferences, applied as one decides at the time to be appropriate—or, more to the point, what one *wants* to be appropriate. Friend, this condition is prevalent among "Christians" as well as "the world." There is, on the other hand, nothing about the Bible's principles that is relative or circumstantial. Friend, *principles* do not change with the whims of society. *Principle* is defined by *Webster's* as "**1** a fundamental truth, law, etc. upon which others are based; **2** *a*) a rule of conduct *b*) adherence to such rules; integrity."[2] The principles in God's Word are the *fundamental* truths that all other laws and rules of conduct, including our personal ones, need to be based upon. These principles have long been the rules for life in honorable societies. Even "uncivilized" tribes in wild areas of the earth, who never heard the Scriptures, have been found to have moral codes based upon the principles found in God's Word, just as the Bible says they would in Romans 2:14-15. Only in recent history have these principles been abandoned *en masse* (read also Romans 1:19-22). And all we have to do is open our eyes in order to see the results of this folly. God's truths are as valid, and as valuable, today as they ever were—and be sure of this: they, not these modern, "enlightened" ideas, will judge us in the last day: "He that rejecteth me, and receiveth not my words, hath one that judgeth him: the word that I have spoken, the same shall judge him in the last day" (John 12:48).

Webster's defines *truth* as "**1** a being true; specif., *a*) sincerity; honesty *b*) conformity with fact *c*) reality; actual existence *d*) correctness; accuracy **2** that which is true **3** an established fact."[3] And *fact* is "**2** a thing that has actually happened or is really true **3** reality; truth."[4]

Think about these definitions. There is no way truth, then, can be whatever one wants it to be. *Truth* is reality, what actually is;

119

it is established fact, what is really true. If something is true, then everything that counters, or opposes, it must be false. Someone may say, "Can't something be true sometimes but not all the time?" Well, the statement "It's raining today," can be true in Chicago but not true in Phoenix, or it can be true in Chicago at 5 a.m. but not be true in Chicago at 9 p.m., so *in that sense* something can be true sometimes but not all the time. But "It's raining today" and "It's not raining today" cannot both be true in the same spot at the same time. Likewise, "we can live holy in this life" and "we cannot live holy in this life" (the same place at the same time) cannot both be true. Both can *not* be accurate, or correct, or realistic. That God is the all-powerful, all-knowing Creator, or that the devil is real, cannot be both true and untrue. Whichever is true, those who believe the opposite *believe a lie*. Those 81 percent of "Christians" believe lies. Can you see how we cannot make truth relative, bending it to suit ourselves, without simply destroying it?

Another example: "Two plus two equals four" is true. Since it is, "two plus two equals three" cannot also be true, or even be true in certain situations. If we based our economy on such *situational ethics*, businesses that were experiencing financial difficulties could decide that, *in their circumstances*, two plus two could equal five for their income, and three for their expenses. If this were the case, our world would be in utter chaos (much more so than it is). Everyone could manipulate the figures as his condition warranted. Buying, selling, paying taxes, earning a paycheck, leaving our wealth to our heirs, saving and investing—it would all be massive confusion, and that's exactly what is going on in the religious/moral realm! Be certain of this: it's a far greater disaster morally and spiritually than it could ever be in the financial world.

The same would be true in manipulating the laws of nature. Air and space travel, automotive science, the construction industry, medical science, and on and on—all of these *have* to accept certain truths when it comes to natural laws. If they did not, who would want to board an airplane or drive a car or go to the dentist? Absolute truth is the only thing that gives order and sense to life, in whatever realm you may want to consider. But, I say again, nowhere is this more important than in the realm of moral truth. If you board an airplane that was built with no regard for the natural laws governing gravity and aeronautics, it may cost your life. But if you go into eternity having ignored or manipulated *moral laws*, it will cost your soul, dear one. Forever!

It boggles my mind how otherwise right-thinking people can accept absolutes along natural lines without any trouble, yet reject them on moral and spiritual issues. This is incompatible with believing; it is altogether unbelief. The Bible says "this" or "that," but they've become "wiser." My dear reader, *that* is more than dangerous!

Let's study, briefly, what God, Himself, says about absolute truth. Someone may say, "Is that really important?" and my answer is, "*Yes, it most certainly is*. It is *all*-important." Remember, Jesus said *we live* by every word of God (Matthew 4:4). Without absolute truth, our faith has no basis or foundation. When built on mere suppositions, and dependent upon individual human reasonings, it is in vain and can but collapse. Talk about building on the sand! So, to get God's opinion on the matter, lets read Psalm 19:7-11:

7 The law of the LORD is perfect, converting the soul: the testimony of the LORD is sure, making wise the simple.

8 The statutes of the LORD are right, rejoicing the heart: the commandment of the LORD is pure, enlightening the eyes.

9 The fear of the LORD is clean, enduring for ever: the judgments of the LORD are true and righteous altogether.

10 More to be desired are they than gold, yea, than much fine gold: sweeter also than honey and the honeycomb.

11 Moreover by them is thy servant warned: and in keeping of them there is great reward.

In verse 7, *perfect* comes from the Hebrew word **tamiym** (taw-meem') and means, "*entire* (lit., fig. or mor.); also (as noun) *integrity, truth:*—without blemish, complete, full, perfect, sincerely (-ity), sound, without spot, undefiled, upright (-ly), whole."[5]

Wow! Also in verse 7, *testimony* in the Hebrew is **eduwth** (ay-dooth') and means "witness."[6] Friend, whatever God witnesses about any given thing, it is sound, complete, true, and sure. Conversely, any witness that contradicts God's witness, is altogether unsound, lacking, false, and wavering. Let's examine, now, what the Psalmist was teaching:

1) the law of the Lord is *perfect*;
2) the testimony of the Lord is *sure*;
3) the statutes of the Lord are *right*;

4) the commandment of the Lord is *pure* and brings *enlightenment*;
5) the fear of the Lord is *clean, and enduring;*
6) the judgments of the Lord are *true and righteous altogether;*
7) these convert the soul, make wise the simple, rejoice the heart, and enlighten the eyes; they endure forever, are better than gold, and are sweeter than honey;
8) keeping them brings great reward.

Friend, that which is perfect needs no improvement; that which is sure needs no debate; that which is right needs no correction; that which brings light needs no enlightenment; that which is clean needs no scrubbing; and that which is true and righteous altogether needs no tampering, defies contradiction, and cannot be refuted. That's quite absolute if you ask me. And look at the benefits of following these: conversion, wisdom, rejoicing, enlightenment, endurance, treasure, and sweetness. Why would anyone want to tamper with God's truth, or even doubt it, and cast these blessings aside?

Number two in our list says that the testimony, or witness, of the Lord is *sure*. Dear one, when God witnesses to us in His Word on any subject, it is sure; it cannot be shaken, moved, or changed. It will stand, Jesus said, *forever* (Matthew 24:35, Mark 13:31, Psalm 119:89). It can never be supplanted by the faulty reasonings of mere men (1 Corinthians 1:25).

Number three says that *the statutes of the LORD are right*. Anything, then, that contradicts God's statutes must be *wrong*. There can only be *one truth* about any particular issue.

Did you know that God's Word has something to say about human reasoning in relation to truth? Well, it does. First of all, adding our ideas and feelings to God's principles, or claiming that these principles are not relevant to us today, and thereby "adjusting" them, has already been covered in this book. God hates anyone's adding to or taking from His sacred Word. God's Word is *absolute*, and needs no adapting, because it comes from a God Who knows everything, and Who changes not. He knows what works and what doesn't. He knows every possible circumstance that can come up in life, and His Word, *as is*, covers it all. How do I know? Because He knows the end from the beginning and, so, knew what was needed, and what would work, for all of time, before He ever established the world and created mankind (Isaiah 46:10). Also, I know because "He is the Rock, his work is perfect" (Deuteronomy 32:4). Here, the same Hebrew word for *perfect* is used. Because He is perfect, His Word is perfect; He and it never need to change. Improvement is not necessary, and in fact, is not possible. And, since His Word is *perfect*, His Word is the only *perfect guide* for living—the only complete, unimpaired, and enduring, truth!

What, then, *does* the Bible say about human reasoning and truth? Look at Jeremiah 10:23, which says, "O LORD, I know that the way of man is not in himself: it is not in man that walketh to direct his steps." *Wow!* It isn't *possible* for mankind to find the way, or the truth, on his own! This is simply not *in* himself! It is not *within* mankind to find the right direction! No matter how brilliant or wise he may become, *it is not within him!* And, friend, to try to direct one's own steps only shows what a fool one is. Isaiah 30:21 reads, "And thine ears shall hear a word behind thee, saying, This is the way, walk ye in it, when ye turn to the right hand, and when ye turn to the left." Clearly, in ourselves, we cannot find the way. In our own wisdom, we will but "turn to the right, or the left, hand," and it takes God to get us back on track. This book is trying to broadcast that "word behind thee" that is saying you are off track, friend, if you've been taken in by false Christianity. God's Word is clear about "the way" you ought to "walk in." I urge you to heed that Voice!

Again, Proverbs 3:5 says, "Trust in the LORD with all thine heart; and lean not unto *thine own understanding* (emphasis added)." Then, Proverbs 8:1 and 6-7 instruct us:

1 Doth not wisdom cry? and understanding put forth her voice?

6 Hear; for I [wisdom] *will speak of excellent things; and the opening of my lips shall be right things.*

7 For my mouth shall speak truth; and wickedness is an abomination to my lips.

Again, Proverbs 2:5-9 reads:

5 Then [when one follows verses 1-4] *shalt thou understand the fear of the LORD, and find the knowledge of God.*

6 For the LORD giveth wisdom: out of his mouth cometh knowledge and understanding.

7 He layeth up sound wisdom for the righteous: he is a buckler to them that walk uprightly.

8 He keepeth the paths of judgment, and preserveth the way of his saints.

9 Then shalt thou understand righteousness, and judgment, and equity; yea, every good path.

Friend, there is no good path to be found outside of God's Word, no matter how *relative* it may be to our *situation*. To think so is to be deceived. We need to look nowhere else to find a good way to walk in through life. God, Himself, is the only source of true wisdom and right understanding (read Job 28:12-28; it is *beautiful*). Now let's read 1 Corinthians 1:25-27a:

25 Because the foolishness of God is wiser than men; and the weakness of God is stronger than men.

26 For ye see your calling, brethren, how that not many wise men after the flesh, not many mighty, not many noble, are called:

27 But God hath chosen the foolish things of the world to confound the wise . . . .

"The foolishness of God is wiser than men." How utterly unwise, how *absurd*, and how futile, it is for any man or group of men to suppose that they can improve on God's Word. How audacious it is for them to purport to know, better than He, what is and what should be, when it comes to being successful spiritually. I tremble for those who make any such claim. I wouldn't want to be in their position at the final Judgment!

First Peter 2:22 says, "neither was guile found in his mouth" [Christ's, verse 21]. *Guile* is taken from the Greek word **dolos** (dol'-os), and according to *Strong's Greek Dictionary*, it means "a *trick* (*bait*), i.e. (fig.) *wile*:—craft, deceit, subtilty."[6] So, if there was no guile in Jesus' mouth, He never said anything deceitful or sly or crafty or untrue. Therefore, everything He did say, in the flesh or through the written Word, is *absolute truth* and absolutely enduring.

Hebrews 6:18 and Titus 1:2 tell us that it is impossible for God to lie. Also, Psalm 33:4 says, "For the word of the LORD is right; and all his works are done in truth." No matter what the controversy is about, *the Word of the Lord is right*, and any other opinion or application is *wrong*. The Psalmist added, in verse 11, "The counsel of the LORD standeth for ever." It will never, ever, be replaced by situational ethics or the idea that truth is relative or subjective. All other, contradicting, counsel is futile! Paul made this fact conclusive in Romans 3:4, when he said, "Yea, let God be true, but every man a liar; as it is written, That thou mightest be justified in thy sayings, and mightest overcome when thou art judged."

We are not to judge God, such as saying His Words fall short and need updating; if we try to, *He* will overcome. Indeed, God will judge *us*, and He will do so according to His immutable Word. So, friend, modern Christendom has failed because, after centuries of "proclaiming the Gospel," its own elite—the "born again"—do not believe the essential things it takes to be a Christian. That means—alas—that most of its "converts" are not converted. Its "born-again" ones are not saved.

Next, and which is the subject of this book, nominal Christianity has failed mankind by inventing false "Jesuses" and preaching them to the people. The people, then, believing in these false "Jesuses," suppose they are saved when they are not, and they hope in vain for an eternity of rest and bliss. How sad. How utterly distressing. How horribly tragic! What could be worse? What could be more terrible than dropping into hell when one expected Heaven? This is serious business. The devil is having a heyday while he deceives souls, and he can do much more damage through "Christianity" than he can through outright evil. Many good people who would never be duped by blatant evil are caught in the trap of this "Christianity" that falls short of real Bible salvation. But Satan's tactics haven't, in themselves, really changed. He deceived Eve by asserting that God didn't really mean what He said, and he has seduced 81 percent of today's "born again" by convincing them that the Bible is not all that accurate in what it teaches. That's saying, again, that God doesn't really mean what He says. It's the same devil, using the same tactic, friend, and he is doing this in large part, today, through so-called "Christianity"! Don't let him do that to *you*!

God had said that in the day Adam or Eve ate of the forbidden fruit, he or she would die. What did the devil say? "Ye shall not surely die" (Genesis 3:4). So it is in nominal Christianity today. God says, "The soul that sinneth, it shall die" (Ezekiel 18:20a), and, "The wages of sin is death" (Romans 6:23), but again Satan (through these modern "Christian" leaders) says, "Ye shall not surely die when you sin. You're a *believer.*" Friend, God never made any such exception. Adam and Eve, after all, were believers too. They spent hours of sweet communion with God, walking and talking with Him, and they were holy, but their sin broke their relationship with God and brought spiritual death. And they had only one sin. *Only one!*

Again, God tells us we must be born again of the Spirit of God, but Satan (through today's church leaders) says, "You don't *have* to be born again. Joining church is just as good." God said that to love the world is enmity with God, but Satan (through modern Christendom) says, "Just don't go too far. No one completely escapes the influence of worldly things." Church leaders fail to preach and demand a separation from the world. "Believers" look and act just like "Vanity Fair." They follow the same amusements, adhere to the same fads, seek the same pleasures, follow the same styles, partake in the same pop culture. In short, they march to the same drum. There is little, if anything, that distinguishes them in a crowd from "the sinners." And, because of false prophets, they think this is perfectly normal living for the saved.

Jesus rebuked the religious leaders of His day for doing this same thing. God's commandments said "thus and thus," but they taught their own ideas as being just as good. Let's read it. Notice how these words of Jesus sound a lot like the foregoing paragraphs: "God said 'this,' but ye say 'that.'" Matthew 15:1-9 read:

1 Then came to Jesus scribes and Pharisees, which were of Jerusalem, saying,

2 Why do thy disciples transgress the tradition of the elders? For they wash not their hands when they eat bread.

3 But he answered and said unto them, Why do ye also transgress the commandment of God by your tradition?

4 For God commanded, saying, Honour thy father and mother: and, He that curseth father or mother, let him die the death.

5 But ye say, Whosoever shall say to his father or his mother, It is a gift, by whatsoever thou mightest be profited by me;

6 And honour not his father or his mother, he shall be free. Thus have ye made the commandment of God of none effect by your tradition.

7 Ye hypocrites, well did Esaias prophesy of you, saying,

8 This people draweth nigh unto me with their mouth, and honoureth me with their lips; but their heart is far from me.

9 But in vain they do worship me, teaching for doctrines the commandments of men.

Friend, this indictment fits today's so-called Christian leaders like their skin. They are always saying that what the Bible teaches is not necessary in this modern time, or that it simply does not mean what it says—but Jesus, Himself, said that those who lay the actual Word of God aside, and substitute their own ideas, are hypocrites. The hearts of those who teach for doctrines the commandments of men are *far from God*. It doesn't matter how many followers they have (except that it means a lot more blood will be on their hands), how many seminary degrees they have, how much they're revered as eminent leaders, *or how dear they are to you*, these teachers of tradition, instead of God's sure Word, actually hinder souls from finding redemption. Jesus addressed these scribes and Pharisees again, in Matthew 23:13, with these words, "But woe unto you, scribes and Pharisees, hypocrites! for ye shut up the kingdom of heaven against men: for ye neither go in yourselves, neither suffer ye them that are entering to go in." In verse 15, He added this searing charge: "Woe unto you, scribes and Pharisees, hypocrites! for ye compass sea and land to make one proselyte, and when he is made, ye make him two-fold more the child of hell than yourselves." Modern "Christian" leaders do the *exact same thing* by adding to or taking from the pure words of God and substituting their own ideas.

Some holiness fighters may try to use Paul's words in Galatians 2:18 to persuade their people not to pay attention to things like this book. There, Paul said, "For if I build again the things which I destroyed, I make myself a transgressor." Or they may quote Galatians 1:8-9:

8 But though we, or an angel from heaven, preach any other gospel unto you than that which we have preached unto you, let him be accursed.

9 As we said before, so say I now again, If any man preach any other gospel unto you than that ye have received, let him be accursed.

They might say something like, "Now, [put your own name here], you know that if you accept this holiness doctrine, you'll be building up what you had destroyed, and that will make you a transgressor. And remember, Paul said if anyone preached any Gospel but the one you've received, let him be accursed."

Paul did *not* say "any other Gospel than the one *you've* received," friend. He wrote this to the *Galatians* about what *he* had preached to *them*. And in verses 11-12 he certified that the Gospel he had preached unto them was not after man, but of Jesus Christ. I can turn this around on these modern leaders and tell you that if *they* preach to *you* any other Gospel than the one Paul preached—and Paul's message plainly taught holiness—let *them* be accursed.

Neither did Paul say that if *you* build up what *you* once destroyed, you make yourself a transgressor. Many people have worked hard to destroy the teaching of holiness, and it would please the Lord tremendously if they would see the light and start building it up. Paul was talking about what *he* had destroyed. The context of this statement deals with the Old Testament ceremonial Law; if Paul built up the Law again, after preaching that it had been done away in Christ (2 Corinthians 3:11, 14), he would make himself a transgressor. That has nothing at all to do with denouncing a false doctrine by walking in the light. These leaders that misuse Paul's words are, again, adding their own ideas to the Word of God. After all, Paul was right then building up the Church of God, which he said he had previously "wasted" (1 Corinthians 15:9, Galatians 1:13, Philippians 3:6). He wasn't making himself a transgressor in that! Correct interpretation of these statements must take account of what Paul was really saying as seen in their contexts. Friend, *every* Scripture must be interpreted in light of its context.

Dear reader, try to grasp just how serious it is when religious leaders add their own opinions to the sacred Word or "explain away" what God says. Look at Deuteronomy 12:32: "What thing soever I command you, observe to do it: thou shalt not add thereto, nor diminish from it." Now read Proverbs 30:5-6:

5 Every word of God is pure . . . .

6 Add thou not unto his words, lest he reprove thee, and thou be found a liar.

Lastly, read Revelation 22:18-19:

18 For I testify unto every man that heareth the words of the prophecy of this book, If any man shall add unto these things, God shall add unto him the plagues that are written in this book:

19 And if any man shall take away from the words of the book of this prophecy, God shall take away his part out of the book of life, and out of the holy city, and from the things which are written in this book.

Refusing to submit to what God's Word teaches, and telling others that it doesn't mean what it says, then adding one's own ideas to it, is very terribly dangerous!

Let's go on. Again, God said, "Be ye holy, for I am holy," but Satan (through these false prophets) says, "Merely do your best. God understands that you're human. No one can live like that in this world." They leave believers in their sins. What, pray tell, are these believers saved from? Don't forget that Jesus came to "save his people from their sins" (Matthew 1:21). The only way Jesus saves is *from sin.* Anyone who is "saved" and is not saved from sin, does not have Bible salvation. If your "Jesus" did not save you *from sin,* you do not believe in the Jesus of the Bible. I say this kindly, but I say it with conviction. And I mean it when I say I tell you this kindly. I say these things in love. I love souls too much to look the other way while they hurtle toward eternity with a false hope. If you believe in a false "Jesus," *I want you to find it out while you can do something about it!*

You may say, "Well, my preacher teaches us that we must be born again. He doesn't just promote joining church." Okay. But what *kind* of being born again does he teach? Just as there is a Bible Jesus and a false "Jesus," there is a Bible "born again" and a false "born again." We saw this in the fact that 81 percent of those who claim to be born again, do not believe the Bible. Being born again according to the Scriptures produces real believers, and it brings a life that is free from sin. Look at 1 John 3:9, which says, "Whosoever is born of God doth not commit sin; for his [God's] seed remaineth in him: and he cannot sin, because he is born of God." When you were born again, were you saved *from* sin, or *in* sin?

You may ask, "Are you saying that born-again people *can't* sin?" Friend, *I* didn't say this. John, inspired by the Holy Ghost, said it. But, yes, John said that born-again people can't sin. They cannot sin, because sinning and being a child of God cannot go together. They are polar opposites of each other. They are mutually exclusive. If you are one, you cannot be the other. So, as long as one is born of God, he cannot sin, because sinning destroys his born-again experience. To put it another way, *it is impossible for the truly born again to live a sin-more-or-less-day-by-day experience!*

This text is not referring to the *ability* to sin. Certainly God doesn't take away our free moral agency, our right to choose, when we get saved. Christians can leave God's will and go back to sin if they want to, but John was simply telling those he wrote to that no one can be a *sinning Christian.* If we're Christians, we live above sin, and if we sin, we are no longer born again. We don't sin and stay saved (more on this in chapters ten and eleven). I repeat, born-again people cannot sin because when they sin, they abandon their born-again experience. But as long as they stay committed to God, and *Christ remaineth in them,* they will not sin. The Psalmist said, "Thy word have I hid in mine heart, that I might not sin against thee" (Psalm 119·11). Since Calvary, we can "hide" Jesus in our hearts, for Christ is the Word made flesh (John 1:14). So, to summarize this point, we cannot be born again and be living in sin, and we cannot be living in sin and be born again. It cannot happen, John said—and it's just that simple.

We have learned that there is, of course, a spiritual infancy, when newly-born-again babes have to grow and develop. While they are new in their walk with Christ, it is possible for them to fall while in temptation or during trial, just as a human child doesn't just get up one day and start walking without some mishaps. If these will immediately come to Christ in repentance, and seek His strength for the future, they can continue in their lives as Christians. This is not—I repeat, *it is not*—the same as sinning more or less day after day. It is a very temporary situation, with complete victory following—unless that individual gives up in his failure. But God is gracious with newborn babes and struggling souls as long as those souls are not just being careless or uncommitted. He does not condone, put up with, excuse, or overlook, these sins, but He forgives them and gives strength, so the babe can learn and grow through them, and have victory in the future.

Friend, modern, nominal, "Christianity" has failed because, instead of leading people to this deliverance from sin, they say no one can obtain it. These two positions, also, are polar opposites. These preachers and teachers are not just a little bit off target; they're *100 percent* off target. To be sure, it is almost impossible for people to find deliverance from sin where judgment is not poured out on sin. Therefore, since modern Christendom doesn't put judgment on sin, but rather makes room for it, its "converts" aren't obtaining this deliverance. But it's not because Christ hasn't provided it; it's because those who profess to preach the Gospel stand in the way! Oh, they talk a good talk, about how terrible sin is, but they certainly don't put judgment on it in the lives of their people, or themselves, and they insist that a lot of sins are not even sinful, such as the aforementioned love of the world. The Apostle Paul said that he was "set for the defense of the gospel" (Philippians 1:17), but today's "Christian" ministers spend their time defending sin instead. Instead of exercising themselves unto godliness, as commanded in 1 Timothy 4:7, they exercise themselves in opposing godliness. I repeat, they're 100 percent off target. They have completely missed the mark.

Missed the mark? Dear reader, the word *sin* is taken from the Greek words *hamartano* (ham-ar-tan'-o), *hamartema* (ham-ar'-tay-mah), and *hamartia* (ham-ar'-tee'-ah). The latter two are derived from the first, which *Strong's* says means "to *miss* the mark (and so *not share* in the prize)."[7] So, missing the mark is sin, and those who miss it *will not share in the prize.*

America is in crisis today, far more than ever before in her history, and the bulk of the problem is because of the letdown in the pulpits. Were they still "crying aloud and sparing not" when it comes to sin, things would never have deteriorated to the point they have. Let's look at those words in the Bible: "Cry aloud, spare not, lift up thy voice like a trumpet, and shew my people their transgression, and the house of Jacob their sins" (Isaiah 58:1). Most of today's "Christian" leaders can't "blow the trumpet." They don't "spare not" when it comes to sin; rather, they *do* spare, making room for sin in the believer, and for "sinning Christians" in the church. When they do show the people their sins, it's of no avail, because they do not require them to stop sinning, and, in fact, they tell them they can't.

A test sometimes put on people, at least in the past, to help determine whether or not they were insane, was to put them into a room with a spigot that is turned on and running. They were then handed a mop and a bucket, and told to clean up the water. If they started mopping without turning off the spigot, they failed the test. This is exactly what Christendom is doing today. They are trying to deal with all the problems sin wreaks on society—crime, drug addiction, teen pregnancy, sexually transmitted diseases, violence, drunk driving, out-of-control divorce, etc., etc.—but they won't "turn off the spigot" and put judgment on sin itself. Instead, they tolerate it, defend it, and make excuses for it. *This is spiritual insanity.*

Modern "Christianity" has failed because it has only "healed the hurt of the daughter of my people slightly, saying, Peace, peace; when there is no peace" (Jeremiah 8:11; also 6:14). Jesus tells us in John 16:8, "And when he [the Holy Spirit, verse 7] is come, he will reprove the world of sin, and of righteousness, and of judgment."

The word *reprove* comes from the Greek word *elegcho* (el-eng'-kho), which means, "to *confute, admonish:*—convict, convince, tell a fault, rebuke, reprove."[8] It is the task of the Holy Ghost to:

1) convince, or convict, people of sin;
2) show them that they ought to, and can, be righteous through salvation;
3) warn them of the judgment awaiting sinners.

In bringing an awareness of their sins to men and women, the Spirit of God urges them to repent of those sins and be saved. Be sure of this: *the Holy Spirit is faithful!* He is doing what He is supposed to do. He brings conviction of sin to hearts. But, alas! Today's "Christian" ministers offer these convicted sinners a faulty remedy! They tell them that they can be delivered from the *penalty* of their sins without being delivered from sin itself. They "heal sinners' wounds" slightly. People get enough religion to salve their consciences, but not enough to save their souls. But because they get a counterfeit salvation, they stop searching for the true. Because they are told they are "saved," they no longer worry about being lost. The Holy Spirit's conviction is salved over by a false security, and His work on the hearts of men and women is made *of none effect.* They believe they have made peace with God, *when there is no peace.* These anti-holiness preachers and teachers are actually found to be undoing the work of the Holy Ghost! This is a very serious offence, friend, in the sight of a God Who is not willing that any perish, and Who requires the blood of the deceived at the hand of the deceiver.

The Psalmist wrote, "Mercy and truth are met together; righteousness and peace have kissed each other" (Psalm 85:10). Peace and righteousness go together. They fit hand-in-glove. We will never have peace with God unless we have righteousness. And remember, righteousness, in the New Testament sense, means victory over sin. Again, Romans 6:18 says, "Being then made free from sin, ye became the servants of righteousness." And verse 19 says, " . . . even so now yield your members servants to righteousness unto holiness." *Holiness.* Without it there is no peace with God.

I touched on this earlier, but now I want to go deeper into the fact that modern "Christianity" has failed to keep the world out of the church. A good example of this failure is Christendom's attitude toward movies and TV. *Wait!* Please hear me out. You may think I'm really radical, here, but let me show you why I say this, okay? Church leaders continually bemoan the filth in these media, right? They fret about what this trash is doing to our youth, our marriages, our society in general, right? In so doing, they are openly admitting that these things are unfit for the eyes, ears, and hearts, of their flocks. Yet, for the most part, they go right on watching them. They go right on condoning them in the homes of their people and themselves. For decades, now, Christendom has conducted campaigns to "clean them up," yet they have had no real effect on them. Instead, their content is growing ever worse and *worse*! But rather than clean movies and TV out of their hearts and homes and habits, these "Christians" hang onto them as if they were necessary to life. Anything I said was that corrupt, I would certainly not welcome right into my home! David wouldn't have, either: "I will walk within my house with a perfect heart. I will set no wicked thing before mine eyes" (Psalm 101:2-3).

Get rid of my TV and my VCR/DVD player? Why, that's unheard of! How right that statement is; it *is* unheard of. Modern preachers won't ask anyone to do it. No matter that the stuff TV and movies bring right into their homes is unfit for sinners, let alone Christians. No matter that it contradicts, and even mocks, everything they claim to believe in and cherish. No matter that it saturates them with a worldly spirit that numbs their sensitivity to the Holy Spirit. No matter that their vulnerable children are exposed to every shade and nuance of evil imaginable. How can they reconcile exposing their children to all of that in light of the Bible edict to bring them up in the nurture and admonition of the Lord? In spite of all the sick content in movies and on TV, those who profess to love Christ supremely still can't banish them from their lives. Many professed Christians even say things such as, "Oh, I don't even watch that thing. It's horrible." Yet they cannot get rid of it. They just have to have it. Talk about bondage! Modern "Christians" are, as a whole, almost entirely in bondage to movies and TV. Some churches even have TVs within their walls and/or show movies there. These two archives of evil receive the ardent, unrelenting devotion usually given to a *god*. Yes, that's my point. Movies and TV have become gods to many, if not most, of today's "believers," but, my friend, having any god before the Lord Almighty is idolatry, and no true Christian can be an idolater.

The early Christians turned the world upside down (right-side up) in a few years, yet, I repeat, the nominal "church" has been "cleaning up" the entertainment industry for decades while it has only grown horribly worse. (A real impact they're having, huh?) The Apostles did not try to "convert" worldliness, rather, they converted people *from* worldliness. They didn't "christianize" evil. They didn't try to. Evil will always be evil. They realized that they were to hate the world and its evil and turn their backs on it. They declared a "come out" message to the masses and people came out of the world. What people need to do is accept the fact that movies and TV, and all other strongholds of worldliness are, *by nature*, evil, off limits, and against God, and then *forsake* them. Remember, dear one, friendship with the world is *enmity* with God (James 4:4), and loving the world *bars God's love* from your heart (1 John 2:15)! This is true, no matter how loudly modern "Christian" leaders cry the opposite.

And they do. Today's "apostles" are themselves under the spell of the world. No wonder their disciples are. Instead of withstanding sin and worldliness, these leaders are swept away in its current, trying to shed a little "positive influence" around them as they tumble downstream. This is so *far* from what God called His ministry to be and to do.

Try to get nominal "Christians" to give up their TVs, their movies, their music, their conformity with popular culture, and we would hear their howl around the world! The truth is that the nominal "Christian" is in love with the world, and the nominal "church" aids and abets this love. You have to travel far and wide to find a preacher who separates his people from the pop culture of this world. The Bible, however, demands this, and James actually said that friendship with the world is spiritual adultery! Oh, let's just read it. James 4:4 says, "Ye adulterers and adulteresses, know ye not that the friendship of the world is enmity with God? whosoever therefore will be a friend of the world is the enemy of God."

Then, look at the Apostle John's words:

1 John 2:15 Love not the world, neither the things that are in the world. If any man love the world, the love of the Father is not in him.

16 For all that is in the world, the lust of the flesh, and the lust of the eyes, and the pride of life, is not of the Father, but is of the world.

How much plainer can anything be than that? Oh, friend, did you get it? *Loving the world is actually being an enemy of, and committing spiritual adultery against, our divine Husband, Jesus Christ!* Yet modern "Christianity" fails to require this separation from the world; it says, instead, "Well, now, it's all right to have *a little* of the world. Just don't go overboard." This is adding to and taking away from the Scriptures. They add that "a little" is okay, and they take away the eternal truth that no one loving the world can possibly be saved! Friend, let me hit it again: God condemns this adding to and taking from His sacred and immutable Word. The verses I just quoted leave no room for a little of the world. If we love the world, period, we do not have the love of God in us, period. If we are friendly with the world, period, we are adulterers or adulteresses and enemies of God, period. It's just that simple. Do not let anyone complicate it for you. And please let me ask you, dear one—do you love the world? If you do, you are not God's child; you are His . . . . Oh, what a sad situation! Please come to the truth so you can be His friend!

Although Christendom, today, fails to hold this standard for the people, this is the standard of the Bible, and it is the standard of the *Jesus* of the Bible. Any "Jesus" who allows the world in the "church" is a false Jesus, and preachers who do so are false prophets. If you do not have the love of God in you, and if you are an enemy of God (in other words, if you are a "worldly Christian"), no amount of "faith" is going to carry you into Glory, precious soul.

I know this is shocking to you, friend, but I don't want your blood on *my* hands. I don't want you to be lost. I must tell you the truth, and I love you enough to tell you the truth, even though I expect this book will make a lot of enemies for me and even bring persecution my way. But the very fact that it is shocking only proves how modern "Christianity" has failed you. What I'm sharing in this book is the explicit teaching of the Scriptures, yet the people don't hear it preached. Preachers are supposed to "hear the word at my mouth, and give them warning from me" (Ezekiel 3:17), but instead they are preaching "smooth things . . . [and] deceits" (Isaiah 30:10). Modern Christendom's "preacher factories" (seminaries) don't crank out preachers who "preach the Word." They produce ministers who preach that which soothes the fleshly whims and lusts of the people. They cringe at the thought of preaching something that "ruffles someone's feathers."

Jesus set the Church in the world to be "the salt of the earth" (Matthew 5:13), but He went on to say that "if the salt have lost his savour, wherewith shall it be salted? it is thenceforth good for nothing, but to be cast out, and to be trodden under foot of men." Salt preserves, but, sadly, today's churches have lost their ability to preserve society, as we've already shown. Salt also makes thirsty and *this* salt is supposed to make people thirsty for salvation and then draw them to the Fountain of living waters. Yet the savorless salt that is found in modern Christendom cannot make people thirsty for righteousness. All it offers is a watered-down "gospel" that doesn't cost much, if anything, and all it draws to are broken, polluted, cisterns that can hold no water (Jeremiah 2:13). And, hey, did you hear what Jesus said about salt that has lost its savor? If the salt—or we could say, the *"church,"* for Jesus was talking to His disciples—have lost his saltiness, it is *good for nothing!* Hey, Jesus said this; I'm only repeating it. Don't be like the Jewish leaders in Jesus' day and hate Him for telling it like it is.

The Apostle Paul wouldn't be welcome in today's nominal pulpits. Look at what he said in 2 Timothy 3:1-5:

1 This know also, that in the last days perilous times shall come.

2 For men shall be lovers of their own selves, covetous, boasters, proud, blasphemers, disobedient to parents, unthankful, unholy,

3 Without natural affection, trucebreakers, false accusers, incontinent, fierce, despisers of those that are good,

4 Traitors, heady, highminded, lovers of pleasures more than lovers of God;

5 Having a form of godliness, but denying the power thereof: from such turn away.

Here Paul gave a list of horrible sins, and although they were terrible in themselves, he then said they were found in people who *had a form of godliness.* Friend, today's churches are full of people who love themselves and are covetous, people who are proud and boastful, heady and highminded. They are running over with folks who are or were disobedient to their parents and many other forms of authority. And they are certainly crowded with those who love pleasure. Paul said these love pleasure more than they love God.

You may cry, "I don't know how you can say the churches are full of people who love pleasure more than they love God!" Friend, I didn't say it; I only quoted Paul's words to Timothy and brought it up to date. But you can test it, yourself. It's easy. Just tell them God is against all forms of worldly entertainment, and see how fast they rise up against you. See how fast they make excuses for their pleasure seeking, how fast they make room for it under the garb of being "Christians." Tell them that God demands a separation from these, and you will see outright rebellion. You will see what they truly love.

Paul said these people would be *unholy*, and that this was a sign of conditions that were dangerous. In saying this, he let us know that unholiness is *not the norm* for Christians. I don't need to tell you that the modern "Christian churches" are full of people who are unholy. They *admit* that they are. They even get angry if someone says that they, therefore, can't be saved!

Again, all of these conditions were found in people who had a form of godliness, Paul said, and he added that this produced a perilous situation. Sin in "the church," my friend, is perilous indeed. Why? Because God will not tolerate sin. If sin is in "the church," *God will not tolerate "the church."* Don't think for one minute that God will put up with sin in "Christians" just because they claim to be His people. In fact, sin in those who profess to be His people stirs God's wrath a lot more than sin in outright sinners. Remember what He told the Laodiceans? He said, "So then because thou art lukewarm . . . I will spue thee out of my mouth." And He told the Ephesian church this: "Repent . . . or else I will come unto thee quickly, and will remove thy candlestick" (Revelation 3:16, Revelation 2:5). When a church loses its candlestick—symbolic of its being the light of the world and the Lord's Church (Revelation 1:20)—it goes into darkness and is His Church no longer. He said He would come quickly. He does not put up with such conditions very long. He warns, and if people do not shape up, He leaves. Friend, churches that won't line up with the Word are abandoned by God! And most so-called Christian "churches" of our time have lost their light—along with their salt—a long time ago. Just remember, God did not leave or forsake them until after they left and forsook Him!

Next, Paul made a very profound statement. He said that these sin-laden professors of Christianity, who indeed had a form of godliness, *denied the power of godliness*. This is, for sure, a description of almost all of modern Christendom. What is the power of godliness? It is that divine power whereby God enables us to live godly lives ("in this present world," Titus 2:11-12). It is that by which godliness reigns, in us, over evil, that which much more abounds than sin's power.

Modern Christendom absolutely denies this power. These words of Paul describe to a "tee" the condition found in today's so-called

Christian churches. You know it's so. Modern Christendom is full of people who claim to be God's people—they have the *form*—right while they live in sin and vehemently deny that anyone has power to live a godly life.

Modern "Christianity" has failed, and it has failed *you*, dear reader. It fits perfectly into 2 Timothy 3:1-5 and is in a perilous condition indeed. Why? Because God is nowhere near it. The masses who worship in its assemblies Sunday after Sunday are deceived. But while Paul, in these verses, gave a perfect description of *fallen* Christianity, and for sure, *today's* "Christianity," you can read a description of the Church that meets God's approval in Ephesians 5:25-27:

25 Husbands, love your wives, even as Christ also loved the church, and gave himself for it;

26 That he might sanctify and cleanse it with the washing of water by the word,

27 That he might present it to himself a glorious church, not having spot, or wrinkle, or any such thing; but that it should be holy and without blemish.

Friend, God's Church is holy and without blemish. Paul even said, "or any such thing"! And if you would be a part of it, you must obey God's Word. What is God telling you to do? Well, for one thing, He instructs you, through the Apostle Paul, to *avoid* people who deny the power of godliness. Read 2 Timothy 3:5 again. It ends with the words, "from such turn away." Friend, I was part of nominal "Christianity" once. I was, indeed, saved there, but I had a hard time holding onto my experience and was in and out. Then "I heard [a] voice from heaven, saying, Come out of her, my people" (Revelation 18:4), and I obeyed! I am not "preaching" what I have not practiced. I am not issuing a challenge that I have not been given, myself. But I praise God with every breath, that I was given that challenge! It opened up more clearly the living way, and brought me a far more abundant life!

Are you wondering *how* one becomes a part of God's holy and spotless Church, if the assemblies of so-called Christianity are fallen, and we need to turn away from such? (I *hope* you are.) Dear reader, all you need to do is humble your heart before God, confess and forsake your sins, believe as the Word of God instructs, get a true born-again experience, and live a godly life, by the power of God. It is *all* by the power of God. This is, simply put, being *saved* as the Bible promises to believers in the real, actual, Christ. Acts 2:47 tells us that "the Lord added to the church daily such as should be saved." Since the Church is the household of God (see 1 Timothy 3:15), we're born into it when we become His child; no joining is needed or desired. Nowhere in the Bible are we instructed to join a church. Once you have found this true salvation, you are in His Church; He has added you to it; just ask God to direct you to a congregation of His true people. He will!

Someone may say, "But 'without spot or wrinkle' refers to when the church gets to glory. That's when she is made pure." No, friend; when the end comes, Jesus will deliver up the kingdom to the Father, not to Himself: "Then cometh the end, when he shall have delivered up the kingdom to God, even the Father; when he shall have put down all rule and all authority and power" (1 Corinthians 15:24). Presenting the Church to Himself is *not* at the end of time. It happens *daily*. Also, making the Church spotless includes that continual washing of water by the unadulterated Word of God (Ephesians 5:26). Read it! That takes place in this life, friend, and it is why Jesus called a ministry. Look at Ephesians 4:11-13:

11 And he gave some, apostles; and some, prophets; and some, evangelists; and some, pastors and teachers;

12 For the perfecting of the saints, for the work of the ministry, for the edifying of the body of Christ:

13 Till we all come in the unity of the faith, and of the knowledge of the Son of God, unto a perfect man, unto the measure of the stature of the fulness of Christ.

From what we have studied, so far, we see that believers are saved and made holy at conversion, then they are kept holy by the continual washing of the Word of God. That is the purpose of the ministry. So, as understanding comes through the faithful preaching and teaching of the Word, believers learn how to be more like Christ. Up to that understanding, they have not sinned, because there was no knowledge. They were holy before, and when they measure up to the new understanding, it makes them more holy. Jesus' Church is without spot or blemish, or any such thing, right now, in this present world!

Are you beginning to see how far nominal Christendom has fallen from the position the Church of God was initially, and is continually, called to? Instead of today's pulpits calling believers to an ever-greater holiness, really washing them in the Word and bringing them to the full measure of Christ, modern "Christianity" hides the Scriptures about what Jesus' redemption really produces, and tells everyone that they *can't* reach perfection till they get to Heaven. No; if they don't reach it here, they won't *get* to Heaven. Hear again Paul's words: *He gave some, apostles; and some, prophets; and some, evangelists; and some, pastors and teachers; For the perfecting of the saints . . . till we all come . . . unto the measure of the stature of the fulness of Christ.* Friend, Christ is holy, and for us to reach His full measure, we must be holy. This, again, is the reason Christ called a ministry. This perfecting takes place in this world. Since Christ gave a ministry to bring the people to all that He is, any professed ministry that fails to produce a holy people is not the ministry Christ gave.

Nominal Christianity has failed, also, in its very *believing*. While it claims to believe that living for Christ is better, higher, and grander, than living in sin, many do not really believe it. Show the masses that truly living for Christ demands this separation from all sin, and, I repeat, they will rebel. They will take the world; they will cling to their sins. The truth is that the majority of them do not want to be free from sin. It is not Christ that they believe, and it is not living for Him that they love. What they love is a religion that allows them to have the world and their sins and still, supposedly, escape the consequences of these. So, while claiming to live for God, and loving it, they are actually in rebellion against Him. They don't believe that living holy lives, above this sinful world, is the best way to live. They'd rather have their easy-on-the-flesh religion. They'd rather go their own way.

Notice that I just said, "many," "the masses," and "the majority." Thank God, there *are* those out there who hate their sins. They long to be able to truly and fully obey God. Like Paul, in Romans 7, they are wretched and miserable, but, alas, they do not know that they can be delivered. *It is for these that I labor to bring the truth to light in this book!*

Also, nominal Christianity fails *in its believing* because, while claiming to believe that Christ is the all-powerful, all-sufficient, Lord of all, in practice it denies that He is. It denies that He has sufficient power to really handle the sin problem. Indeed, while it claims to believe that Jesus is Lord, and while it *calls* Him Lord, it does not do the things He says, for it does not believe He can give the power to do so. But Jesus said, "And why call ye me, Lord, Lord, and do not the things which I say" (Luke 6:46)? According to the Bible Jesus, there is *no use* in calling Him Lord, when you do not do as He says. So, while today's nominal "Christians" call Jesus "Lord," they fight His lordship over their own lives, and they fight His lordship over Satan and sin. He simply cannot handle these, according to them, so His followers have to be overcome by them. *Not so, my friend!* It is ludicrous to say that Jesus' followers have to commit sin! Christendom fails in its believing because all such "believing" is futile. It is fruitless. It is a mockery of Jesus Christ. He *is* Lord. He commands and the devil flees. And it works in the lives of His followers yet today!

Though we examined 2 Timothy 3:1-5 closely, there's another thought there that we need to consider, and that is this: the key to this whole list of perils is pretty much summed up in the first indictment: men shall be lovers of their own selves. This thing of *self* is the culprit behind all sin. Isaiah revealed this to us in Isaiah 53:6, where he said, "All we like sheep have gone astray; we have turned every one to his own way . . . ." Having our own way is the downfall of every one of us. That's why Jesus carefully instructed us that the very first rung on the ladder of salvation is self-denial. Let us review His words in Matthew 16:24-25:

24 If any man will come after me, let him deny himself, and take up his cross, and follow me.

25 For whosoever will save his life shall lose it: and whosoever will lose his life for my sake shall find it.

Luke 14:26-27 confirms this:

26 If any man come to me, and hate not his father, and mother, and wife, and children, and brethren, and sisters, yea, and his own life also, he cannot be my disciple.

27 And whosoever doth not bear his cross, and come after me, cannot be my disciple.

Here, self-denial is clearly set forth as an absolute requirement for discipleship. Romans 6:6, remember, tells us just how we are to deal with self—we are to crucify it. That is why Jesus said we must take up our cross and follow Him. In other words, we must die out to self. We do this by entirely yielding our *self* to God, surrendering our all, and our will, to His will and control. Anything less will absolutely fail to make one a disciple of Christ. Jesus said that without it, we *cannot* be His disciples, no matter how much we "believe." He said our trying to preserve "our life" would only result in our losing it. It's in dying that we live; it's in losing that we gain. But so-called Christianity does not set this total self-denial, this *killing* of self, before the people; it does not come close to setting it forth as *absolutely required*, and that's why the perilous times Paul spoke of are with us today. You may be sure that if you die out to self and truly believe the Gospel, God will give you victory over your flesh every day! Again, the choice is ours, but the power, the miracle, is of God.

In Luke 19:12-14 Jesus said:

12 A certain nobleman went into a far country to receive for himself a kingdom, and to return.

13 And he called his ten servants, and delivered them ten pounds, and said unto them, Occupy till I come.

14 But his citizens [not his servants] *hated him, and sent a message after him, saying, We will not have this man to reign over us.*

Nominal Christendom, today, will talk about Jesus. They will sing about Jesus. They will hold retreats about Jesus. They will host conferences about Jesus and set up web sites about Jesus. They will write books and newsletters about Jesus. They, supposedly, work hard for Jesus. But it's that *reigning* they have a problem with. They don't want preachers to tell them God cares how they dress, where they go, or what they watch and listen to. And the preachers don't want to tell them, either. It costs too much. They are afraid they will lose their people. Instead, they lose their souls, and cause their people's souls to be lost as well. Preachers and people alike are willing to "deny" themselves the really vile stuff, but they balk at watching everything they do. The Bible commands this, however. Read it: "Whether therefore ye eat, or drink, or whatsoever ye do, do all to the glory of God" (1 Corinthians 10:31). Now read Colossians 3:17: "And whatsoever ye do in word or deed, do all in the name of the Lord Jesus, giving thanks to God and the Father by him." Hey, did you get that? Indeed, God requires that we watch everything we do and everything we say, and when our heart is right, we'll thank God while we're doing it. But we'd better beware if we're doing anything we cannot do in His Name and for His glory, no matter how much we claim Him as our Lord.

Be honest with yourself, dear friend. Can you really say that you do all you do in Jesus' Name and to the glory of God? Is all of your entertainment and recreation glorifying to God? There are many "Christians" who know fornication, adultery, and homosexuality, are wrong, but they watch it all the time on the screen. They really hate to miss their soap operas. *Do you really think Christians can watch this filth on a day-by-day basis to the glory of God?* What about the Scripture that talks about finding pleasure in those who do wrong (Romans 1:32)? Are these "Christians" not enjoying this trash? Why else would they watch it? Surely no one is forcing them to. And are they not sympathizing with their favorite characters, even though their actions are evil? Are they not actually hoping the illicit affairs work out, because they *like* the characters involved in them? No doubt some of you who read this actually cringed when I called such "entertainment" filth, and trash, and garbage. Well, what would you call it, if you were honest? I ask you, being myself honest, how can Christians be entertained by such evil?

You may ask, "Well, do *you* never, ever, watch such things?" Dear one, I do not have a TV; we've never allowed one in our home, and I don't run over to someone else's house to watch it. The only movie I have watched, in decades, was *The Ten Commandments*, which I threw away after I watched it, because it was so lewd, and it was not faithful to the Bible account. I did purchase *The Passion of the Christ* a few years ago, thinking it would be beneficial to see such a graphic portrayal of what Christ went through for me. To this day, though, I've never watched it. Even though it's supposedly biblical, it was still created by Hollywood, a cesspool of sin and worldliness, and I'm afraid it will reek of lewdness as well.

Beyond those two, I do not buy, rent, download, or attend movies. I actually hate the world, as I'm supposed to do, because I've found the real, true, Jesus of the Bible, and He fills my soul with such sweetness that the things of this world are but hollow and worthless in comparison. Dear one, when we die to sin, self, and the world, the new life Jesus brings is joy unspeakable and full of glory!

Someone may ask, "Are you never tempted by the world?" Oh, yes, of course. Honestly, I'm human. But from the depth of my heart, I can say, "I'd rather have Jesus!" because I truly would. He surpasses all I ever found while I chased after the world!

Paul said we are to "abstain from all appearance of evil" (1 Thessalonians 5:22), and in Ephesians 5:3 he told us, "But fornication, and all uncleanness . . . let it not be once named among you, as becometh saints." He went on, in verses 11-12:

11 And have no fellowship with the unfruitful works of darkness, but rather reprove them [that's what I'm doing].

12 For it is a shame even to speak of those things which are done of them in secret.

Of course, today many of these things are done *openly,* but that doesn't change the shamefulness of their finding a place in the conversations, or entertainment, of those who are called by Christ's Name. I'm sure some "Christians" talk animatedly about their "soaps." And what about so many video games? Let me make this clear up front: I do not play shady or questionable—let alone vile and violent—video games. How can Christians who know assaulting, killing, destroying property, running someone down or beating someone up, is wrong, *do it themselves* all the time through video games? And what about the lewdness and sexual innuendoes that one finds in them? Does this glorify God? *What kinds of passions do these things stir up within the players?* In some video games the players even have to commit rape to move to the next level. In others, they have to kill every last "enemy"—and even innocent bystanders—to move up a level. Even in "milder" games, they have to run over people, crash into cars and buildings, leaving behind them a wake of terrible destruction, and be the fastest one to do all of this. How, I ask you, can Christians get so caught up in acting out such violence to the glory of God? Furthermore, many games—very many, in fact—revolve around the idea of a supernatural, magic, and occult, *force* to enable the player to gain his goals. Friend, supernatural power that is not of God is *of the devil.* And God's Holy Spirit is *not* the inspiration behind games created by unregenerate men. Can Christians play, with reliance on "the force" for their success and victories? Is this not a subtle form of having another god? "Oh, come on," someone may say. "They're only games! Loosen up a little." Well, friend, have you never read God's opinion of these very real spirits that people take so lightly today and play around with? Get a good concordance and study it. There is just no way a saved person can play with demonic power to the glory of God! The occult is creeping into American culture at an alarming rate, and many good people don't even realize that they are playing right into this devilish system. Do you use words like "karma," or "mantra"? These are straight out of the occult world.

Many are taking yoga and martial arts classes and don't know that these are very much a part of the occult world. Dear friend, just because something is "common," it doesn't make it any less wrong. A terrible amount of the occult has sneaked into children's books, games, and activities. It's downright scary! And just because these things may offer "benefits" (yoga, for example), that doesn't make them one bit less dangerous. Satan always, *always*, presents benefits when he tempts us! (Remember Eve?) What all these things are, in reality, are other "chains of darkness," and they will "reserve you unto judgment" just as surely as did those Peter and Jude spoke of.

I'm absolutely sure that many who watch movies and TV, or play around with these corrupt video games, books, and music, etc., have to battle their consciences to indulge in them; unfortunately, their consciences lose the battle and, in time, are silenced. They are silenced until folks can toy with such evil, and *enjoy* it, without a care, all the time claiming to love Jesus. Tell me, how can anyone do these things to the glory of God and in Jesus' Name?

As you were reading the paragraphs above, friend, did you feel resistance toward the thought of God's requiring you to give up your worldly, and/or corrupt, entertainment? Did (even a wee bit of) rebellion raise up? Well, please remember what Jesus gave up for you—and be assured that He never asks you to give up anything that is good for you. "No *good* thing will He withhold from them that walk uprightly" (Psalm 84:11b; emphasis added). And when we follow the Lamb whithersoever He goeth (Revelation 14:4), we will *never* regret it. You just cannot beat God when it comes to giving. The more you give up for His sake, the more of Heaven's riches He will pour into your soul! You talk about joy! You do not know joy like you will know it when you put Him before your own desires. But one reason we have all these ungodly things infiltrating the lives of so-called Christians is because . . .

Modern "Christianity" has failed. It will not set forth a Bible standard for personal conduct. Instead, it allows sins of every kind to overrun professed believers' lives, defile and harden the heart, and sear the conscience. In short, it *calls* Jesus Lord, but it will not let Him *be* Lord, it will not let Him reign over it, and, for sure, it will not demand this of its people. I am quite confident that many preachers will tell their people that "that woman [me] is crazy. Avoid her like the plague!" I just ask you, please, as you indulge in your sinful activities, look inward and ask yourself, "Can I really do this to the glory of God and in the holy name of Jesus?" God will be true to your soul, dear one; will you be true to Him?

The next failure we will consider in this study is that Christendom fails in its worship. Jesus said, in John 4:23-24:

23 But the hour cometh, and now is, when the true worshippers shall worship the Father in spirit and in truth: for the Father seeketh such to worship him.

24 God is a Spirit: and they that worship him must worship him in spirit and in truth.

Psalm 51:6 says, "Behold, thou desirest truth in the inward parts." Psalm 5:9 speaks of those whose "inward part is very wickedness." We have proven that when we are not pure in heart, we are not truly Christ's followers. And if we do not have Christ in our hearts, we do not have *truth* in our inward part. Neither is our *spirit* right. How, friend, can such a one worship the Lord in spirit and in truth? God promised, in Ezekiel 36:26, that He will give penitents a new heart and a new spirit. Without these—a right spirit and truth in our inward parts—there is no way we can properly worship God. Remember verses 11-15 of Isaiah the 1st Chapter, where God told Israel how He looks upon the worship of those who do not worship in (a right) spirit and in truth. To bring this vividly to mind again, let's reread God's judgment on such worship, given in verse 15:

15 And when ye spread forth your hands, I will hide mine eyes from you: yea, when ye make many prayers, I will not hear: your hands are full of blood.

Are modern Christendom's hands full of blood? Yes, they are. First Corinthians 11:27 says, "Wherefore whosoever shall eat this bread, and drink this cup of the Lord, unworthily, shall be guilty of the body and blood of the Lord."

"Worship" without a pure heart is an abomination to God, friend. Isaiah was addressing those who professed to be God's people but were willfully disobedient. Worship offered from such hearts made God sick then, and it makes God sick today. All over this nation, and indeed, around the world, millions are regularly offering to God so-called worship that does not go any higher than their heads. Why? Because their hearts and spirits are not holy. *They that worship the*

Father must *worship Him in spirit and in truth*! True worship requires a spirit that is abiding in God's truth, and God's truth demands holiness of life. Modern "Christianity" is failing to offer acceptable worship to God, and it is instrumental in causing millions of people to offer unacceptable worship to God. And in the process, often every Sunday, those millions are eating and drinking of the communion supper of the Lord unworthily and bringing His blood upon their heads. Let me press upon you yet *again* that this is very serious business.

Modern "Christianity" is failing the souls of men and women, boys and girls, by providing them with a false refuge. We can read about this in Isaiah 28:14-18:

14 Wherefore hear the word of the LORD, ye scornful men, that rule this people which is in Jerusalem.

15 Because ye have said, We have made a covenant with death, and with hell are we at agreement; when the overflowing scourge shall pass through, it shall not come unto us: for we have made lies our refuge, and under falsehood have we hid ourselves:

16 Therefore thus saith the Lord GOD, Behold, I lay in Zion for a foundation a stone, a tried stone, a precious corner stone, a sure foundation: he that believeth shall not make haste.

17 Judgment also will I lay to the line, and righteousness to the plummet: and the hail shall sweep away the refuge of lies, and the waters shall overflow the hiding place.

18 And your covenant with death shall be disannulled, and your agreement with hell shall not stand; when the overflowing scourge shall pass through, then ye shall be trodden down by it.

Whew! That's strong stuff, isn't it? But this is exactly how God feels about those who "rule His people" with a scornful attitude toward His holiness within men. Look at what these vain leaders said: *We have made a covenant with death and an agreement with hell.* This *hell*, in Hebrew, is **sh'owl** (sheh-ole'); in the Old Testament, the word *hell* is always translated from the word *sh'owl*. *Strong's Hebrew and Chaldee Dictionary* says it means, "*hades* or the world of the dead . . . includ. its accessories and inmates:—grave, hell, pit."[9] Then, there are three Greek words translated *hell* in the New Testament: **geenna** (gheh'-en-nah) or **gehenna**, **Hades** (hah'-dace), and **tartaroo** (tar-tar-o'-o) or **Tartaros**. The first, *gehenna*, was "used (fig.) as a name for the place (or state) of everlasting punishment."[10] The third,

Tartaros, means "(the deepest *abyss* of Hades); to *incarcerate* in eternal torment,"[11] and *Hades*, which the Hebrew *sh'owl* refers to, means "the place (state) of departed souls:—grave."[12] Notice that, even though *Hades* refers to the grave, it also refers to the place of departed souls. Clearly, then, souls do not cease to exist at physical death; they merely *depart*. Solomon told us where they depart to in Ecclesiastes 12:7: "Then shall the dust return to the earth as it was: and the spirit shall return unto God who gave it."

"Oh," someone may say, "then every spirit gets to dwell with God in eternity?" No. Each spirit will return to God for *distribution* according to what it did while in its physical body. God alone, as Supreme Judge, will have control over that distribution! Some will be told "Welcome to my home!" and some will be told "Depart into everlasting torment!"

I said all of that to say this: although the term *hell* in Isaiah 28 may not be referring to the place of punishment, the very thought of death and the grave, for those whom God is displeased with, rings of eternal terror. And that Hebrew word, *sh'owl*, does mean "the world of the dead" *with its inmates*! For certain, the souls of the dead will still live beyond death! At any rate, when those Jews said they had made a covenant, an agreement, with death and the grave, they were saying that they were no longer afraid of them. The fear of God had been lifted off of them because of their false refuge. I've heard of people who said, "Well, God and I have an understanding. We've worked everything out." Because of this, they aren't worried about eternity. This is nonsense! For sure, God has worked out a Plan of Salvation, but if we refuse to line up with it, He won't make any side deals with us.

Because of those Jews' "covenant" with death, they had confidence that *when the overflowing scourge shall pass through, it shall not come unto us*. What did their "covenant" consist of? *We have made lies our refuge, and under falsehood have we hid ourselves.*

How utterly foolish! How completely futile! Who in his right mind would deliberately rest his eternal welfare on lies, on falsehood? But, friend, this is a picture parallel to what we find among so many who claim to be Christ's followers today. Those Jews wanted to do their own thing, go their own way, yet be safe from God's judgment. So they deceived themselves into thinking they could be. Remember, they told the prophets to prophesy *not* right things, but to prophesy *deceits*! Most modern "Christians" want to, and are *taught that they can*, do the same thing, that they can displease God on a day-to-day basis, and still escape His wrath. But, just as God had the last word with old Israel, He will have it with those who make lies their refuge and hide under falsehood today.

"What lies, what falsehood?" you may ask. Well, I've already explained some of these, but let's review them again: the lie that you can be a Christian, that you can "believe unto salvation," but that God cannot deliver you from your sins; the lie that, even though you sin from day to day, you're still acceptable to God and will go to Heaven when you die. These, and all others like them, comprise "covenants" and "agreements" with death and hell that are handed out in false Christianity today. They provide a "refuge" and a "hiding place" under which multitudes are finding solace.

The "only" problem with this solace is that it *is* a lie, it *is* a falsehood. *It will never hold up; it will never work.* When you stand before God to give an account, and you call upon your covenant and your refuge, they will not be there. They will have burned up in the consummation! I said God had, and will have, the last word. What is it? He gave it in verses 16-18. Let's read 17 and 18 again:

17 Judgment also will I lay to the line, and righteousness to the plummet: and the hail shall sweep away the refuge of lies, and the waters shall overflow the hiding place.

18 And your covenant with death shall be disannulled, and your agreement with hell shall not stand; when the overflowing scourge shall pass through, then ye shall be trodden down by it.

Again, this is strong stuff. In the construction industry, a line and a plummet enable the builders to make straight, even walls. God's line is judgment, and His plummet is righteousness. These enable God to make, and keep, the Church straight. In Isaiah 1:27, we read, "Zion shall be redeemed with judgment, and her converts with righteousness." That this "Zion" (as well as "Jerusalem") often referred, in prophecy, to the New Testament Church, is found in the following texts:

Isaiah 62:1 For Zion's sake will I not hold my peace, and for Jerusalem's sake I will not rest, until the righteousness thereof go forth as brightness, and the salvation thereof as a lamp that burneth.

11 Behold, the LORD hath proclaimed unto the end of the world, Say ye to the daughter of Zion, Behold, thy salvation cometh; behold, his reward is with him, and his work before him.

12 And they shall call them, The holy people, The redeemed of the LORD: and thou shalt be called, Sought out, A city not forsaken.

Matthew 21:4 All this was done, that it might be fulfilled which was spoken by the prophet, saying,

5 Tell ye the daughter of Sion, Behold, thy King cometh unto thee, meek, and sitting upon an ass, and a colt the foal of an ass.

Hebrews 12:22 But ye are come unto mount Sion, and unto the city of the living God, the heavenly Jerusalem, and to an innumerable company of angels,

23 To the general assembly and church of the firstborn, which are written in heaven, and to God the Judge of all, and to the spirits of just men made perfect,

24 And to Jesus the mediator of the new covenant, and to the blood of sprinkling, that speaketh better things than that of Abel.

"Ye are come," not "ye shall come." These verses are not referring to the literal Zion or Jerusalem, but to the *heavenly Jerusalem*. Neither are they referring to some future time. It says "You are here." Verse 23 says this Mount Zion, this Heavenly Jerusalem, is the *Church*. Isaiah prophesied that the Church would be redeemed with judgment and righteousness. "Bible thumping" judgment on sin and the demand for righteousness among the believers is what makes and keeps the Church clean. How clean? Without spot and blemish! Do you have a problem with "judgment preaching"? Friend, God loves it (Isaiah 30:18, Isaiah 61:8). Why? Because it is the only thing that will redeem Zion.

Did you notice that Isaiah said *hail* would sweep away that refuge of lies? What is hail, as used here in the Bible? Well, Deuteronomy 32:2 says, "My doctrine shall drop as the rain." Hosea 6:3 tells us, "He shall come unto us as the rain, as the latter and former rain unto the earth." Just as the rain brings life and vibrancy to creation, God's doctrine, His Word, brings these to the soul. Rain is water and hail is ice—frozen, or solid, water. Just as God's doctrine falls like rain on the soul, His *solid doctrine*, or judgment, falls like *hail* on the false refuges and sweeps them away. That's what I am striving to do in this book—bring God's solid truth to the fore so the false refuges in which millions are hiding can be exposed and swept away. So you, dear friend, can run for your life and find a true refuge in the real Jesus of the Bible. If you feel the things I'm saying are "hard," it's because God is sending *hail* your way to tear up your false refuges. It's not *you* that God is hammering; it's the lies that will damn your soul if you stay hidden in them.

Are holiness-fighting preachers and teachers God's men and women? Are they called, of Him, into the ministry, given the charge to feed His flock? Or—"perish the thought," you say—are they the "false prophets" that Jesus and the Apostles warned us to beware of? I know you don't want my opinion, and you're wise if you don't; my opinion is no better than anyone else's. But let's see what God, Himself, said about prophets who do not teach His Word correctly. Jeremiah 23:14-17, 21-22, and 30-32 will tell us. I know this is a lengthy reading, friend, but it is vital:

Jeremiah 23:14 I have seen also in the prophets of Jerusalem an horrible thing: they commit adultery, and walk in lies: they strengthen also the hands of evildoers, that none doth return from his wickedness: they are all of them unto me as Sodom, and the inhabitants thereof as Gomorrah.

15 Therefore thus saith the LORD of hosts concerning the prophets; Behold, I will feed them with wormwood, and make them drink the water of gall: for from the prophets of Jerusalem is profaneness gone forth into all the land.

16 Thus saith the LORD of hosts, Hearken not unto the words of the prophets that prophesy unto you: they make you vain: they speak a vision of their own heart, and not out of the mouth of the LORD.

17 They say still unto them that despise me, The LORD hath said, Ye shall have peace; and they say unto every one that walketh after the imagination of his own heart, No evil shall come upon you [Those refuges of lies].

21 I have not sent these prophets, yet they ran: I have not spoken to them, yet they prophesied. [Emphasis added.]

22 But if they had stood in my counsel, and had caused my people to hear my words, then they should have turned them from their evil way, and from the evil of their doings.

30 Therefore, behold, I am against the prophets, saith the LORD, that steal my words every one from his neighbour [emphasis added].

31 Behold, I am against the prophets, saith the LORD, that use their tongues, and say, He [God] *saith.*

32 Behold, I am against them that prophesy false dreams, saith the LORD, and do tell them, and cause my people to err by their lies, and by their lightness; yet I sent them not, nor commanded them [emphasis added]: *therefore they shall not profit this people at all, saith the LORD.*

Friend, this is so solemn that it left me, for two or three minutes, immobilized. I am *serious.* It really did. I hardly knew what to say next.

But, with God's help, I'll move on, now, as it is certainly His will that you *hear His words.* Dear one, you can *tell* when your preachers and teachers are speaking at God's command; you can *know* when they are called and sent by Him: they will turn you from your sins, not talk "peace" when there is no peace.

By God's grace, I have given numerous instances of how Christendom, today, is failing to represent God and His Word. My friend, do not let them lead you away from God any longer. *They shall not profit you at all, saith the Lord!*

God has commissioned His followers to go and preach the Gospel to every creature because He wants everyone to know the truth. It is truth that sets us free (John 8:32). How sad that so many who claim to be His ministers don't preach *the Gospel.* One reason these preachers prophesy deceits is because the masses want it that way. Thank God, there are honest hearts around, but most people want a watered-down "gospel," an easy way to Heaven. Friend, Jesus said we have to abandon our way and Paul said we must crucify our flesh. There is no "easy" way to Heaven; that is why Christ admonished us to count the cost—there *is* a cost. What does it cost? Our all; but Paul said, in Romans 12:1, that this is reasonable service. After all, look at what our redemption cost Jesus! In exchange for our all, God gives us *His* all, and His riches are unsearchable, His joy is unspeakable, at His right hand are (clean and wholesome) pleasures forevermore, and we can taste and see that the Lord is good. We surely get the best of the trade. By the way, that verse also says that part of our reasonable service is to present *holy bodies* to God in order to be acceptable to Him. How can we do this if we don't have holy bodies?

We mentioned Isaiah 30:10 earlier in this chapter, but let's look at its context:

Isaiah 30:1 Woe to the rebellious children, saith the LORD, that take counsel, but not of me; and that cover with a covering, but not of my spirit, that they may add sin to sin:

8 Now go, write it before them in a table, and note it in a book, that it may be for the time to come for ever and ever:

9 That this is a rebellious people, lying children, children that will not hear the law of the LORD:

10 Which say to the seers, See not; and to the prophets, Prophesy not unto us right things, speak unto us smooth things, prophesy deceits:

11 [This is still the people speaking to the prophets] *Get you out of the* [right] *way, turn aside out of the* [right] *path, cause the Holy One of Israel to cease from before us.*

Now look at what God said in Jeremiah 5:30-31:

30 A wonderful and horrible thing is committed in the land;

31 The prophets prophesy falsely, and the priests bear rule by their means; and my people love to have it so: and what will ye do in the end thereof?

Did God excuse the prophets for not "getting the Word at His mouth and warning the people from Him," since the people loved to have it that way? Not at all, my friend. People don't like to have their "feathers ruffled," and the vast majority of professed ministers don't want to ruffle them, but neither of these will ever get away with this. Look at what God told Ezekiel in 3:17-18:

17 Son of man, I have made thee a watchman unto the house of Israel: therefore hear the word at my mouth, and give them warning from me.

18 When I say unto the wicked, Thou shalt surely die; and thou givest him not warning, nor speakest to warn the wicked from his wicked way, to save his life; the same wicked man shall die in his iniquity; but his blood will I require at thine hand.

"Their hands are full of blood."

Let me remind you that God told Adam he would surely die if he ate the fruit of the tree of knowledge of good and evil, but Satan said, "You won't die." God is still giving the Word, "The soul that sinneth, it shall die," but Satan is still saying, through his false prophets, "No, you won't; not if you're a believer."

Friend, what you need to *believe* is that the soul that sinneth, it shall die. If, instead, you listen to, and take refuge in, lies, *you* will die in your iniquity, and God will require your blood at *your ministers'* hands. Most people won't take the pure, unadulterated Word of God, and most of those who profess to preach it would rather please the people than to please God. But I pray that you are not one of those who want "smooth things and deceits." I pray that you are an honest heart who truly wants to serve Christ and will rejoice to find the truth. And if you are one of these ministers or teachers that fight holiness, I pray that you will accept the truth, find a real experience of salvation, and then help in the rescue of others from this deception. Jesus told us that the Holy Spirit would guide us into all truth (John 16:13). He is striving to guide *you* into all truth. That is why God sent this book your way, to help you see if *your* Christianity is genuine or not, and to help you find the real thing if you don't have it. It is not His, or my, intention to merely steal away your confidence. It *is* His, and my, intention to make sure you have your confidence in the right thing.

Friend, you can enjoy the real thing. That is God's desire, and it is mine. Jesus set up only one redemption Plan. It is a fallen "Christianity" that has muddied the waters and made it so hard for men and women to find the strait and narrow way. I know it sounds harsh and judgmental to say that modern Christendom has fallen short of leading souls to Christ, but, friend, this is simply the truth. The "Jesus" they are leading millions to is not the Jesus of the Bible.

Alexis de Tocqueville was a famous French statesman, social philosopher, and historian, who lived from 1805 to 1859. In 1831 he, with Gustave de Beaumont, began traveling through America. Their aim was to observe the American people and the institutions they had set up. De Tocqueville then wrote *Democracy in America*, a two-part treatise published in 1835 and 1840. His work has been called "the most comprehensive and penetrating analysis of the relationship between character and society in America that has ever been written."[13]

Here are some quotations attributed to de Tocqueville's *Democracy in America* (I'm told that the book is no longer in print):

"Upon my arrival in the United States the religious aspect of the country was the first thing that struck my attention; and the longer I stayed there, the more I perceived the great political consequences resulting from this new state of things.

"In France I had almost always seen the spirit of religion and the spirit of freedom marching in opposite directions. But in America I found they were intimately united and that they reigned in common over the same country."

"Religion in America . . . must be regarded as the foremost of the political institutions of that country; for if it does not impart a taste for freedom, it facilitates the use of it. Indeed, it is in this same point of view that the inhabitants of the United States themselves look upon religious belief.

"I do not know whether all Americans have a sincere faith in their religion—for who can search the human heart?—But I am certain that they hold it to be indispensable to the maintenance of republican institutions [the institutions of the Republic]. This opinion is not peculiar to a class of citizens or a party, but it belongs to the whole nation and to every rank of society."

"In the United States the sovereign authority is religious, . . . there is no country in the world where the Christian religion retains a greater influence over the souls of men than in America, and there can be no greater proof of its utility and of its conformity to human nature than that its influence is powerfully felt over the most enlightened and free nation of the earth."

Let me digress, here, for a minute. Many, today, insist that America was not founded as a Christian nation. They distort, and misquote, our historical documents to support their lies. But this Frenchman, who traveled all over America, did not say merely that "religion" shaped our entire national life, but that the *Christian* religion did. His observances of American life gave him this conclusion. Read our historical documents, yourself, and you will see this as well. Let's look, now, at some more of de Tocqueville's words.

"The Americans combine the notions of Christianity and of liberty so intimately in their minds, that it is impossible to make them conceive the one without the other."

"In the United States the influence of religion is not confined to the manners, but it extends to the intelligence of the people . . . .

"Christianity, therefore reigns without obstacle, by universal consent; the consequence is, as I have before observed, that every principle of the moral world is fixed and determinate . . . ."

This is what this Frenchman found in America in her early days! How sad that she has lost that intimacy between Christianity and freedom. And how tragic that her "Christians" no longer see moral principles as fixed and determinate. Let us look, next, at *these* solemn words of Alexis de Tocqueville:

"I sought for the key to the greatness and genius of America in her harbors . . . ; in her fertile fields and boundless forests; in her rich mines and vast world commerce; in her public school system and institutions of learning. I sought for it in her democratic Congress and in her matchless Constitution.

"Not until I went into the churches of America and heard her pulpits flame with righteousness did I understand the secret of her genius and power.

"America is great because America is good, and if America ever ceases to be good, America will cease to be great."[14]

Friend, I am made to wonder what this great Frenchman would write if he were to have visited America in our times. Today's governmental leaders are trying to banish God from our highest institutions, and this once-revered Christianity is now being scoffed at and scorned. It is even being attacked as irrelevant to, and contrary to, our society's needs or well being. Indeed, it is becoming refuse, or garbage, *despised* among America's elite today. Instead of our once-cherished freedom *of* religion, many today seek to foist upon the entire nation a freedom *from* religion.

But far worse than the disdain for Christianity found in America's higher echelons today, is the stark loss of her "pulpits flaming with righteousness"! Indeed, were our pulpits still ablaze with righteousness, political and other "leaders" with disdain for God could never get anywhere. Hear, again, from our French statesman:

"In the United States, if a political character attacks a sect [denomination], this may not prevent even the partisans of that very sect, from supporting him; but if he attacks all the sects together [Christianity], every one abandons him and he remains alone."[14]

Sadly, today's pulpits cringe from declaring righteousness and, instead, make room for sin in both the world and the church. What the Bible calls *adultery*, is now "having an affair." *Fornication* is nothing more or less than people doing what's "natural." The cry that is heralded all over the country is no longer "Repent or perish!" but "If it feels good, do it!" Oh, I'm not saying this is being heralded from *the pulpits*, but neither are they heralding, "The soul that sinneth, it shall die." And the letdown of that cry by the church is why the other cry is widespread in our society.

Lying is no longer condemned by many; instead they allow that some lies are "white." Some even claim that *everyone* lies sometimes. And, for sure, many who profess to be Christ's followers lie now and then, when it's convenient or "helpful," and they think it's all a part of their not being able, after all, to live without sin. I wonder if they've ever been told that "without [the City of God; see context] are . . . whosoever loveth and maketh a lie" (Revelation 22:15), or that "all liars, shall have their part in the lake which burneth with fire and brimstone: which is the second death" (Revelation 21:8). This does not say, "unbelieving liars"; it says *all* liars. Remember, the Gospel is simple. When it says *all* liars, it means *all* liars.

Sin of every kind and description and shade is rampant today. These religious leaders are right, indeed, when they say that sin is so "everywhere" and so powerful. But they are the reason it is powerful, and they are the reason it is everywhere. When the pure Gospel is preached under the anointing of the Spirit of God, and people embrace and live it, it casts down sin's strongholds. It produces the condition de Tocqueville found. It is because our pulpits no longer flame with righteousness that society has unraveled. De Tocqueville did not find such chaos pervading everything as we see today. In every part of America, he found people of all ages and backgrounds who really lived lives of honesty and integrity, and who believed in and practiced righteousness. For the most part, even those who were not religious respected those who were, and the God they honored, and they followed closely the *principles* of righteousness, as a general rule.

Friend, face it: modern "Christianity" expends far more of its time, resources, and energy, excusing sin than it does in proclaiming true righteousness. Alas for the loss of those days when the pulpits flamed with righteousness and godly principles dictated the behavior of all levels of American life and society! Alas for the loss of godliness in those entrusted with church, governmental, or societal, leadership!

Have you ever read one of the "Rules of Conduct" sheets that the schools required teachers of America's children to live up to in bygone years? Oh, many would laugh at them today, but people of those times never heard of sexual molestation or involvement between teachers and their scholars. They were never dismayed over sexual scandals among school system staff. High moral values reigning over society resulted in such tranquility and civility and chaos-free living. Even those who were enduring hard times didn't worry about being further exploited by their fellow men. Remember, although there were incidents where evil things happened, de Tocqueville spoke of the conditions that *prevailed* over American society from coast to coast.

Again, look at what he found in America in the 1830s:

"I do not question that the great austerity of manners that is observable in the United States arises, in the first instance, from religious faith . . . . its influence over the mind of woman is supreme, and women are the protectors of morals. There is certainly no country in the world where the tie of marriage is more respected than in America or where conjugal happiness is more highly or worthily appreciated . . . ."[14]

"Righteousness exalteth a nation . . . ." That's exactly what de Tocqueville found true in America. But what are we finding today? " . . . but sin is a reproach to any people" (Proverbs 14:34). "The wicked shall be turned into hell, and all the nations that forget God" (Psalm 9:17). My heart weeps when I think of how righteousness exalted this nation—God said it would, and de Tocqueville found it had—and of how this letdown in America's pulpits has brought her to a place where greed and corruption, dishonesty and fraud, crime and cruelty, and, oh, such immorality, are raging from the White House to the cardboard house. If de Tocqueville were observing us today, what a different work his treatise would have been. Instead of praising our steadfast righteousness, in government and all levels of society, because of our flaming pulpits, he might have written something like this: "Throughout America, society seems to be unraveling. Factions here and there are at each others' throats, and chaos is seen in streets where once tranquility and decency reigned. Her schools no longer educate their students; instead they are bent on controlling their ideas and shaping their opinions. Worse, and no doubt the cause of it all, her ministry seems afraid to upset those in their flocks who want to indulge themselves in sinful habits and pleasures. Where righteousness had reigned in every aspect of national life, the pulpits are now afraid to 'cry aloud' for fear of disturbing the sleeping masses so filled with apathy and indifference. Indeed, they are almost silent regarding what the demands of Christianity are. Government has all but totally rejected moral integrity, and it is no wonder. So have most of the churches. No longer is America great, because she is no longer good."

Ah, dear reader, America's former moral and societal success reaped deep respect from other nations, but now they mock and scorn her. Why? Almost total abandonment of the true message of the Gospel of Jesus Christ has brought her down, and it will ultimately bring her *to hell*. Think, again, of how Paul told Timothy that having a form of godliness but denying the power of godliness would bring perilous times. About all that's left in Christendom today is a form—and perilous times are, indeed, upon us from sea to shining sea.

The blame for this fall, in the "church" and, consequently, in our nation, must be laid at the feet of those who claim to be ministers of Christ and yet fail to preach *the Gospel*. It must be laid to those who offer to the people a "Jesus" that is not the true Jesus of the Bible. Today's so-called Christianity has failed God, our society, and *you*, my friend.

CHAPTER EIGHT

"Jesus Is Too Good to Send a Soul to Hell"

It is almost impossible to go to a funeral where the deceased isn't said to be in a better place, out of his misery, and at peace, no matter what kind of life had been lived. No one seems to be able, or willing, to accept the thought that Christ might send someone to hell. Some who profess to be Christians come right out and say it, and many others believe it: *Jesus is too good to send a soul to hell.* Even those who say they believe in hell, and that some will go there, usually don't believe it in practice. It would appear that hell is only for the really horrid people, such as Adolph Hitler, Jeffrey Dahmer, Ted Bundy, Saddam Hussein, etc. Certainly ordinary people don't end up there. *God wouldn't do that. He's a God of love.*

May I jar you up really good again? The truth is that what the Bible Jesus is too good to do, is to take sinners to Heaven. And by "sinners" I mean anyone who does not live a holy life, anyone who sins more or less day by day. No matter how much we loved a deceased party, God did not take that person to Heaven if he or she had sin in their heart. Does this seem harsh to you? It shouldn't. This is the clear teaching of the Word of God. But, alas, modern "Christianity" no longer preaches the clear Word of God, and the truth comes as a shock to the benumbed ears of the masses!

This is a tragedy. Why? Because if the pulpits still blazed with the true Gospel, the deceased could have been prepared for death. And, because, when people go to funerals where just anything passes the test and is "accepted into Heaven," it lifts the fear of God right off of their hearts. They feel confident that they, too, will be accepted into the portals of Glory, regardless of how they live while on earth. But they

160

will not. Dear reader, it is not cruel to proclaim the truth about this; it is cruel not to.

People are so far removed from the pure Gospel that, I say again, the thought of God putting judgment on them for their sins shocks them. But God is holy. Christ is holy. He cannot, and will not, tolerate sin. Oh, He allows us to choose it, as I already showed when dealing with His giving us a free will. He allows it in our lives *if we want it*. But He does not allow it in His people after they're saved (in His Church), and He will not allow it in His eternal abode.

Think about this: for God to take sinners to Heaven would be to *reward* sin. Wait; do not hurry on. Please *do* think about this. Friend, God will never reward sin! Someone may say, "No, He doesn't reward it; He forgives it and no longer punishes the believer for it." I know this is a cherished belief, but there's more to it than that. Remember that the *reward* will be given based upon our *deeds in this life*, what we *did* here, not on our "faith." And the only sins that are forgiven are sins that are repented of, or *forsaken*. If we continue in sin from day to day, we definitely have not forsaken sin. In a sin-day-by-day lifestyle, one is sure to commit a number of sins over and over. Dear one, this is not repentance. Therefore, our nightly prayers for forgiveness are futile. If you still do not understand this, please reread chapters one through three of this book.

Again, dear one, for God to reward sin is impossible; to do so would mar His own holiness. *It would!* How could a holy God reward sin? He will not do that. He will never stoop to the point of rewarding sin. Even *tolerating* sin in His presence would mar His holiness, let alone *rewarding* it. Why? Because holiness, by its very nature, must exclude sin. It must! If it does not exclude sin, it is not, itself, holy. I must repeat it: God does not tolerate sin in His presence, and He certainly never rewards it. That's why He tells us so expressly that "the soul that sinneth, it shall die," and that "the wages of sin is death." Jesus said, "Ye shall . . . die in your sins: whither I go, ye cannot come" (John 8:21). I beg you, do not choose to be deceived. Take the pure Word of God. You will not sin from day to day in this life and reap Heaven for it.

Not only must holiness exclude sin, but it must *condemn* it. Holiness *must* condemn sin. And God does condemn it. Does the Bible say this? Yes. Let's read, again, a portion of Romans 8:3-4:

3 God . . . condemned sin in the flesh:

4 That the righteousness of the law might be fulfilled in us . . . .

Where sin is not condemned, righteousness cannot exist. How, then, can sin and righteousness coexist in saved people? How can they coexist in *you*? How could they coexist in Heaven? Sin must be condemned *in us* (in our flesh), for righteousness to exist *in us*. Then, when we come in repentance and faith, that condemnation is lifted off of us, but it is never lifted off of sin itself. Again Paul's words ring clear:

Romans 8:1 There is therefore now no condemnation to them which are in Christ Jesus, who walk not after the flesh, but after the Spirit.

2 For the law of the Spirit of life in Christ Jesus hath made me free from the law of sin and death.

"Oh," someone may say, "God doesn't take sin to Heaven. The sinner is cleansed of sin before he enters Heaven." But you mean *just* before he enters Heaven, right? In other words, the sinner is cleansed of sin in, or through, death. This is not true, friend. When Romans 6:23 says that the wages of sin is death, it does not mean the wages of sin is life. "Christians" cannot sin, here, and expect eternal life there. We must be delivered from sin before death overtakes us. The verse we quoted a moment ago proves that God does not put up with sin while we are *in the flesh*, then give us righteousness at death and take us to Heaven. It says that *God condemned sin in the flesh* that we could be righteous. Without righteousness *here*, we won't be righteous *there*, for 1 Corinthians 6:9 says, "Know ye not that the unrighteous shall not inherit the kingdom of God?" Dear one, it's absolutely true: we cannot even get into the kingdom, here, until sin is condemned in our flesh and we are made the righteousness of God in Christ! Look at Luke 16:16; we get into the Kingdom here in this world: "The law and the prophets were until John [the Baptizer]: since that time the kingdom of God is preached, and every man presseth into it." And Paul told the Roman Christians that this Kingdom *is* righteousness:

Romans 14:17 For the kingdom of God is not meat and drink; but righteousness, and peace, and joy in the Holy Ghost.

18 For he that in these things serveth Christ is acceptable to God, and approved of men.

Please look at Ecclesiastes 11:3b, where it says, "And if the tree fall toward the south, or toward the north, in the place where the tree falleth, there it shall be." In the Bible, trees are often used as a symbol of people. See Isaiah 61:7, Jeremiah 17:8, and Ezekiel 17:24. Remember, also, that Nebuchadnezzar was spoken of figuratively as a tree. The context of Ecclesiastes 11:3b is a series of simple metaphors, setting forth many gems of wisdom and truth. So, we can take this simple statement for the individual truth that it is: wherever a tree falls, that's where it will lie. But I'm sure God had more in mind, when He inspired Solomon to write these words, than stating the obvious about a tree falling in a field or forest. Since trees represent people, whatever state we are in when our "tree falleth"—when death overtakes us—such shall be our state in eternity.

If you're not convinced, however, read with me the Apostle Peter's admonition "to them that have obtained like precious faith with us," in his second epistle:

2 Peter 3:10 But the day of the Lord will come as a thief in the night; in the which the heavens shall pass away with a great noise, and the elements shall melt with fervent heat, the earth also and the works that are therein shall be burned up.

11 Seeing then that all these things shall be dissolved, what manner of persons ought ye to be in all holy conversation and godliness,

12 Looking for and hasting unto the coming of the day of God, wherein the heavens being on fire shall be dissolved, and the elements shall melt with fervent heat?

13 Nevertheless we, according to his promise, look for new heavens and a new earth, wherein dwelleth righteousness.

14 Wherefore, beloved, seeing that ye look for such things, be diligent that ye may be found of him in peace, without spot, and blameless.

These are very sobering words, filled with both warning and great promise and hope. But in this passage, Peter lets us know that we have to be holy *before* this life ends for us, or for the world as a whole, if we want to lay hold on that hope. *What manner of persons ought ye to be in all holy conversation and godliness, looking for and hasting unto the coming of the day of God?* Here, it is clear that we must be holy while we're looking for His coming. We are not made that way *after* He comes. The Greek word for *conversation*, here, is the same as quoted earlier in this book, and means "behavior."

Seeing that ye look for such things, be diligent that ye may be found of him in peace, without spot, and blameless. When Jesus comes, friend, He must *find* us without spot and blameless; He will not come and *make* us that way. Again, oh, let me stress it: on Judgment Day, we will be accepted or rejected, by Christ, according to what we *did* here, in our bodies, and not according to our *faith* here. Peter was talking to the Church in these verses. Please notice that he in no way inferred that their faith would secure for them a holiness when Jesus comes again. They had to have it already, and he urged them to diligence in keeping themselves holy as they looked for such things! Please do not go into eternity expecting to be made holy then, my precious reader. If you are not holy here and now, you will not be found in peace "over there." I beg you, be diligent, today, about what manner of persons ye ought to be while *awaiting* the Day of the Lord! There is no such thing as continuing to sin here and being made righteous during or after death, then gaining a place in Heaven.

Consider these verses:

2 Corinthians 5:10 For we must all appear before the judgment seat of Christ; that every one may receive the things done in his body, according to that he hath done, whether it be good or bad [good *or* bad, not some of each].

11a Knowing therefore the terror of the Lord, we persuade men . . . .

1 Peter 1:17 And if ye call on the Father, who without respect of persons judgeth according to every man's work, pass the time of your sojourning here in fear.

Did you notice that these texts emphasize the words "every man" and "every one"? And that second Scripture text tells us that God will deal with mankind without respect of persons. God will not give special treatment to anyone, just because that one was "religious" while on this earth. *Everyone* will be judged, not by his "faith," but by his works, by his deeds, done while in the body. If those deeds done in the body were not righteous, that soul will not be made righteous after leaving the body. I know I'm repeating, but I want you to get it. Each person's judgment will be *according to that he hath done,* not according to that he hath "believed." Peter said, if you call on the Father, pass your time in this world in *fear,* because you will be judged by your works! Friend, this means you. *You* will be judged by what you do here on earth, not by whether or not you had a Christian profession. Don't be deceived by those who pervert the Gospel! Remember that reverent, godly, fear is the beginning of wisdom (Job 28:28, Psalm 111:10). You do not need to be afraid of God if you are living according to His Word, but if you are not, "it is a fearful thing to fall into the hands of the living God" (Hebrews 10:31).

"What," you may ask, "is the purpose of believing in Jesus, if our faith doesn't matter at the judgment?" Our faith *does* matter; the purpose of believing, dear one, is that we will be saved *from* our sins when we confess and repent. When our faith grips God's promise, we are given a new heart and spirit, made a new creature, and enabled to live in obedience to everything we know to be God's will. Because of this, because of our faith, we will have righteous deeds for which to be judged in the end. However, any "faith" that does not secure these benefits will, indeed, not matter at the judgment.

Remember the simplicity of the Gospel? Remember how the Apostle Paul was afraid people's minds would be corrupted and they would lose sight of that simplicity? Well, when the Bible says we'll all be judged for what we *did in the body*, it means exactly that. The sad truth is that modern Christendom corrupts people's minds by making this simple truth so obscure and telling them these Scriptures don't mean what they say. We *all* will be judged by what we did here, and no one will get special treatment over there. If we don't get rid of our sins while in this time world, we need not expect to get rid of them after death comes to us, just because we were "believers." Again, what we need to *believe* is the Bible. If you believe you will be made holy in or after death, and then received into Heaven, you either have not *heard* the true Word of God before, or you aren't really *believing* it. Tragically, what you believe is a lie, friend. The "Jesus" you trust in, the one who cannot make you holy until you die, is a false Jesus, not the One of the Bible.

What Does *Good* Mean?

Does being good mean to tolerate just anything, to just "live and let live," to let others do anything they want to do, refraining from ever offending offenders by being "judgmental"? That is certainly the definition modern society has given the word. They go so far as to say that putting judgment on some sins constitutes a hate crime. But this kind of being "good" is, in reality, not good at all. Life itself demands a standard of right and wrong, and whenever a civilization begins to erase the line between the two, whenever a civilization begins to mix the "black" and the "white" into a murky gray, that civilization has begun to deteriorate. Sin leads only downward, and given enough time, such a civilization will cease to exist.

Early in the last century, Joseph Daniel Unwin, a British anthropologist, studied at least eighty civilizations that spanned some 5000 years of history. Going into this study, he held some pretty "liberal" ideas, but he found the evidence so overwhelming that it radically changed his own view. He found that moral decline always resulted in a society's demise. That's *always*, by the way; there were *no* exceptions. He outlined cycles that those civilizations had passed through, which were, roughly, as follows: first, being under tyranny; second, gaining their independence through moral revival; third, reaping prosperity; fourth, becoming materialistic; fifth, seeking pleasure and becoming indifferent; sixth, declining morally; seventh, disintegrating; eighth, going back under tyranny. Friend, did you locate where America is in this process? I'd say we've passed number six and are already quite into number seven. In fact, I believe we are actually into number eight.

Unwin's findings were quoted by Reb Bradley in his outstanding book, *Born Liberal, Raised Right* (which I *urge* every American to read). Here are Bradley's words: " . . . Unwin determined that the loss of self-restraint, culminating in unlimited sexual expression, precipitated each empire's demise. Either the individuals in those societies became personally ruled by their passions, resulting in lawlessness and social chaos, or in their hedonism they lost the moral fiber necessary to successfully protect themselves militarily. *America on both fronts has great reason for concern* [emphasis added]."[1]

Politicians of all stripes are shredding the Constitution, and, I repeat, I believe we are even already in the early stages of number eight. And please let me reiterate that in all of Unwin's study, there were no exceptions to this pattern. Scary, isn't it! And with modern "Christianity" aiding and abetting the downward slide, it's even scarier.

What is "good"? Well, good is not condoning, or even overlooking, evil. Whenever "good" becomes tolerant of evil, it ceases to be a virtue and becomes, instead, a vice. It becomes, itself, evil. This idea that God is too "good" to send a soul to hell is an oxymoron. It is because God is good that He sends sinners to hell. That is where sinners deserve to be. God has given Heaven's best to provide a means for mankind to be saved. Christ's sacrifice was a tremendous one. What He suffered is indescribable. He willingly went to Calvary and gave His life, going through all that He endured, to save your soul and my soul from hell. If we fail to follow Him and obey His Word, we deserve to go to hell. It is God's goodness that provided for us the way to escape hell, but if we do not receive His gift of eternal life, we certainly have no valid claim by which to escape eternal death. It is not a lack of "goodness" on God's part to send us there.

Whenever preachers and teachers are so "good" that they fail to call sin, sin, and warn people about its consequences, it is, again, no virtue on their part. It is not *goodness*. It is grossly unfair. It is unkind. It is not a love for souls, but a love for the flesh. It is cowardice, a willingness to please man rather than to please God. It is selfishness, preferring to let souls be lost rather than to be, themselves, unpopular. At the very least, it is ignorance of the truth, and such an ignorance that it renders them unfit to be preachers or teachers. Why? Because they are instruments by which souls are being destroyed! This is not goodness, dear one. It is slaughter—and since this condition prevails in Christendom today, it is *wholesale* slaughter.

What is "good"? *Goodness* is benevolence, certainly, but *goodness* is also righteousness. And whenever benevolence overrides righteousness, it becomes unrighteousness and is no longer good. God will be benevolent whenever possible, but when righteousness is at stake, He will preserve righteousness at the expense of benevolence. The Bible is full of examples of this, and they start at the very dawn of time. God gave Adam and Eve a very wonderful existence. The Garden of Eden was, indeed, a paradise. They wanted for nothing. They had utopia. God was, for sure, good to them, and He was more than just their God; He was their friend and companion. And this paradise condition was to continue as long as they abode in righteousness. However, when they turned from right and committed sin, as much as God loved them, He did not let "benevolence" overrule. He did not reward evil. He cast them out.

Look at the story of Jonah. God pronounced destruction on Ninevah. Why? Because the people of Ninevah were unrighteous. Their sins provoked God to anger and that righteous anger demanded judgment. *It was only because they repented and turned to righteousness that God became, again, benevolent toward them.*

We know, of course, that God is good to sinners. The Bible says He lets the rain fall on the just and the unjust alike (Matthew 5:45). God loves being good to mankind. He pleads with us to obey His righteous laws because they are, whether we want to believe it or not, *for our own good* (Deuteronomy 6:24, 10:13; Ezra 8:22; Job 22:21; Proverbs 13:21, 14:22, 16:20; Jeremiah 5:25, 32:39, etc.). But God is not good to sinners because He doesn't care that they are sinners. He is good to sinners in hopes of turning them from their sins to Him. He wants to win them by, and to, His love. Look at what the Apostle Paul said about this in Romans 2:3-4:

3 And thinkest thou this, O man, that judgest them which do such things [listed in Romans 1], *and doest the same, that thou shalt escape the judgment of God?*

4 Or despisest thou the riches of his goodness and forbearance and longsuffering; not knowing that the goodness of God leadeth thee to repentance?

God's goodness should lead us to repentance. This is God's design, His goal, His aim, His desire. His goodness was never intended to make us complacent in our sins. It was never intended to imply that God was overlooking our sins. It was never showered upon us to indicate that we could get by with our sins. God's goodness was directed toward us *to turn us from our sins*. And if we had a true ministry at large out here, preaching "hellfire and brimstone" against *sin* so people could tremble under conviction, but then showing *sinners* that God wants to forgive them and save them from both sin and its consequences, God's goodness would bring a lot more people to repentance. History proves this. Remember what de Tocqueville found as he traveled America? Instead, sadly, we now have a so-called ministry that pats sin on the back, and gives "believing" sinners a free pass into Heaven. This has perverted the concept of God's goodness, making people feel that because God is good, He will overlook their wrongdoings. May God have mercy on these ministers' souls; they are in serious trouble with God!

This does not just apply to "formal" Christendom; it applies to "fundamental" Christendom as well. It applies to multitudes who claim to be born again. These may not teach that God overlooks sin in *sinners*, exactly, but they do teach that He overlooks sin in *Christians*. The truth is that God does not overlook sin in *anyone*. And that does not mean

He is not "good." It means He *is* good. He is too good to condone sin, to sympathize with it, to fraternize with it, to become an ally to it. God will never do that. Doing so, I say again, would mar His own holiness. And, friend, if righteousness is of such paramount importance to God, shouldn't we count it important ourselves? Shouldn't we see *un*righteousness for the horrid thing that it really is?

What is "good"? *Goodness* tells people the truth. *Goodness* won't fail to be honest with souls, even when those souls don't want to hear what honesty delivers. *Goodness* loves God, and men and women, enough to deal squarely with eternal issues, to deal squarely with sin and its consequences. *Goodness* hates evil. That is why God hates evil. If you do not hate evil, you are not really good. And if you are lightly living in sin, and professing to be a Christian, you certainly do not hate evil. If that is your condition, and you stay in that condition until you die, you are going to be lost forever. God is going to send you to hell. He is too good to take you to Heaven. And, dear reader, dear eternity-bound soul, He is good enough to tell you the truth about it. I entreat you, let His goodness lead you to true repentance and salvation.

Frustrated Justice

Justice, according to *Webster's*, is "**1** the quality of being righteous; rectitude **2** impartiality; fairness **3** the quality of being right or correct **4** sound reason; rightfulness; validity **5** reward or penalty as deserved; just deserts **6** *a)* the use of authority and power to uphold what is right, just, or lawful."[2] *Rectitude* is defined as "**1** conduct according to moral principles; strict honesty; uprightness of character **2** correctness of judgment or method."[3]

We are living in a society that is wandering further and further from being one of justice. I want to reiterate what I said earlier: being so "good" that we condone evil is not a virtue. Real good demands some standards of conduct. When society is increasingly lenient with those who violate those standards, chaos soon reigns. We are seeing this all around us today. The courts shy away, many times, from really punishing crime—unless it's a crime that is in the public eye for one reason or another and punishing it severely is politically correct. The tendency is toward treading lightly on those who tread recklessly on our laws. We even have organizations that protest anyone's really suffering for doing wrong. They passionately champion these lawbreakers' "cause." The term "cruel and unusual punishment" is a crusade cry for the "rights" of criminals. Even those who are responsible for grave acts of violence and terrorism against their fellow men are said to be deserving of leniency. No one, these crusaders believe, should be given more than a "slap on the wrist." But what does this slap on the wrist really produce? It produces bad guys who sneer at the law. It produces good guys who fear for their safety. Oh, let's be realistic. It produces good guys who just aren't safe. It produces war zones in our schools. It produces repeat offenders who freely roam the streets with intent to commit another crime. It produces overloaded court rosters and overcrowded jails and prisons. It produces "plea bargaining" that releases lawbreakers from the proper consequences of their deeds. It produces an apathy among youth so that they don't fear to do wrong. Why should they? When I was young, "Crime does not pay!" was a truth etched into our souls, but today crime pays folks quite well and in many ways (except spiritually).

This kind of softness toward wrongdoing erodes civility and frustrates honest, law-abiding citizens. There is little that is harder to take than to see these miscarriages of justice occurring time and time again and to see society unraveling in the process. And now it has invaded the basic foundation of civilization, the home. Today it is "abusive" to correct one's children. How in the world can we expect people to behave out in our communities when they do not learn to behave in the home? It is no wonder the school rooms are scenes of chaos. And from there it rolls out into our streets. It is a basic, foundational principle of life: wrongdoing should be punished. Not just "whipped with a wet noodle," but punished severely enough to end the wrongdoing. Any correction that does not curb the wrong behavior is not severe enough. May I repeat that? I must. *Any correction that does not curb the wrong behavior is not severe enough.* It's just that plain and simple. It is my humble opinion, based in part on first-hand observation, that most of the children who are being poisoned with drugs for ADHD are simply in need of loving discipline.

What does the Bible say about justice and injustice? Well, let's look:

Deuteronomy 16:20 That which is altogether just shalt thou follow, that thou mayest live, and inherit the land which the LORD thy God giveth thee.

Psalm 82:2 How long will ye judge unjustly, and accept the persons of the wicked? Selah.

3 Defend the poor and fatherless: do justice to the afflicted and needy.

Proverbs 21:3 To do justice and judgment is more acceptable to the LORD than sacrifice.

Isaiah 56:1 Thus saith the LORD, Keep ye judgment, and do justice: for my salvation is near to come, and my righteousness to be revealed.

Colossians 4:1 Masters, give unto your servants that which is just and equal; knowing that ye also have a Master in heaven.

Leviticus 19:15 Ye shall do no unrighteousness in judgment: thou shalt not respect the person of the poor, nor honour the person of the mighty: but in righteousness shalt thou judge thy neighbour.

Malachi 2:9 Therefore have I also made you contemptible and base before all the people, according as ye have not kept my ways, but have been partial in the law.

God is a God of justice. He hates injustice. He hates partiality when dealing with offenders, and He hates partiality when dealing with the victims. It is God Who ordained civil authority to order men in ways of right behavior. Romans 13:3-4 states:

3 For rulers are not a terror to good works, but to the evil. Wilt thou then not be afraid of the power? do that which is good, and thou shalt have praise of the same:

4 For he is the minister of God to thee for good. But if thou do that which is evil, be afraid; for he beareth not the sword in vain: for he is the minister of God, a revenger to execute wrath upon him that doeth evil.

Civil authorities are *ministers of God.* What's their job? "To execute wrath upon him that doeth evil"! Whenever civil authorities fail in this mission, or whenever they show partiality in carrying it out, they are failing God. God demands justice of His followers, He demands justice among civil governments, and He certainly holds parents accountable for being just in the home and requiring right behavior out of their children:

Proverbs 13:24 He that spareth his rod hateth his son: but he that loveth him chasteneth him betimes.

171

[*Betimes* comes from the Hebrew word **shachar** (shaw-khar'), which means "prop. to *dawn,* i.e. (fig.) *be* (up) *early* at any task (with the impl. of earnestness)."[4] Those who truly love their children chasten them *early* and *earnestly.*]

Proverbs 19:18 Chasten thy son while there is hope, and let not thy soul spare for his crying.

Proverbs 22:15 Foolishness is bound in the heart of a child; but the rod of correction shall drive it far from him.

Proverbs 23:13 Withhold not correction from the child: for if thou beatest him with the rod, he shall not die.

24 Thou shalt beat him with the rod, and shalt deliver his soul from hell.

Does the New Testament agree with this idea of bringing children into subjection to parental authority? Yes. Paul taught that those who would lead God's people must be in control of their children, and we are to follow our leaders as they follow Christ (1 Corinthians 4:16, 1 Corinthians 11:1). In Titus 1:5-6, in setting forth the requirements for elders, Paul said this:

5 For this cause left I thee in Crete, that thou shouldest set in order the things that are wanting, and ordain elders in every city, as I had appointed thee:

6 If any be blameless, the husband of one wife, having faithful children not accused of riot or unruly.

And, in 1 Timothy 3:4, he covered the same thing, stating that a bishop should be "One that ruleth well his own house, having his children in subjection with all gravity."

God wants parents to bring their children into subjection to the laws of the home. He wants them to administer justice in the home. When a child does wrong, he should be corrected; and correction is only *correction* when it *corrects* the behavior. Friend, when children are trained in submission to the law of the home, they will have little trouble submitting to the law of the land or the Law of God. Another Scripture showing that God's attitude about children's obedience hasn't changed under the New Testament is Colossians 3:20. It says, "Children, obey your parents in all things: for this is well pleasing unto the Lord." *In all things.* Parents who fail to require this obedience set their children up for failure and, perhaps, eternal destruction.

Just a word on the matter of corporal punishment: God tells us to use it, and He is to be obeyed in this, just as in anything else. However, when the Proverb writer spoke of "beating" children with the rod, remember that some words used in 1611, when the *King James Authorized Version* of the Scriptures was translated, have different meanings, or shades of meaning, today. (You can read Shakespear, who lived from 1564 to 1616, and find the same thing true about his writings.) This just reflects the way language evolves over time. Look in any standard dictionary, and you will find some definitions that have "arc." or something similar, which stands for "archaic," or outdated. Just as *hating* our parents, siblings, and children requires us to "love them less" than God, so the term *beat* means physical discipline, but it does not mean to be brutal. God *hates* real child abuse; but He also hates it when proper discipline is neglected. I repeat, His Word says we need to have our children *in subjection*, or under control.

Even though I said children who disobey should be *punished*, I prefer the term *corrected*. When a parent truly disciplines a child from a heart of love, in order to prepare that child for life and eternity, it is more to correct than to punish. Discipline should be administered before the parent becomes angry, and the child should be reassured of the parent's love at all times. The child needs to know the "punishment" is directed at the wrong behavior, not at him as a person. The parent is *correcting* the child for his own good. If this is done properly, and done from the very start, it will usually keep rebellion out of our children; if, however, a little rebellion breaks out, then *adequate punishment* will subdue it. If we love our children as we ought, we will be diligent in seeing to it that it does.

God is a God of justice, and it follows that He will render justice, without partiality, without wavering, when it comes to our sins. This, in itself, is a truly sobering realization (and one that nominal believers are being robbed of). The Bible says the wages of sin is *death*. There is only one way to escape the just reward for our sins. Jesus Christ met the demands of God's justice when He took our sins upon Himself on the cross. Since He did that, when we forsake our sins and give control of our lives to God, He can be "faithful and just" to give us mercy and forgiveness (1 John 1:9). It is only through Christ's loving sacrifice that this blessed mercy can be ours, but, praise God, it can be. But, again, it follows that, when we fail to claim this mercy, or fail to qualify for it by true repentance, we will abide, still, under divine justice and wrath. The blood of Christ is the only cover that protects us from that wrath, and His blood only covers those who obtain true Bible salvation that delivers from sin's power, as well as its penalty. If the "Jesus" you believe in leaves you in your sins, after you become a believer, he will also leave you under the divine wrath of God. He has no precious blood to cover you, and you abide, still, under divine justice. You will reap the due reward of your deeds. I urge you to cast away your false "Jesus," your false believing, and come to the real Christ for real deliverance!

CHAPTER NINE

Objections to Holiness

Because holiness fighters have their Scriptural "proofs" that no one can live a holy life in this evil world, not even "Christians," I want to look at some of their objections to holiness. We will consider the Bible texts they use, and examine these in the light of their contexts. As we have already seen, taking Scriptures out of context can completely alter their meaning and miss their intended message altogether. But, friend, the Word of God is not a collection of God's random musings that He allows us to interpret as we see fit or to "take it or leave it." The Word of God is *absolute truth*, remember, and it was inspired by the Holy Ghost with specific meaning that we need to allow Him to teach us.

On the other hand, don't let anyone tell you its interpretation needs to be left to theologians alone. Certainly, true ministers have a special anointing for teaching and leading God's people. Certainly, God reveals many things to them that He doesn't reveal to others. However, it is your and my responsibility to become intimate with God's Word and Spirit, and to make sure that what we are being taught is the truth. Jesus told *us* to beware that no one deceives us, and this would be impossible if we didn't have biblical knowledge of our own.

Too often men with divinity degrees are thought to have exclusive access to the "real knowledge" of God. The Bible, however, gives us a totally different picture. It's not what is in the head that opens up the Word of God to men, but what is in the heart. Today's theological seminaries are "cranking out" preachers who have been schooled in a "social gospel" and have learned to be good "mixers." However, God wants good *separators*. These seminarians will not stand up and declare what "thus saith the Lord," and they leave people in their sins and in their worldliness. There is no way they can teach God's Word, for they cannot see it (John 3:3). The natural man, one who is not spiritually minded, cannot receive the things of the Spirit of God, because the things of God are spiritually discerned. In other words, they are learned through a spiritual connection with the divine Teacher (1 Corinthians 2:14-16). Intellect is not the key to divine revelation. I, myself, have a 4.0 cumulative college GPA (not from a seminary), but I learned God's truth by being willing to obey it and studying the Book to find God's doctrine, not prop up my own. Before He could teach me, I had to own that I didn't know anything. The Apostle Paul, who *was* highly educated, counted all of his natural credentials as worthless, and became as a child (Philippians 3:4-9). Because of this, God taught him many deep truths. Let's read Paul's own words about his earthly wisdom, in 1 Corinthians 2:1-5:

1 And I, brethren, when I came to you, came not with excellency of speech or of wisdom, declaring unto you the testimony of God.

2 For I determined not to know any thing among you, save Jesus Christ, and him crucified.

3 And I was with you in weakness, and in fear, and in much trembling.

4 And my speech and my preaching was not with enticing words of man's wisdom, but in demonstration of the Spirit and of power:

5 That your faith should not stand in the wisdom of men, but in the power of God.

Are you wondering, "Does God really give His deep truths to the 'unlearned'?" Isaiah 29:11-12 tells us that "learning" doesn't have a thing to do with receiving divine revelations of truth:

11 And the vision of all is become unto you as the words of a book that is sealed, which men deliver to one that is learned, saying, Read this, I pray thee: and he saith, I cannot; for it is sealed:

12 And the book is delivered to him that is not learned, saying, Read this, I pray thee: and he saith, I am not learned.

Here in this text, we can see that it makes no difference whether one is learned or unlearned, when it comes to gaining understanding of God's sealed Book, the Word of God. How do we know the Word of God is sealed? Read Matthew 11:25, where Jesus said, "I thank thee, O Father, Lord of heaven and earth, because thou hast *hid these things* [emphasis added] from the wise and prudent, and hast revealed them unto babes." Do you want to understand the Scriptures? Become, and remain, a "babe." In this context, being a "babe" is not about growth and maturity, but about humbly acknowledging that any understanding we may get from God, comes directly from Him, and not by or through any intellect on our part. So, don't claim to know anything, or how to discover anything, in yourself. Please don't get offended, friend, but you don't. No one does.

Deuteronomy 29:29 tells us "The secret things belong unto the LORD our God: but those things *which are revealed* [emphasis added] belong unto us and to our children for ever, that we may do all the words of this law." For anyone to grasp biblical truth, it *must* be revealed by God. Otherwise, it is *hidden*. No amount of "head knowledge" will open it up; the only One Who can reveal it is God, Himself, and He has chosen to *hide* it from the wise and prudent and *reveal* it to His babes. His babes, of course, are those who have been born again, into His family, and whosoever is born of God doth not commit sin (1 John 3:9). And, look at God's *purpose* in revealing His truths to us: *that we may do all the words of this law.* Friend, with all the degrees, and titles, and knowledge, and prominence, these theologians attain, they still only believe, and they only teach, that we *can't* do all the words of God's law, or Word. Isn't that amazing? Think about it. Scholars who are considered *eminent* in their Bible knowledge, and practically infallible in their Scriptural interpretations, don't even know the reason God reveals His Word to us! In fact, their very teachings *thwart* that purpose! God reveals to us, that we may *obey* Him, and these theologians say He's revealed to them that we *can't* obey Him. Come on, it's true. Partial obedience is disobedience in God's eyes, remember. That's something God *has* revealed!

When Moses wrote those words just quoted, and mentioned keeping "all the words of this law," don't forget that the ceremonial Law was fulfilled in Christ, but the moral Law is everlasting.

"Does God really give His deep truths to the 'unlearned'?" Paul taught that intellectuality, education, and theological degrees do not determine who understands God's Word. Look at 1 Corinthians 1:26-29:

26 For ye see your calling, brethren, how that not many wise men after the flesh, not many mighty, not many noble, are called:

27 But God hath chosen the foolish things of the world to confound the wise; and God hath chosen the weak things of the world to confound the things which are mighty;

28 And base things of the world, and things which are despised, hath God chosen, yea, and things which are not, to bring to nought things that are:

29 That no flesh should glory in his presence.

High-ranking theologians are, for the most part, "wise men after the flesh," for they "walk in the flesh and not in the Spirit." Oh, yes, they do. Remember Paul's words in Romans, Chapter 8? He said those who are in Christ Jesus walk not after the flesh, but after the Spirit (verse 1), *because* they have been made *free from the law of sin* (verse 2). And in verse 4 he said the righteousness of God is *fulfilled in these*. When today's religious leaders insist that the law of sin is over us as long as we are in this world, even after we "believe," they are actually proclaiming themselves to be after the flesh. Therefore all of their "wisdom" is fleshly wisdom, and it has not opened the sealed Book to them.

Isaiah 35:8 tells us, "And an highway shall be there, and a way, and it shall be called The way of holiness; the unclean shall not pass over it; but it shall be for those: the wayfaring men, though fools, shall not err therein." To understand the Word of God, we don't need to be wise in this world or in the eyes of people. All we need to do is "become fools," or to admit we don't know anything. Remember how Jesus said those who would obey it would know the doctrine? It just takes a heart that's willing to humbly "follow the Lamb whithersoever he goeth" (Revelation 14:4), even when He "goeth" against what we've always believed.

An highway shall be there. Someone may ask, "Where?" Well, verse 4 says that God "will come and save you." Verses 5-7 describe, in metaphors, what happens when He does that, then verse 8 says, "And an highway shall be there." Friend, when one is truly saved, by the Bible Jesus, the highway is right before him. The next step he takes will be on the highway of holiness!

Let's call the Apostle Paul back to the witness stand. He has so much to teach us. I urge you to read the entire 2nd Chapter of 1 Corinthians, but for now, let's look at verses 7-12:

7 But we speak the wisdom of God in a mystery, even the hidden wisdom, which God ordained before the world unto our glory:

8 Which none of the princes of this world knew: for had they known it, they would not have crucified the Lord of glory.

9 But as it is written, Eye hath not seen, nor ear heard, neither have entered into the heart of man, the things which God hath prepared for them that love him.

10 But God hath revealed them unto us by his Spirit: for the Spirit searcheth all things, yea, the deep things of God.

11 For what man knoweth the things of a man, save the spirit of man which is in him? even so the things of God knoweth no man, but the Spirit of God.

12 Now we have received, not the spirit of the world, but the spirit which is of God; that we might know the things that are freely given to us of God.

"The things of God knoweth no man." This shuts us out, friend; it leaves us in total ignorance about God—unless He reveals Himself to us. Well, praise God! "He hath revealed them unto us (His babes) by His Spirit." One thing is sure, though. May I say it again? I will: *no man can know what is not revealed!* Dear one, this text makes it plain that worldly wisdom does not open to us the mysteries of God. And if you still think the wisdom meted out in seminaries today is not worldly wisdom, let me say this: it *cannot* be spiritual wisdom, for if they had that, they would not fight holiness! The hidden things of God are revealed to man by the Spirit of God, and we already proved that only the holy have the Spirit of God within them (Romans 8:1-14). Generally speaking, the only things that God reveals to unregenerate men are things they need to know in order to see their need of salvation and what they need to do to be saved.

Let's look, again, at Romans 7:5 and 8:8-9:

7:5 For when we were in the flesh, the motions of sins, which were by the law, did work in our members to bring forth fruit unto death.

8:8 So then they that are in the flesh cannot please God.

9 But ye are not in the flesh, but in the Spirit, if so be that the Spirit of God dwell in you. Now if any man have not the Spirit of Christ, he is none of his.

How simple the Gospel is! It's when we're in the flesh that sin works in us, it's when we're in the flesh that we cannot please God, but truly saved people are not in the flesh; they are in the Spirit. If any have not the Spirit, he is not one of His. Therefore, in spite of their educational advancements, theologians who do not live holy lives cannot perceive spiritual things. First Corinthians 2.14-16 adds still more confirmation that this is so:

14 But the natural man [one in the flesh] *receiveth not the things of the Spirit of God: for they are foolishness unto him: neither can he know them, because they are spiritually discerned.*

15 But he that is spiritual judgeth all things, yet he himself is judged of no man.

16 For who hath known the mind of the Lord, that he may instruct him? But we have the mind of Christ.

It's no wonder nominal Christendom calls the idea of living holy lives "foolishness." If your preacher, or teacher, tells you what's in this book is foolishness, dear soul, you can know without a doubt that he is a natural man and not a spiritual one. Since Christendom is full of natural men, rather than spiritual men, they cannot discern these truths. But true believers have the mind of Christ, thank God, and the Great Teacher is right in their hearts (John 14:26 and 16:13). I want to reiterate, friend, it's not what's in the head that makes us able to rightly understand the Word of God; it's what is in the heart. As long as we are willing to obey it, Jesus promised that we would know His doctrine. A pure heart and a hunger and thirst after righteousness open the way.

"Does God really give His deep truths to the 'unlearned'?" Well, Peter and John were known as ignorant and unlearned men (Acts 4:13), yet their understanding of God was such that God included their writings in the holy Scriptures, in order to teach us. And when reading their epistles, one would certainly never guess that they were ignorant or unlearned. Before we look into nominal Christianity's arguments against holiness, let me stress, again, that divine revelation doesn't depend on our intellect or level of learning; it depends on the condition of our hearts.

All right, have we all checked our hearts to be sure we're ready to accept, and obey, God's will? Then we're fully qualified to understand what that will is, so let's examine these objections to holiness. We'll start with the fact that anti-holiness teachers claim that all God sees, when He looks down on sinning "Christians," is the blood of Jesus; that since their sins are covered by that blood, He cannot see any sins and, therefore, doesn't hold sin against these "Christians." Their sins will not keep them from being His children or going to Heaven. Some even portray this as a big umbrella these believers have over them, with Jesus' blood on the umbrella, hiding their sins from God's eyes. Hence, these people are "safe in the arms of Jesus."

This sounds really good—to the flesh; it sounds sweet and lovely and protective. And Ephesians 1:7 does say, "In whom we have redemption through his blood, the forgiveness of sins, according to the riches of his grace." The problem with this "blood umbrella" is that it won't stand the test of Scriptural scrutiny. That hail of judgment totally shreds it. You see, God's Word does not say Christ's blood keeps sinning "Christians" continually covered. *No Scripture says, or implies, that,* but there is a lot in the Bible that says it does not. Look at 1 Peter 1:2: "Elect according to the foreknowledge of God the Father, through sanctification of the Spirit, unto obedience and sprinkling of the blood of Jesus Christ: Grace unto you, and peace, be multiplied." Here Peter declares that being sprinkled with Jesus' blood is connected with obedience; so are *grace* and *peace* and our being *His elect.* Every one of the blessings mentioned in this verse is dependent on obedience. This verse also says the Blood application actually *follows* obedience. And *Strong's Greek Dictionary* says the term *sanctification* in this verse comes from the Greek word *hagiasmos* (hag-ee-as-mos'), which means, "*purification,* i.e. (the state) *purity*; concr. (by Hebr.) a *purifier:*—holiness."[1] This means, then, that to claim the blood of Jesus as a cover for our sins is only the right of those who are made pure and holy. Being holy implies total obedience, remember? Friend, God knew, before He made the world, that man would sin and need to be redeemed, so He lovingly provided His Plan of salvation for us. Through His foreknowledge, and that Plan, we're called back from sin to obedience (and thereby holiness) through Christ's blood and the divine operation of the Holy Ghost in our hearts. You just cannot separate the cleansing, or covering, by the Blood from being made holy and obedient! This absolutely refutes any idea that Christians can go on sinning after being saved, but the "blood umbrella" covers them.

Let's turn, now, to Hebrews 13:12: "Wherefore Jesus also, that he might sanctify the people with his own blood, suffered without the gate." Here we learn that having Christ's blood applied *sanctifies* us, and the Greek word for *sanctify* is *hagiazo* (hag-ee-ad'-zo), and means "to *make holy.*"[2] *Hagiazo* comes from the word *hagios* (hag'-ee-os), which means to be physically pure and morally blameless.[3] Paraphrased, this verse would read, "Wherefore Jesus also, that he might make the people holy through his own blood, suffered without the gate." The very purpose of Jesus' death was that His blood might make us holy! Again, this text leaves no room, whatsoever, for the claim that one can sin day by day and have the Blood cover them.

We examined Acts 26:18 in chapter three of this book, but please allow me to bring it up again, for it clarifies our present thought: "To open their eyes, and to turn them from darkness to light, and from the power of Satan unto God, that they may receive forgiveness of sins, and inheritance among them which are sanctified by faith that is in me." In this verse, we have words that Jesus spoke to the Apostle Paul when He met him on the Damascus Road. This was *Paul's calling*—to turn the Gentiles to God so they could be forgiven and receive an inheritance through Christ. But, friend, the Gentiles' salvation—and, if you're reading this, you are probably a Gentile (nonJewish)—was not a spiritual smorgasbord, where each convert could pick and choose a custom-made experience. Salvation, like Jesus Himself, is the same, yesterday, today, and forever (Hebrews 13:8). We can't select the results we want and leave behind what we don't want. It's a "package deal." Turning to God brings forgiveness of sins *and* inheritance, Jesus told Paul. Then He said the inheritance is *expressly* for those "which are sanctified by faith that is in me." The term *sanctified*, here, comes from that same Greek word (*hagiazo*), meaning "pure and blameless."[4] Friend, if your being "saved by faith" did not include this being "sanctified by faith," or being made holy, your faith was not really in the Bible Jesus. Jesus' words, here, definitely show that only those who are *made holy* by faith in Him receive this forgiveness and this inheritance. Only the holy have the "blood cover."

Some may try to argue that "darkness" doesn't necessarily refer to sin, and I will be the first to tell you that none of the words translated *darkness* in the New Testament come from Greek terms that mean sin or unrighteousness. However, when you carefully consider what Jesus and the Apostles said about darkness, you can clearly see that darkness is equated with sin. Let's examine a few more of these texts, and you will understand this.

Luke 22:53 When I was daily with you in the temple, ye stretched forth no hands against me: but this is your hour, and the power of darkness.

182

John 3:19 And this is the condemnation, that light is come into the world [1:4, 6-9], *and men loved darkness rather than light, because their deeds were evil.*

2 Corinthians 6:14 . . . for what fellowship hath righteousness with unrighteousness? and what communion hath light with darkness?

Ephesians 5:8 For ye were sometimes darkness, but now are ye light in the Lord: walk as children of light:

10 Proving what is acceptable unto the Lord.

11 And have no fellowship with the unfruitful works of darkness, but rather reprove them.

12 For it is a shame even to speak of those things which are done of them in secret.

Ephesians 6:12 For we wrestle not against flesh and blood, but against principalities, against powers, against the rulers of the darkness of this world, against spiritual wickedness in high places.

Colossians 1:13 Who hath delivered us from the power of darkness, and hath translated us into the kingdom of his dear Son:

14 In whom we have redemption through his blood, even the forgiveness of sins.

1 Peter 2:9 But ye are a chosen generation, a royal priesthood, an holy nation, a peculiar people; that ye should shew forth the praises of him who hath called you out of darkness into his marvellous light.

I'm sure those who believe and teach that Christians still sin claim that the Apostles' writings support their position, but these texts certainly show that they do not. The Apostles taught the exact opposite! The experience Jesus came to bring takes us out of darkness and it takes darkness out of us. In other words, it makes us holy. Only those who are holy have received forgiveness of sins, been brought into the Kingdom of God, and have part in that divine inheritance. Notice what else Jesus told Paul his ministry to the Gentiles would do. As well as turn them from darkness to light, it would turn them from the *power* of Satan to God. When the true Gospel is preached, and believed, it still turns people from Satan's power to a life lived through the power of God.

Jesus told Paul that *faith in Him* brings this experience. Again, this refutes the idea that "believing in Jesus" saves, yet leaves the believer under the power of sin. Twice in the last several verses we have quoted, deliverance from sin's, or Satan's, power is specifically referred to—once in Acts 26:18, and again in Colossians 1:13. Dear one, if your believing fell short of securing a holy life for you, if it (supposedly) gave you an escape from the penalty, but not the power, of sin, please allow God to show you that, up to now, your believing has not saved you. And, *please*, meet God's conditions, now, and believe the actual Gospel, and let Him save your soul!

First John 1:7 says, "But if we walk in the light, as he is in the light, we have fellowship one with another, and the blood of Jesus Christ his Son cleanseth us from all sin." Here someone may say, "See! *After* we start walking in the light, Jesus' blood cleanses *us* from *our* sins. How can you say we can't sin and still be saved?" You know, that's a good point; I appreciate honest inquiry. Let's see if we can find the answer.

First, if this verse means what you believe it means, it would be contrary to all the Scriptures we have studied throughout this book that teach the opposite. It definitely counters what Paul taught in Romans, Chapters 6-8. We examined that verse by verse and proved that Paul taught holy living as not only possible, but very much required of us. In light of the fact that all those texts definitely refute the idea of sinning Christians, and in light of the fact that God's Word never crosses itself up, there has to be a clear solution to this problem. So let's dig a little deeper.

First of all, as already studied, just a few verses farther down (2:1), John said he wrote that first chapter so "that ye sin not." Therefore, he clearly wasn't teaching anything therein that condoned sin in the saved. Second, John was writing about walking in the light as Christ is in the light. So, what can we learn from that, that will help us? How is Christ in the light? Well, in John 8:12, Jesus said, "I am the light of the world: he that followeth me shall not walk in darkness, but shall have the light of life." So, Jesus *is* the light. Walking in light as He is in light has to mean being totally in light, as there is no darkness in Him (1 John 1:5). Since we already learned that Christ and the Apostles used the term *darkness* to refer to the realm of sin and Satan, and since Jesus said those who follow Him shall not walk in darkness, it is evident that walking in light as Christ is in light simply does not allow for being saved and still sinning from day to day.

What, then, could John have meant when he said that Jesus' blood cleanses the sins of those who *are* walking in light? Well, for any of us to realize that we are sinners, and that we must repent and believe the

Gospel to be saved, God has to give us that much light. Otherwise we would abide in total darkness about sin and salvation, and God Himself. Obeying that revelation, then, *is* walking in light, the first light God gives us. Yes, my friend, the answer to our dilemma really is that simple. John said we cannot walk in darkness, in sin, and walk with Christ, but if we walk in that first ray of light, through faith, and turn from darkness and sin, His blood cleanses us, and from then on we walk in fellowship with Christ.

What we have learned, then, is that the promise of cleansing, the promise of being covered by Jesus' blood, is only for those who walk in the light as Christ is in the light, and to do that, we must leave all darkness, all sin, behind. It cannot be otherwise, dear one. Paul taught the Ephesians (5:11) to "have no fellowship with the unfruitful works of darkness, but rather reprove them." And to the Corinthians, Paul wrote, " . . . for what fellowship hath righteousness with unrighteousness? and what communion hath light with darkness" (2 Corinthians 6:14) Since it is impossible to have fellowship with Christ while having fellowship with darkness, Christ's blood only covers the *past* sins of those who are now in light as Christ is in light. And, not only are we told to forsake darkness, but we are told to *reprove* the works of darkness. How can we reprove sinful works when we ourselves commit them from day to day? To try to do that would be mockery.

First John 1:7, then, is a transitional step. When that step is taken, when we stop walking in darkness and step into light, we are cleansed from every sin of our past, and afterward we continue to walk in the light as Christ is in the light. Really studying this text, in light of other Scriptures on the subject, solves the problem. Praise God!

Now let's read Romans 3:25, which says, "Whom God hath set forth to be a propitiation through faith in his blood, to declare his righteousness for the remission of sins that are past, through the forbearance of God." There it is! This verse talks about what faith in Jesus' blood does for us. It does not, however, say anything about it covering the day-to-day sins of "Christians." Read it again and see if you can find that. You didn't, right? No, dear one. It says Christ's blood remits *sins that are past*. That is all it remits. Present sins are not automatically included under any "umbrella." Why? Simply because only those who have *forsaken* sin are covered by Jesus' blood, and forsaken sin doesn't continue from day to day. Some may argue that

"God is merciful to His believers; His forbearance and longsuffering provide this cover for their sins." Well, I must reply, "Not so!" This Scripture says, and I repeat, that it is the remission of sins that are *past* that God's forbearance, or longsuffering, provides.

To summarize this point, friend, Christ's blood absolutely does not cover day-to-day sin in the lives of believers, and, since it does not, when God looks down on them, there is no umbrella; what He sees is their sins!

Let's move on. Holiness fighters love to quote Romans 3:10, which reads, "As it is written, There is none righteous, no, not one." What they do *not* tell you is that this text's *context* shows that it is not referring to life under the Gospel but life under the Law of Moses. Remember, this is *Romans*, where Paul made a contrast between what the Law produced and what the Gospel produces. Let's look at the context of Romans 3:10. Verses 10-18 talk about the wickedness that is in *unregenerate* man, and all of this is being quoted or paraphrased by Paul from the *Old Testament*. Did he not say, "As it is written"? Well, where was this written? Some of it comes from Psalm 5:9, some comes from Psalm 10:7, some comes from Psalm 14:1-3, some from Psalm 36:1, some from Psalm 140:3, and some from Proverbs 1:16. Search it out. It is very true that those in Old Testament times could not be righteous as Christ is righteous. We have already covered this, but let's look further at this context:

Romans 3:20 Therefore by the deeds of the law there shall no flesh be justified in his sight: for by the law is the knowledge of sin.

21 But now [emphasis added] the righteousness of God without the law is manifested, being witnessed by the law and the prophets;

22 Even the righteousness of God which is by faith of Jesus Christ unto all and upon all them that believe: for there is no difference.

The Law could not justify man, and, therefore, under it "there [was] none righteous, no, not one." But Paul teaches us, here, that true faith in Christ Jesus brings the *righteousness of God* unto and upon all them that believe. Friend, this is what Bible believing does. It does it to and for *all them* that believe. Therefore, verse 10 does not prove that Christians sin; if read together with its context, it proves that they *do not*! That's the shape the Law left people in, but thank God, we have something greater than what the Law could give: the righteousness of God, by faith in Christ. To clinch the fact that Paul was *not* talking about Christians in verse 10, look at verse 17—"And the way of peace have they not known."

We can find more about the difference faith in Christ makes in Romans, Chapter 5:1 and 9-10:

1 Therefore being justified by faith, we have peace with God through our Lord Jesus Christ.

9 Much more then, being now justified by his blood, we shall be saved from wrath through him.

10 For if, when we were enemies, we were reconciled to God by the death of his Son, much more, being reconciled, we shall be saved by his life.

Friend, here we see two aspects of salvation. First, when we were enemies, we were reconciled by Jesus' death; second, being reconciled, we shall be saved by His life. Modern Christendom accepts the first part, that of being saved from sin's penalty because Jesus' blood brings us reconciliation with God, and we are no longer enemies. However, they deny the second part—what Jesus' *life* imparts to us. What is it? Being saved from sin's power. *We shall be saved*, Paul said, and this is the same *saved* (**sozo**) as that in our opening Scripture text, Acts 16:31, and others that we have covered—that of being saved *from* sin. False Christianity, today, says believers are "saved" by Christ's death, but cannot be *saved* by His life within us. How they miss the mark!

Furthermore, earlier in Romans 3, Paul wrote about the difference between the Jew and the Gentile. In verse 9, he asked, "What then? are we [the Jews] better than they [the Gentiles]? No, in no wise: for we have before proved both Jews and Gentiles, that they are all under sin." And, *then*, he quoted that "There is none righteous, no, not one." Under the Law, the Jews were accepted, as a nation, while the Gentiles were "aliens from the commonwealth of Israel, and strangers from the covenants of promise, having no hope, and without God in the world" (Ephesians 2:12). But, as verse 9 states, under the Gospel God lumped them all together, all under sin. Look next at Galatians 3:21-22:

21 Is the Law then against the promises of God? God forbid: for if there had been a law given which could have given life, verily righteousness should have been by the law.

22 But the scripture hath concluded all under sin [emphasis added], that the promise by faith of Jesus Christ might be given to them that believe.

Because all were "concluded under sin," whether Jew or Gentile, salvation in Jesus Christ comes unto all in the same manner—by faith. So the statement, "there is none righteous, no, not one," applies, as well, to the fact that, under the Gospel, no one is "righteous" by virtue of being born into a particular nation. Everyone, the world over, is equally a sinner. And among unregenerate men and women, there is, indeed, none righteous. The next verse, verse 23, clinches this point: "For all have sinned, and come short of the glory of God."

Jesus taught us, in Matthew 7:21-23, that we cannot be His disciples unless we do God's will. This is true no matter how much we call Him "Lord," or profess to be Christians. Look at it:

21 Not every one that saith unto me, Lord, Lord, shall enter into the kingdom of heaven; but he that doeth the will of my Father which is in heaven.

22 Many will say to me in that day, Lord, Lord, have we not prophesied in thy name? and in thy name have cast out devils? and in thy name done many wonderful works?

23 And then will I profess unto them, I never knew you: depart from me, ye that work iniquity.

All right. What's another favorite Scripture of those who defend sin in believers? Well, they love 1 John 1:8, which reads, "If we say that we have no sin, we deceive ourselves, and the truth is not in us." Oh, how false teachers just lift verses out of their settings and try to build up their pet theories with them. Here, they claim that since it is John talking, and talking to the Church, this definitely means no Christian should try to claim that he has no sin. Well, certainly, if this verse is lifted out and isolated, it appears to say that. But, friend, the only way anyone can use this verse to condone sin in the life of a Christian is to completely ignore what John was discussing here. What was it? Well, let's just read it and see. We'll begin with verse 5:

5 This then is the message which we have heard of him, and declare unto you, that God is light, and in him is no darkness at all.

6 If we say that we have fellowship with him, and walk in darkness, we lie, and do not the truth:

7 But if we walk in the light, as he is in the light, we have fellowship one with another, and the blood of Jesus Christ his Son cleanseth us from all sin.

8 If we say that we have no sin, we deceive ourselves, and the truth is not in us. [But . . .]

9 If we confess our sins, he is faithful and just to forgive us our sins, and to cleanse us from all unrighteousness.

10 If we say that we have not sinned, we make him a liar, and his word is not in us.

Reading these verses carefully reveals to us what John's burden was. He said the blood of Jesus (unlike the blood of bulls and goats) cleanses from all sin, but if we say we have no sin, we deceive ourselves, for all have sinned. However, if we confess our sins, He will forgive them and cleanse us from all unrighteousness. Then John repeats that if we refuse to confess that we have sinned, we are but making God a liar. Isn't this simple, really? John was merely addressing the fact that, if we want Christ's blood to cleanse us and bring us *into* fellowship with God (not after we're there), we must confess that we have sin to be cleansed from. We can know beyond a shadow of a doubt, by reading the context, that John was not saying Christians still live in sin. First, John started these verses out with the statement that we can't have fellowship with God if we walk in darkness. So, there is *no way* the saved still have sin that must be continually confessed. Look at verses 8 and 10 together. The Apostle was talking about past sins.

How can I be so sure? Read the next verse, Chapter 2, verse 1. This is the second point in this context that disproves this doctrine that Christians sin from day to day. I touched on it before, but let's read it: "My little children, these things write I unto you, that ye sin not." What he was writing, in Chapter 1, was not to condone sin in believers. It was not to "prove" that Christians still sin, and must continually confess it, after being saved. It was written for the express purpose of teaching Christians that sin is not acceptable in their lives! The rest of 2:1 deals with what to do *if* a Christian sins, but the burden and purpose of John's words in Chapter 1 was "that ye sin not." And for sure, the things he said in Chapter 3 totally condemn this sin-you-will-from-day-to-day idea.

What's another "proof text" these false leaders use? One is in Matthew 19:17, where Jesus spoke to the rich young ruler and said, "Why callest thou me good? there is none good but one, that is, God." Anti-holiness teachers claim that Jesus' words, "there is none good but God," prove that no one can live a holy life. But do His words prove that? No, my friend, they do not. All they prove is that goodness, or righteousness, or holiness, does not come from or through man. No mere man is good. Paul said, there in Romans 7:18, "For I know that in me (that is, in my flesh,) dwelleth no good thing." God's goodness, however, dwelt within his soul. Goodness comes from God and God alone, but He lives His goodness within us.

If this argument were valid, with Jesus asking, "Why callest me good," one could build a doctrine claiming that Jesus, Himself, wasn't good. But, just as surely as He meant no such thing, neither did He mean that men and women can't be made good *in Christ!*. Jesus asked the man why he *called* Him good. He did this to focus the young man's attention on where goodness comes from. This young Jew had, after all, kept the commandments from his youth up. Jesus was ushering in the New Covenant, which brought righteousness right within the heart of true believers, and He was moving this young man's attention from his own to God's righteousness. After all, this man had just asked Jesus, "What lack I yet?" Remember how the Apostle Paul said that as "touching the righteousness which is in the law, [he was] blameless," yet he wanted to "be found in him [Christ], not having mine own righteousness, which is of the law, but that which is through the faith of Christ, the righteousness which is of God by faith" (Philippians 3:6, 9)? Under the Law, mankind could only attain to *ceremonial* righteousness, but under the Gospel, the very righteousness *of God*—the only One Who is, in and of Himself, righteous—is *lived within* those who are born again. How? By His Spirit! The bottom line? No *man* is good, but God within him is.

Let's look at some other texts that bear this out. Romans 10:3-4, 8-10, says this:

3 For they [the Jewish nation, verse 1] *being ignorant of God's righteousness, and going about to establish their own righteousness, have not submitted themselves unto the righteousness of God.*

4 For Christ is the end of the law for righteousness to every one that believeth.

8 But what saith it? The word is nigh thee, even in thy mouth, and in thy heart: that is, the word of faith, which we preach;

9 That if thou shalt confess with thy mouth the Lord Jesus, and shalt believe in thine heart that God hath raised him from the dead, thou shalt be saved.

10 For with the heart man believeth unto righteousness; and with the mouth confession is made unto salvation.

From these verses we can see, first of all, that Christ brought an end to the Law *for righteousness* to those who believe in Him. Since, under the Law, no one could be made righteous, Christ fulfilled, and thereby ended, the (ceremonial) Law in order to bring God's righteousness to men. Note that Paul said those who believe will be saved, and that this being saved by faith, contrary to modern teachings, brings the believer to this righteousness, the righteousness of God. *The righteousness of God.* Friend, did your believing produce God's righteousness in you? Read that last verse again. True believing, the kind that ends with "thou shalt be saved," brings the righteousness of God within the believer. Once more, how is God righteous? *In Him is no darkness at all.* God commanded, "Be ye holy, for I am holy." Again, the righteousness that true Christians have is nót our own. It is God's, lived within us through Christ.

Second Corinthians 5:21 says, "For he hath made him to be sin for us, who knew no sin [Hmmm; 81 percent of *born-again* believers don't believe that Jesus was sinless? How, then, can they call themselves believers?]; that we might be made the righteousness of God in him." These words, *that we might be made,* confirm once more that this righteousness is not from ourselves. We are not righteous, and we cannot make ourselves righteous; only God can. But, again, we are made *the righteousness of God* (verse 3) when we believe on Bible terms and in the Bible Jesus. Friend, I tell you again, this is specifically what Jesus came to do. He will never make us anything but the righteousness of God, and the righteousness of God is holiness.

Romans 5:17 tells us, "For if by one man's offence death reigned by one [Adam]; much more they which receive abundance of grace and of the gift of righteousness shall reign in life by one, Jesus Christ." Dear reader, those who receive God's grace also receive *this gift* of righteousness; and by it we reign in this life through Jesus Christ.

Verses 20-21 of Romans, Chapter 5, part of which we quoted in the beginning of this book, go on to say this:

20 Moreover the law entered, that the offence might abound. But where sin abounded, grace did much more abound:

21 That as sin hath reigned unto death, even so might grace reign through righteousness unto eternal life by Jesus Christ our Lord.

Grace much more abounds than sin; so, as sin had reigned, now grace reigns, and It reigns *through righteousness* that comes to us by Jesus Christ. These verses are so plain and clear. We *can* live holy lives in this world, but it's only because Jesus, Who is God and is holy, lives the righteousness of God within us. And please note that it is grace, through righteousness, that brings us eternal life. Not grace that covers sin in believers, but grace that reigns over sin. Without this righteousness, friend, there is no eternal life.

Again, Romans 8:3-4 says that God "condemned sin in the flesh: That the righteousness of the law might be fulfilled in us." This righteousness is not fulfilled *by* us, but *in* us, through God's Spirit living within us. Since this is all true, friend, can you see how insulting it is to God when men cry, "Living holy is impossible." I must reply, "With God all things are possible" (Mark 10:27), and, "Is any thing too hard for the LORD" (Genesis 18:14)? First Corinthians 1:30-31 teaches:

30 But of him [God] *are ye in Christ Jesus, who of God is made unto us wisdom, and righteousness, and sanctification* [same Greek word here, meaning holiness and purity]*, and redemption:*

31 That, according as it is written, He that glorieth, let him glory in the Lord.

Can we glory because we are holy? In ourselves, absolutely not. Jesus is *made unto us righteousness and sanctification* by God. *We* only glory in the Lord, and our *holy lives* only bring glory to Him. Our part is but to submit, to surrender our will and our lives to God. He does the rest, so we deserve no credit.

Look now at Ephesians 4:22-24:

22 That ye put off concerning the former conversation the old man, which is corrupt according to the deceitful lusts;

23 And be renewed in the spirit of your mind;

24 And that ye put on the new man, which after God is created in righteousness and true holiness.

Dear one, remember that in 2 Corinthians 5:17, Paul said that any man who is in Christ is a new creature, that old things pass away and everything is new. Well, in this text we see Paul telling the Ephesian Church pretty much the same thing. Again he mentions the "old" being exchanged for the "new," but his words here certainly amplify the meaning. These terms, *creature* and *created*, add more proof that it's nothing that springs from man himself. Only God is the Creator, but look: He makes this new creature *after Himself, in righteousness and true holiness!*

Colossians 3:9-10 agrees:

9 Lie not one to another, seeing that ye have put off the old man with his deeds;

10 And have put on the new man, which is renewed in knowledge after the image of him that created him.

This new man, which we must put on, is made after the image of God. I think these Scriptures are sufficient to show that, while it's true that there is none good but God, when God is in the true believer, *His* goodness is seen in all that we do.

Other texts used to argue against living holy in this life are 1 Kings 8:46 and Ecclesiastes 7:20:

1 Kings 8:46 If they sin against thee, (for there is no man that sinneth not,) and thou be angry with them . . . .

Ecclesiastes 7:20 For there is not a just man upon earth, that doeth good, and sinneth not.

These words, in both texts, were spoken by Solomon, and, again, Solomon lived under the Law, about a thousand years before Christ's perfect sacrifice for sins was offered. We've already found that it was "not possible that the blood of bulls and of goats should take away sins" (Hebrews 10:4). But we have also found that the blood of Jesus can and does. Let us look at some other verses in Hebrews 10 for yet more understanding:

5 Wherefore when he cometh into the world, he saith, Sacrifice and offering thou wouldest not, but a body hast thou prepared me:

7 Then said I, Lo, I come . . . to do thy will, O God.

10 By the which will we are sanctified through the offering of the body of Jesus Christ once for all.

14 For by one offering he hath perfected for ever them that are sanctified.

Again, the Greek word for *sanctified,* in both verses above, is the same one I referred to earlier, and it means to be made holy. Jesus came to do God's will, which was that we would be made holy through His perfect sacrifice. Unlike those of the Old Covenant, it does take away our sins. First John 3:5 adds: "And ye know that he was manifested to take away our sins; and in him is no sin." Someone may say, "That means there's no sin in Jesus. It does not say there's no sin in us." Oh, but the next verse does: "Whosoever abideth in him sinneth not." In Jesus is no sin, so If we're in Him, there's no sin in us. On the other hand, if we have sin in us, we can't be in Him.

The sacrifices of the Old Covenant could not take away sins, so in that dispensation, indeed, there was "no man that sinneth not." But we are not in that dispensation, and the Book of Hebrews most certainly sets forth how much better things are under the New Covenant. *The Thompson Chain-Reference Bible* even says that the key word in Hebrews is "*better*."[5] It speaks of better promises, better Blood, better hope, better sacrifices, a better testament (or covenant). How, friend, could the New Covenant be better, if it left us in pretty much the same condition those under the Old Covenant were in? They could not get rid of sin, but through their sacrifices, offered in faith in Christ's future perfect sacrifice, they obtained *atonement* for sin. Today's holiness fighters claim that Jesus' perfect sacrifice does no more than that for us! But the Scriptures tell us differently. Hebrews 7:19 says, "For the law made nothing perfect, but the bringing in of a better hope did; by the which we draw nigh unto God." And verse 25 adds, "Wherefore he is able also to save them to the uttermost that come unto God by him, seeing he ever liveth to make intercession for them."

Let's read Hebrews 9:22-26 now:

22 And almost all things are by the law purged with blood; and without shedding of blood is no remission.

23 It was therefore necessary that the patterns of things in the heavens [the types and figures of the New Covenant's spiritual realities] *should be purified with these; but the heavenly things themselves* [the fulfillment of the types] *with better sacrifices than these.*

24 For Christ is not entered into the holy places made with hands, which are the figures of the true; but into heaven itself, now to appear in the presence of God for us:

25 Nor yet that he should offer himself often, as the high priest entereth into the holy place every year with blood of others;

26 For then must he often have suffered since the foundation of the world: but now once in the end of the world hath he appeared to put away sin [emphasis added] *by the sacrifice of himself.*

Verse 23 says *the patterns* of heavenly, or spiritual, things—those ceremonial types and shadows under the Law and the prophets, which foreshadowed the coming of Christ and His perfect salvation—were purged by animal sacrifices. The spiritual realities, however, which cast those shadows, and that come to us through the Gospel, are purified by *better sacrifices*. In other words, what the Old Covenant sacrifices could not do, Christ's sacrifice of Himself accomplished. The old sacrifices could not take away sins, but Christ is able to *put away sin* and save *to the uttermost* those who believe in Him.

Webster's defines *uttermost* as "utmost,"[6] which he then says means "*adj.* 1 most extreme; farthest 2 of the greatest degree, amount, etc.—*n.* the most possible."[7] So, "saved to the uttermost" doesn't mean saved a little bit, or saved from the worst sins, or saved from the penalty, but not the power, of sin. It clearly means fully, totally, and completely saved, saved to the *greatest degree*. Shame on these false prophets who belittle God by saying He isn't able to do this! God said He *is* able! We just read it. And I believe it. And, having believed it, I now live it! You can too.

While writing this book, I read a number of commentaries on Romans 8:1-4. To refresh your mind, this Scripture text tells us that there is no condemnation for those who are in Christ Jesus. God condemns sin in the flesh, but when one repents and believes, the Spirit of life in Christ Jesus sets him free from that "law of sin and death," and therefore from its condemnation.

Most Bible teachers claim, however, that this text only means freedom from condemnation, because God put all our condemnation on Christ, when He died, and believers are therefore released from it, even though they go on sinning. One even taught that, as a "Christian" progresses, his growing closeness to Christ makes him keenly aware of *his sins*, causing him to abhor sin, and even himself. So, he then needs to *mature* yet more and *learn to shed* his condemnation. Because *his sins* are covered by Christ's blood, he doesn't need to feel condemned over them.

Friend, that is ridiculous! If it is being close to Christ that makes one aware of his sinfulness and, therefore, his condemnation, how could getting even closer, take it away? As long as he is sinning, which this teacher affirms that he is, the closer he gets to God's holy Son, the *more* keenly aware of his sins he should become. And, it is not in growing close to Christ, as a Christian, that we gain a keen awareness of sin anyway. That is the work of the Holy Ghost upon a *sinner* through *conviction*, and that is what alerts him that he needs to come to Christ and be saved in the first place (John 16:7-11).

Furthermore, if Paul was struggling under condemnation at the time he wrote the Book of Romans, as this teacher claims, shouldn't he have matured enough by then to have "learned to shed" it? After all, he was one of the most mature preachers God had at the time! If he hadn't yet shed his condemnation, what about all those other believers? And how can you and I hope to reach enough maturity to do so? Again, this would be another exercise in futility! We'd be constantly striving for something that apparently stays just out of reach. In effect, then, all Jesus provided for us is a spiritual wild goose chase, like the legendary dog running after the hot dog on the end of a pole, taking his young master for a nice ride. And, if these modern "apostles" claim that they have succeeded in reaching that level of maturity that releases them from their condemnation, I have to cry "fowl!" I just do not believe they've reached a higher plane than the Apostle Paul reached. Not a single one of them.

Friend, think about it—if this were what Christ came to bring to us, Paul would not, and could not, have so confidently written that "there is therefore *now* no condemnation to them which *are* in Christ Jesus." Furthermore, how could God, Who is honest and holy, have inspired Paul to write something that simply was not true, expressing the condemnation-free state as a "now" experience, when he was still writhing in his condemnation? How honest would it have been for Paul to say he was *now* free from condemnation, right after saying he was miserable in it, unless he had, in fact, been *now* set free, as he said he was? How could he have said he was *now* free from it when he was *now* struggling to mature enough to shake it off? Dear one, can't you see that these false prophets are always putting complete deliverance and victory off into the future? Not Paul! He said he *had* these *right now*!

The Mosaic Law did put full deliverance and victory out into the future. Those who lived under that Law were given a promise of future redemption. But all that the Law of Moses promised was fulfilled in Jesus Christ! It is not still a future promise. It is, indeed, a "now" experience, and that is exactly what the Apostle Paul teaches us in Romans. Again, he describes what the Law could, and could not, do, and then he portrays what the glorious Gospel brought to man. That was, and still is, complete deliverance from both sin and its condemnation. Remember how clearly Paul taught victory in Romans 6 and Romans 8? Away with the idea that he, himself, didn't have that victory!

If you haven't found this deliverance, friend, it's because the masses of so-called Gospel preachers are cheating you out of it, by proclaiming that it's *still* a future blessing. They're leaving you in the same condition people were in under that old Mosaic Law. Let me repeat, and stress, that all the promises of the Law Dispensation were fulfilled, and brought to present reality, through Jesus' life, death, and resurrection. Look at Luke 24:44: "And he said unto them, These are the words which I spake unto you, while I was yet with you, that all things must be fulfilled, which were written in the law of Moses, and in the prophets, and in the psalms, concerning me."

We can, and must, find total deliverance from sin *now*, if we hope to be saved and to make Heaven our eternal home. Clearly, friend, the idea this Bible scholar set forth is *not* what Romans 8:1-4 teaches. For one thing, anyone who has sin in him can't even *get* close to Christ (Isaiah 59:1-2). But, look at what Paul said in Romans 8:1: "There is therefore now no condemnation to them which are in Christ Jesus, who walk not after the flesh, but after the Spirit." Wouldn't being *in* Christ mean being *close* to Him? How much closer could you get than that?

If this man's interpretation were correct, Paul should have written that those Christians who felt a lot of condemnation over their sins needed to mature so they could shed it. Or, if they, unlike Paul, had already progressed past their condemnation, he should have said that there was now no condemnation to those who *had matured* in Christ. Right? Or, he should have written that there is therefore, now, no *need* to feel condemnation, and that as they matured, they would learn to dismiss it. *But that's not what he said!* What he *said* was that, for those who are *in* Christ, there *is* no condemnation! *There is none.* What is there about that statement that's hard to understand? There is no condemnation, for anyone to mature enough to shake off!

Precious soul, Paul started that verse with the words, "There is therefore," and then he added "now." *Therefore* refers to something already said, and it is like saying "because of." What did Paul say before? Well, we already covered this in chapter four, but briefly, he said, "Who shall deliver me from the body of this death" (Romans 7:24)? He then answered his own question in verse 25, saying, "I thank God through Jesus Christ our Lord." So, in Chapter 8 of Romans, he said there was *now* no condemnation, *because* he had been set *free* from *the law of sin and death* (verses 1-2). Having no condemnation was not the effect of "growing up" spiritually; it was the effect of being made free from that law of sin that *produces* condemnation. Paul said *nothing* about maturity here. He said, very clearly, that the reason he had no condemnation was because he had been set free from the "law," or power, of sin. This professed Bible teacher most surely added his own ideas to the Word, and took from it the very essence of what Paul was telling us. He wrested the Word of God to try to make it support his own ideas, rather than conforming his beliefs to that Word. How tragic! Friend, it's much better to be free from the *cause* of condemnation than to be striving for a higher level of "spirituality"—that Paul, supposedly, had not even reached by then—in order to be able to shake it off! That much better experience is what Jesus brought to us: a better covenant, with better Blood, that wrought in us a better redemption and produced better results.

I promised you a more thorough study of how modern religionists rob this precious Scripture text, Romans 8:1-4, of its true, and glorious, meaning by claiming that Paul's deliverance from "the law of sin" was only his deliverance from the Mosaic Law. Let us do that now. It is true that Paul referred much to the *comparison* between the effects of the Mosaic Law and those of the Gospel. It is true that he spent considerable time in setting this comparison before us. However, to say that "law of sin" was the Mosaic Law, is simply not true. By claiming this, these theologians teach that what "the law of the Spirit of life in Christ Jesus" set Paul free from was not sin's power. While the Gospel did, indeed, set mankind free from the ceremonial Law, and its inability to deliver from sin, the "law of sin" that Paul described in Romans 7, was something entirely separate from the Law God gave to Israel of old. Let's look, again, at how Paul portrayed his "law of sin":

Romans 7:5 For when we were in the flesh, the motions of sins, which were by the law, did work in our members to bring forth fruit unto death.

7a What shall we say then? Is the law sin? God forbid.

12 Wherefore the law is holy, and the commandment holy, and just, and good.

13a Was then that which is good made death unto me? God forbid.
14 For we know that the law is spiritual: but I am carnal, sold under sin.
15 For that which I do I allow not: for what I would, that do I not;
but what I hate, that do I.
16 If then I do that which I would not, I consent unto the law that it
is good.
17 Now then it is no more I that do it, but sin that dwelleth in me.
20 Now if I do that I would not, it is no more I that do it, but sin that
dwelleth in me.
21 I find then a law, that when I would do good, evil is present with me.
22 For I delight in the law of God *after the inward man:*
23 But I see another law *in my members, warring against the law of*
my mind, and bringing me into captivity to the law of sin which is in my
members. (Emphasis added.)

What was Paul saying?

a) I delight in *the law of God;*
b) I see *another law* in my members;
c) I'm a captive to the *law of sin* in my members.

God's Law was holy; it was not sin, and it was not *made* sin to Paul. It was not death, and it was not *made* death to Paul. He delighted in the *Law of God*, but that *law of sin* that worked in his members was *another law*! What worked in his members, and made him its captive, and brought him under condemnation, *was not* the Law of Moses! I repeat, that law of sin was *another law*; and it was this *other law*, working in his members, that he found complete deliverance from through the Spirit of life in Christ Jesus (Chapter 8, verse 2). This is the very power of sin that holiness fighters insist that we cannot escape! But just as Paul found release from it, so can you and I!

The Mosaic Law, written on tables of stone, was never in anyone's members. However, praise God, under the Gospel, God does, indeed, write His Law—that moral Law that existed before the Mosaic Law, and will always exist—in our hearts! See Exodus 34:1 and Hebrews 8:10.

Paul makes what he was talking about very clear, if we will just read what he said, so let's go on, now, and do that. Please read it very attentively.

Romans 8:1 There is therefore now no condemnation to them which are in Christ Jesus, who walk not after the flesh, but after the Spirit.

2 For the law of the Spirit of life in Christ Jesus hath made me free from the law of sin and death.

3 For what the law could not do, in that it was weak through the flesh, God sending his own Son in the likeness of sinful flesh, and for sin, condemned sin in the flesh:

4 That the righteousness of the law might be fulfilled in us, who walk not after the flesh, but after the Spirit.

Verse 1 and verse 4 both mention those who walk not after the flesh, but after the Spirit. Clearly neither those who are free from condemnation, nor those in whom God's righteousness is fulfilled, walk after the flesh. Just as clearly, those who have God's righteousness *have no condemnation.* They do not need to grow out of it; they've been delivered from it by being saved *from* sin.

In summary, then, there *is* no condemnation to the saved! Those who walk in the flesh commit sin; those who walk in the Spirit do not. That law of sin is not the Law of Moses, but "another law." The Mosaic Law *was not made sin and death* to Paul or to anyone else. God *condemns sin in the flesh of Christians.* This is not the same as allowing sin in our flesh and just *lifting* the condemnation. Through the work of the Holy Spirit, God's perfect *righteousness is fulfilled in us.*

May God have mercy on those who teach such nonsense as what we just refuted by God's Word—and on those who hear them! This is *not* the doctrine of the Bible, nor of the real Savior. My friend, is *your* Jesus the Bible Jesus?

Let me take the words of that professed Bible teacher and transform them into a true statement. He said, *As a "Christian" progresses, his growing closeness to Christ makes him keenly aware of his sins, causing him to abhor sin, and even himself. So, he then needs to mature yet more and learn to shed his condemnation. Because his sins are covered by Christ's blood, he doesn't need to feel condemned over them.*

What truth would say is, "As a sinner hears the Gospel, the Holy Spirit makes him keenly aware of his sins, and if he doesn't rebel, he will come to abhor sin, and even himself. He then needs to repent and believe, and surrender to Christ, in order to be saved from his sins. Once he does this, his sins are covered by Christ's blood, he has peace with God, and he doesn't suffer under condemnation any longer. Now the righteousness of God, Himself, is wrought within him by Christ's indwelling there."

My friend, if you know of any other Scripture that *seems* to condone sin in the life of a Christian, I invite you to send it to me. I will be happy to study it with you.

CHAPTER TEN

"Well, I Was Saved, So I'm All Right"— Does the Bible Teach This?

No doubt there will be some who read this book who, at one time, really were born again and enjoyed the Lord's work of salvation in their hearts. Because of this, many feel safe now, even though they know they are not following God's will today. They believe, unfortunately, that once they've been saved, they are eternally secure. Whether or not they are presently living right does not concern them.

We refer to this belief as the "once in grace, always in grace," or "once saved, always saved," eternal security doctrine. Millions are staking their eternal welfare on its validity. If you are one of these, dear reader (or if you just need clearer understanding on this subject), will you allow me to examine this doctrine with you? Let me remind you that testing your beliefs by the Scriptures and honest, earnest, prayer will not harm truth; it only polishes truth. But it will expose error, and by doing that, it will set honest hearts free. I know that people's belief in this doctrine is strong. I know it is dear to them. I know they believe anyone teaching that it's not biblical is a heretic and dangerous. If you are one of them, you resist even looking further into my argument. But please carefully and *prayerfully* hear me out. Your soul is at stake! God will never allow unrighteousness to inherit His Kingdom! Never, under any circumstances, will He do so, and I can prove beyond any successful contradiction that eternal security is not a Bible doctrine. It is no more a Bible doctrine than is the teaching that Christians cannot live without sin. But don't take my word for it; my word isn't any better than anyone else's. But, I assure you, I will use God's pure Word to show you that Christians who go back to sin are lost.

To start with, we will look at what Jesus, Himself, said. Luke 9:62 reads, "And Jesus said unto him, No man, having put his hand to the plough, and looking back, is fit for the kingdom of God." This says enough, as far as I'm concerned, but I know that people who have been taught this doctrine think they have Bible to back it up, and I want to be fair, and faithful, to those souls, so let's look at the Scriptures they rest on.

But, first, remember how God created the devil to give man a right of choice? Well, friend, do you think this right of choice is not important to God? If God had made us like the angels (the heavenly ones), and we served Him because we *had* no choice, there would never have been any sin. If there were no sin, God would not have had to sacrifice His only Son as an atonement for sin. Can you see how important our free will was, and is, to God? In creating us with that right to choose whom we will serve, His love compelled Him to provide a Plan for redeeming us when we made the wrong choice. O! What love! He knew what He would have to do, and what Jesus would have to do, to make that remedy available, when our choice to sin condemned us to a horrid and eternal hell.

Remember that we are created in God's image. Even unregenerate man carries within him many attributes of God, our Father by creation, such as a sense of justice, a natural tendency to kindness and caring, etc., and more pertinently, a desire to be loved and cherished. Well, you wouldn't be very thrilled with the prospect of love and marriage, if your life's companion *had* to love you and marry you. But when that special person *chooses* you over all the others around you, *WOW!* It makes you really feel cherished. It fills a longing within you. You crave being loved and wanted, and, just so, God wants us to serve Him because we *choose* Him over all the sinful pleasures and personal ambitions that abound in the world—because we love Him, not because we have to serve Him.

Only service prompted by love was wanted, friend, even though it would come at *extreme cost* to God, and only service prompted by love is accepted. When people get saved, and then turn back to sin, something has certainly happened to their love. Jesus said, "If ye love me, keep my commandments" (John 14:15), and the Beloved Apostle added to this these words in 1 John 5:2-4:

2 By this we know that we love the children of God, when we love God, and keep His commandments.

3 For this is the love of God, that we keep his commandments: and his commandments are not grievous.

4 For whatsoever is born of God overcometh the world: and this is the victory that overcometh the world, even our faith.

Loving God and keeping His commandments are inseparably connected. If we do not keep His commandments, we do not love Him, and if we do not love Him, we will not keep His commandments. The Apostle Paul said, "The love of Christ constraineth us" (2 Corinthians 5:14a). Dear one, *love prompts obedience!*

So we see that God specifically and deliberately set things up so man could choose whether or not to serve Him, and choose to serve Him for only one reason: because he loves Him. Since this is true, since God only wants service that springs from a heart overflowing with love, it makes absolutely no sense to say that once we make a favorable choice, He takes away our free will and we then have to serve Him whether we want to or not. We then have to serve Him even though we don't love Him anymore. Who could get any satisfaction out of service like that? Neither God nor the supposed believer could! That would render our being His child a forced thing, after all He and His Son went through to prevent just that. That is exactly what His plan was established, before the world was, to avoid. Do you doubt that? If God wanted forced service, He would have made us for forced service. Why would He have created us with a free will, so we could choose, and then take it away and force our service after all? God is not foolish. I repeat, dear reader, creating us with a free will was to cost God, and His precious Son, unspeakable grief. He did *not* pay that price just to turn around and force our service after all. Would you sacrifice *your* child? Would you go to that extreme in order to produce something, and then just throw that thing away?

Now stop and consider how *selfish* this "eternal security" notion is. "Because God loves *me*, He'll allow me to scorn Him and make mockery of Him, curse Him, and cast Him away, but He won't cast *me* away. Even if I hate Him, He'll love *me*." Talk about wanting to believe something that is all for *me*, rather than in loving service to *God!* God *is* love, friend, but He's also jealous; He will not tolerate our being His

204

bride but loving the things of sin. Remember, that's spiritual adultery. God is also just, and justice requires judgment on our sins.

Someone may say, "Well, in spite of your boast, you're not using Scripture. You're just using human reasoning. Remember, we have Bible for our eternal security. Lots of it." No, friend, I'm not just using human reasoning. I'm establishing God's purpose in Creation. Then, when I get to the Scriptural proofs that He does not take away anyone's free will of choice, you will understand that, unlike this false doctrine, those proofs fit with His divine purpose from the beginning.

God wants our love first; He only wants service that is prompted by love. Anyone who turns away from keeping God's commandments does not love Him any longer, and God does not want any part of such a thing! He will not have a house full of rebellious children! When we turn from loving Him, and serving Him out of love, we are *deserters*; we have no more part in Him, by our own choice.

Let us now answer the question, "What about all the Scriptures that teach that we can never lose our eternal life?" Well, allow me to say that they only *seem* to teach we can never lose our eternal life, and, once again, that's because they are being interpreted outside their contexts. Remember, the end of the way that seemeth right is death (Proverbs 14:12, 16:25), just as the end of sin is death. Let's study those Scriptures that are used to bolster this once saved, always saved, belief. John 10:27-29 reads:

27 My sheep hear my voice, and I know them, and they follow me:

28 And I give unto them eternal life; and they shall never perish, neither shall any man pluck them out of my hand.

29 My Father, which gave them me, is greater than all; and no man is able to pluck them out of my Father's hand.

"Once saved, always saved" advocates say that these words of Jesus prove that anyone who becomes one of Christ's sheep is eternally secure. They quote the words, "and they shall never perish," and declare that no saved person can ever be lost. They quote, "neither shall any man pluck them out of my hand," and say that, once a soul is in Christ's hand, he can never be taken out. But upon closer examination, we'll find that these verses do not teach eternal security, and the answer is not hard to lay hold of. Again, it's really simple, friend.

Jesus said, "My sheep hear my voice and they follow me." Notice that He did not add, "Well, I have some sheep who used to follow me, but they don't anymore." (Neither did He say, "And I have sheep who hear and follow in some things, but not in everything.") I say again, Jesus' statement is a simple one and easily understood, and nowhere in the context can anyone find exceptions from, or conditions for, His words here. To *hear* and *follow* are fixed principles of, and requirements for, being His sheep! And since Jesus prefaced the rest of this text with this fact, all of the following verses must be interpreted in the light of these words. May I quote them again? "My sheep hear my voice and they follow me." Quite obviously, any who do not hear and follow, are not His sheep. Don't allow your mind to be corrupted, dear one, from the simplicity of the Gospel!

There is no room for controversy here. His sheep hear and follow—and since all the promises in this text are directly spoken about *His sheep,* they can only apply to those who hear (not *used to hear*) and follow (not *used to follow*) Jesus. More specifically, verse 28, "And I give unto them eternal life; and they shall never perish, neither shall any man pluck them out of my hand," only refers to those who hear and follow Him.

Please understand this. Let me repeat it. No one else is given these promises. They are not for anyone who *once* heard and followed. Only *those who hear* (present tense) *and follow* (present tense) have eternal life. Only *those who hear and follow* shall never perish. Only *those who hear and follow* cannot be plucked out of His hand. These blessings are for *no one else.* When any Christian ceases to hear and obey, he ceases to be Christ's sheep, and when that happens, these promises are no longer his.

Someone may say, "But eternal life is *eternal.* How can one who has it ever die? How can anything that is eternal cease?"

The *life* doesn't cease. You are right, eternal life is *eternal,* it is everlasting, it is never-ending. The reason someone who once had eternal life can lose it is simply because eternal life is *in the Son.* When we walk away from the Son, we leave that eternal life behind. It doesn't cease, but *it stays with the Son.* It is only *in Him*! Does the Bible say this? *Yes.* Look at 1 John 5:10-12:

10 He that believeth on the Son of God hath the witness in himself: he that believeth not God hath made him a liar; because he believeth not the record that God gave of his Son.

11 And this is the record, *that God hath given to us eternal life, and this life is* in his Son.

12 He that hath the Son *hath life; and he that* hath not the Son of God *hath not life* [emphasis added in each of these verses].

Do you believe the record God gave of His Son, friend? This text says that record is that God has given us (John was writing to saved people here) eternal life *in His Son.* We cannot find it anywhere else, and if we do not believe this record that God gave of His Son, we make Him a liar. That is serious business, dear one! Those who propagate "eternal security" are giving a different record of Christ than the one God, Himself, gave. People who forsake the *service* of God are forsaking God, Himself, and are no longer *in the Son.* When they leave the Son, I repeat, they leave the eternal life behind.

More on this later, but consider this: eternal existence was there long before man was created, yet it has a *beginning* in human beings. Our eternal spirit only lives in us from the moment we are conceived, and it ceases to live in our mortal frame when we die. Yet our spirit, itself, will live, or exist, forever. Everyone agrees that eternal life, that spiritual life one receives when he is born again, also has a *beginning* in the human soul. Before conversion, we are all "dead in trespasses and sins" (Ephesians 2:1). Is it so hard to conceive, then, that eternal life can cease in our soul when we turn back to sin and experience spiritual death again (the soul that sinneth, it shall die)? Just as our eternal existence lives on after physical death, but not in our mortal body, Christ's eternal spiritual life lives on, when we backslide, but not in us. The argument that we can never perish once we receive eternal life, because that life is eternal, just won't hold up in the light of this fact. *Eternal* goes forever into the past as well as into the future; and, as eternal as eternal life is, if it can have a beginning *in us,* it can also have an ending *in us.*

Dear one, this is not strange to our thinking; it happens all around us, all the time. It's a very simple concept, really. If you quit your job, leave the mall, or graduate from school, those things don't cease to exist. You may not be there, but the action goes on without you. That is how it is when a believer turns away from God. God's Kingdom goes on, His Plan goes on, and His eternal life goes on. The faithful are just as happy and blessed as ever and still enjoying that eternal life. The life goes on—but the backslider no longer has it. Why? Because the soul that sins, dies, and death ends life for the one who dies, even though life goes on for others. Nowhere in God's Word is it said, or even implied, that sin's wages are sometimes life! No; the wages of sin is death.

Are you still not convinced? That's all right. It's difficult, sometimes, to grasp new truths. Just stick with me through the rest of this, and the next, chapters, and by the grace of God, I will prove conclusively that "eternal security" is a false doctrine, used by Satan to destroy millions of souls. Please don't be one of them!

Having eternal life is a lot like using electricity. The power is there whether we use it or not, but when we tap into it, we enjoy its benefits. If, however, we choose to *disconnect* from the power line, no matter how much power is still running through the lines, we won't have any. It's still there, but we cut off our connection with it, so *for us* it is the same as if it wasn't even there. Eternal life is *in the Son*, but if we break our connection with, and no longer have, the Son, we no longer have eternal life. It's just that simple.

"Oh, we *have* the Son," some may argue. "We can never be plucked out of His hand. We just don't obey Him anymore." No, friend; *Jesus* said if we're His sheep, we *do* obey. He has no sheep that don't. Remember James' words? If you're not a *doer* of the Word, you deceive yourself. Since Jesus is specifically referring to those who hear and follow Him, in this text, let's look at His promises in that light:

27 My sheep hear my voice, and I know them, and they follow me:

28 And I give unto those who hear and follow, eternal life; and those who hear and follow shall never perish, neither shall any man pluck those who hear and follow out of my hand.

29 My Father, which gave those who hear and follow to me, is greater than all; and no man is able to pluck those who hear and follow out of my Father's hand.

Reading it this way is entirely correct, friend, because the antecedent of every "they" and "them" in these verses is "my sheep," who hear His voice and follow Him. And reading it this way certainly robs the "eternal security" people of their claim that this Scripture proves no saved person is ever lost, no matter what they do. *Jesus did not teach any such thing!*

Having seen, then, that these promises are only for His sheep—those who *presently hear and follow* Him—let's look at being plucked out of

His hand. Jesus said that "no man" shall pluck His sheep out of His, or His Father's, hand. Advocates of "eternal security" say this has to include *us*, that if *no man* can pluck us out, we ourselves can't. After all, we are men (or women). Certainly we are. But Jesus didn't say we couldn't *walk* out. *Pluck them out* is a verb phrase that denotes action by one person toward another or action by a person toward some thing. *Webster's* says *pluck* means "1 to pull off or out; pick 2 to snatch."[1] *Snatch* means "to try to seize; grab (*at*).[2] And *seize* means "1 to capture; arrest 2 to take forcibly and quickly 3 to grasp suddenly 4 to attack or afflict suddenly."[3] We normally do not refer to things we do to or for ourselves in this manner. If Jesus had been referring to something *we* couldn't do, He would have added, "neither can any of my sheep jump or walk out of my hand."

Yes He would have! We do not pluck, snatch, or seize, ourselves out of anything. If you get out of your car, you do not say, "I snatched myself out of my car," or "I grabbed myself out of my car." And you certainly don't add "forcibly," or "suddenly," etc. No, you say, "I got out of my car." In an extreme case, you might even say, "I leaped out of my car." But you do not, in any sense of the word, say that you plucked, snatched, or seized, yourself out of it. The same is true for getting our of the shower, leaving a building, or anything else that you vacate. And when gardeners or farmers harvest their crops, the produce doesn't *pick itself*. All of these refer to something done *by someone else* to a person or thing!

More important, even, than *Webster's* definition, is the original Greek word used for *pluck* in this Scripture text. According to *Strong's Greek Dictionary*, that word is **harpazo** (har-pad'-zo), and it puts it in even stronger language: "to *seize*" and to "take (by force)."[4] Again, friend, these words *do not* refer to what we do to or for ourselves. Just as you don't snatch yourself by force out of your car or the shower, but, rather, you *get* out, so you can *get* out of God's hand if you *so choose*, even though no one else can snatch you out. It's evident that this Scripture text is referring to someone else's actions, not our own.

Furthermore, Jesus contrasts these persons. That means they aren't the same. He said, "neither shall *any man* pluck *them* out of my hand." The *plucker* and the *plucked* refer to different entities. One is singular, "any man"; the other is plural, "them." The subject in these promises is "my sheep." No *man* can pluck *His sheep* out of His hand. Because these terms do denote violence, the "any man" is set *against* the "them." I repeat, they are not the same. Jesus did not say the "plucking" was on the part of His sheep, but on the part of *a man*. It was not something done *by* the sheep, but *to* them. These facts make it clear that Christ was not saying, "Neither can any man pluck *himself* out of my hand."

What *was* Jesus promising His sheep in these verses? Well, you've heard of people being put out of this church or that church. You've heard about religious leaders denouncing someone and saying he can no longer be a part of them. Jesus, here, is giving us the blessed assurance that, since He is the door, only He can put us out of His Church. Also, since He said He will never leave or forsake us (His sheep), He only puts out those who want to leave. The rest are safe.

To wrap up this part of our study, let's read Hebrews 5:8-9:

8 Though he were a Son, yet learned he obedience by the things which he suffered;

9 And being made perfect, he became the author of eternal salvation unto all them that obey him.

Who is the Bible Jesus the author of *eternal salvation* to? Not those who have served Him, then turned back to sin, but those who *obey* Him. This *obey* is present tense, and does not include those who *once* obeyed Him. When we cease to obey Him, we *walk away from* these promises and lose these privileges. Let me put it this way: no one who was saved but does not presently obey Christ, has eternal salvation promised to him. May I emphasize that? *There is no promise of eternal salvation to those who no longer obey Christ!*

Another argument used to promote this doctrine of eternal security is taken from the following verses:

John 6:39 And this is the Father's will which hath sent me, that of all which he hath given me I should lose nothing, but should raise it up again at the last day.

John 10:29 My Father, which gave them me, is greater than all . . . .

Using this text, these teachers claim that, "God will make sure that a born-again believer is not lost. Even the believer can do nothing to stop *God's will* in the matter, because the believer belongs to Jesus now." So, believers are given to Jesus by the Father, and no longer belong to themselves, and it is the Father's will that Jesus loses none of them; therefore, He never can or will.

"Well," you may say, "that's what it says. How can you refute that?" Oh, dear reader, that's not what it says. And it won't be me refuting it, but God. Certainly it is the Father's will that Jesus loses none of those whom the Father gives Him. But what might be God's will for us and what we actually allow Him to do for us are not always the same, so there is no foundation for the claim that it *must* be so in this case. For one thing, it is *our* will that determines whether He loses us or not. More on this in a minute or two, but if what we do doesn't matter, and we can't change whom we belong to, once we're saved, why would God have inspired Peter to write the following: "Wherefore the rather, brethren, *give diligence* to make your calling and election *sure*: for *if* ye do these things, ye shall never *fall*" (2 Peter 1:10; Emphasis added). Dear one, Peter addressed these words "to them that have obtained like precious faith with us . . . According as his divine power hath given unto us all things that pertain unto life and godliness" (2 Peter 1:1, 3). He was talking to the saved here. For God to put this in the Bible when we *cannot* fall, whether we're diligent or not, would make Him a deceiver! Any time you have an "if," there has to be an "if not." The very meaning of the word "if" insists on the "if not." So Peter's words, without any doubt, let us know that *if* we do *not* act diligently to make our salvation sure, we not only can, but will, fall!

Now, consider this: if God's will *has* to be done in us, once the Father gives us to the Son, how can we thwart His will by turning back to the world and sinful things? What about those who curse His holy Name and defy Him? Or those who rebelliously say they don't even want to go to Heaven? Either we can stop God's will or we can't. The very fact that people can turn again to sinning shows that God's will for them is not always what happens. I find it amazing how anyone can say a once-saved person cannot be lost because God's will, that they never perish, simply has to be carried out, and nothing can alter that—yet, although it is also God's will that they never turn back to sinning, His will in that can be, and often is, altered. How can "whatever is God's will" be inescapable in the one, but be quite resisted and refused in the other? Friend, the truth is that we can, indeed, choose to live in sin again, and it is just as true that the soul that sinneth, it shall die. Away with such nonsense as insisting, on one hand, that God's will has to be done in the saved, and then insisting, on the other hand, that it doesn't have to be done in the saved. Stick with me, my friend, and this will become more clear as we examine God's Word.

Again, these teachers claim that "God will make sure that a born-again believer is not lost. Even the believer can do nothing to *stop God's will* in the matter [emphasis added]." Yet the believer can stop God's will about his turning back to sin. He can stop God's will about his love growing cold. He can stop God's will about his being a light, and salt, and a witness. He can stop God's will about his enduring unto the end. Since he can stop God's will about all of these, and many more, things, it is ludicrous to say he can't stop God's will—in fact, God's *law*—about his reaping what he sows. "*For he that soweth to his flesh shall of the flesh reap corruption; but he that soweth to the Spirit shall of the Spirit reap life everlasting*" (Galatians 6:8).

Beloved soul, there is no promise of everlasting life to those who return to sowing to their flesh! In verse 7, Paul cries, "Be not deceived; God is not mocked: for whatsoever a man soweth, that shall he also reap." This cry is part of the Gospel! God is still heralding this cry through His true ministry today. You will, I will, and everyone else will, reap exactly what we sow! To claim otherwise is to mock God, but God will not be mocked, friend. Those who spread this false doctrine will be!

Remember that all men, everywhere, turn to their own way, or will, and bring spiritual death upon themselves. But 2 Peter 3:9 says, The Lord is . . . not willing that any should perish, but that all should come to repentance." So, if these teachers are correct in their teaching, we have the assurance that everyone will come to repentance, right? *That's God's will in the matter!* So we can all rest our hearts about our unsaved loved ones. They *have* to get saved! Ah, but you and I know that not all of those who have lived up to now came to repentance, and we know that not everyone from now on will come to repentance. If this were the case, Christ would never have given us any warnings about hell. Not one single human being would go there. But God's will certainly can be cast off by man's free will of choice. Remember that man's free will was given to him by God in the first place because God did not then, nor does He now, want forced service. And, friend, to say that Christians can stop His will when it comes to their *conduct*, but they can't stop it when it comes to the *results* of their conduct, would make God *an accessory* to their evil deeds, and that, He will never, ever be!

These teachers add that since believers are given to Jesus by the Father and "no longer belong to themselves," they "cannot choose not to belong to Jesus anymore. *They can no longer decide who they belong to.*" (Emphasis added.) This is ridiculous! Salvation does not make us robots. It does not make us angels, who cannot choose. Dear one, I must ask again, because it's so important: if we "no longer belong to ourselves," and can no longer "choose not to belong to Jesus," how can we choose to go back to sinning? *Think* about how ludicrous this idea is! We cannot choose not to belong to Jesus, yet we can choose to act as if we do not belong to Jesus. We can choose to be rebels. We can deny Him in all that we do, and mock Him at every turn. I'm sorry, but—that's nonsense. How can we possibly choose to stop *obeying* the One we cannot choose to stop belonging to? We either have the right of choice, or we do not have it. If God takes away our right of choice once we are saved, there is no way we can choose to stop obeying Him and go back to sinning!

Since we are talking specifically, here, about *those whom the Father had given Jesus*, we can positively prove that, although it was the Father's will that He lose none of them, He *could* lose some. Look at Jesus' prayer right before He went to the cross, recorded in John 17:

6 I have manifested thy name unto the men which thou gavest me out of the world: thine they were, and thou gavest them me; and they have kept thy word.

9 I pray for them: I pray not for the world, but for them which thou hast given me; for they are thine.

12 While I was with them in the world, I kept them in thy name: those that thou gavest me I have kept, and none of them is lost, but the son of perdition; that the scripture might be fulfilled.

In each of these verses, Jesus again refers to those the Father had given Him. But look! Verse 12 positively says that one of them was lost! Though Jesus had done His best to "keep them," it did not prevent them from being able to *choose* to be lost, as Judas did. Judas started out well; Peter said, in Acts 1:17, that Judas "had obtained part of this ministry," and in verse 25, while praying for a replacement for Judas, the disciples again mentioned "this ministry and apostleship, from which Judas by transgression fell." *Judas, by sinning, fell from his ministry and from his apostleship.* He had been given a high calling, he was one of Jesus' disciples, but His sin caused him to fall, and to become, in Jesus'

213

words, "the son of perdition." The word *perdition* comes from the Greek word *apoleia* (ap o' li-a), which *Strong's Greek Dictionary* says means, "*ruin* or *loss* (phys., spiritual or eternal):—damnable (-nation), destruction, die . . . perish . . . ."[5]

Ruin or loss. If Judas was the son of perdition, friend, and Jesus said he was, then he was ruined and lost. And for him, this involved physical, spiritual, *and* eternal ruin and loss. He received damnation and destruction. Certainly nothing in this definition refers to enjoying eternal reward. For certain, any who are "sons of perdition" cannot be "always saved," as these false teachers claim. They're going to be avenged; they're going to be condemned; they're going to get justice. We defined justice in chapter eight of this book, and justice does not mean rewarding the disobedient by giving them Heavenly bliss and rest in exchange for turning their backs on God! Go back and read that chapter again if you need to.

Perish, according to *Webster's*, means "**1** to be destroyed or ruined **2** to die, esp. violently."[8] And *damnation* is defined as "a damning or being damned."[9] *Damn*, then, is, "*Theol.* To condemn to hell."[10]

In Matthew 10:1 we read, "And when he had called unto him his twelve disciples, he gave them power against unclean spirits, to cast them out, and to heal all manner of sickness and all manner of disease." Verse 2 starts out, "Now the names of the twelve apostles are these . . . ." In verse 4, we read that one of these twelve was "Judas Iscariot, who also betrayed him." Then, verse 5 says, "These twelve Jesus sent forth . . . ."

What do we learn here? That Judas was especially selected and commissioned, and that *he*, as well as the other eleven, had received power to cast out devils and heal the sick. But we find that, after all the warnings and commandments about covetousness in the Scriptures (Exodus 18:21, Psalm 10:3, Proverbs 28:16, Exodus 20:17, Deuteronomy 5:21, etc.), Judas became so full of it that he became a thief (John 12:4-6). Eventually it led to his betrayal of the Lord, and to his being lost forever. He was making choices that he was *free to make,* and it absolutely *changed* his eternal condition. For sure, he never sowed to the flesh and then reaped eternal life. For sure, you and I won't either.

Someone may say, "Yes, but Jesus said the ones the Father gave Him *kept His Word.*" Exactly; but these teachers claim that those whom God gives to the Son don't necessarily *have* to keep His Word.

"Well, why did Jesus say 'they have kept thy word,' when one didn't?" Friend, I think the fact that eleven out of twelve kept it, qualifies Jesus' statement. In verse 12, He also said, "None of them is lost," only He didn't stop there. He added that none was lost *but* . . . . So the entire context is qualified by this "but." Just remember that the one who didn't keep God's Word was *lost*, not eternally saved.

Let's move on. Teachers of eternal security claim that once you are born (again), you cannot become unborn. It's a "done deal." You have God's imperishable seed in you and, because it is imperishable, it can never *die* within you. Okay, what does the Bible say on this point? "It says God's seed is in the born again," you may argue, "and that His seed can never die!" I agree, I agree. But that's not all it says on the subject, and the rest of what it says *qualifies* this point. Let's read it. "Being born again, not of corruptible seed, but of incorruptible, by the word of God, which liveth and abideth for ever" (1 Peter 1:23).

"See," you may cry, "It definitely says that!" Well, it seems to, and John even says that "whosoever is born of God . . . his seed remaineth in him" (1 John 3:9). But I left out several of John's words. Let's look at the entire verse: "Whosoever is born of God doth not commit sin; for his seed remaineth in him: and he cannot sin, because he is born of God."

Peter said "born again," and John said "born of God," and they both mentioned God's seed in relation to this birth, so both of these texts are referring to the exact same thing. Therefore, if Peter's words support the "eternal security" doctrine, so do John's. On the other hand, if John's words do not support that teaching, neither do Peter's. So let's study to see which way it is.

Again, John said that when God's "seed remaineth in him, he cannot sin, because he is born of God." So, while these teachers say God's seed in them prevents their sins from destroying their souls, God says His seed in them prevents their sinning in the first place! If they insist that God's seed remains in us forever, after conversion, then they will have to concede that *they can't do any sin* forever, after conversion. It is absolutely certain, friend, that we either cannot sin, once we're saved, or the saved *can lose that seed*. These people cannot have it both ways, no matter how much they want it both ways!

The conclusion, then, is that, certainly, the Word of God liveth and abideth for ever, but the soul that sinneth, *it* (not the seed) shall die. When sin comes back into the heart, God's seed lives on, yes, but not in that heart!

Let's look at this another way: His seed remaineth in whom? It remains in "Whosoever is born of God," yes, but that is also "whosoever doth not commit sin." John makes it conclusive that these "two" whosoevers are one and the same person. *Read it again.* Since His seed remains in those who do not sin (those born of God), it follows that it ceases to remain in those who do. Friend, this verse *does not say* the incorruptible seed cannot cease to be in us; what it says is that while that incorruptible seed is in us, we *do not sin.* So, when the "eternally secure" go back to sin, that seed just, simply, *cannot* be there! Certainly once born, one cannot become unborn—but one can die. In fact, everyone who has ever been *born* into this world *has died or will die,* unless he is living when Jesus returns. Spiritually speaking, the soul that sinneth, it *shall* die. Peter did not say that one who is born again lives and abides forever, but that the *Word of God* does, and although the Word, or seed, is incorruptible, we are not. Whenever we cease to be the "whosoever doth not commit sin," we cease to be the "whosoever is born of God."

Those who spread this doctrine argue further that if a man's son does wrong and breaks the father's heart, it does not change the fact that they are still father and son. They say the son is a son by birth and will always be a son, no matter what he does, and that it is the same spiritually.

Do I have a reply for this? Well, God does, friend. First of all, even though a wayward son, naturally speaking, is still a son, he is *not so forever.* Marrying and childbearing are of this time world, remember? They relate to our human flesh, not our spirits. We explained this in the chapter on where the devil came from, when we examined the 12th Chapter of Revelation. So wayward sons cease to be sons when they *die* and enter eternity. Jesus told Nicodemus, "that which is born of the flesh is flesh" (John 3:6), and this flesh will not exist in the next world. Paul told us this in 1 Corinthians 15:42 and 44a:

42 So also is the resurrection of the dead. It is sown in corruption; it is raised in incorruption;

44a It is sown a natural body; it is raised a spiritual body.

Just so, God's spiritual sons are no longer His sons when they *die spiritually* (the wages of sin is death). But, since they want to use our "natural" lives to try to prove their point, so will I. When a man and woman marry, they belong to one another. They actually vow to do so as long as life continues for both of them. Jesus said they become one flesh. Not *as* one flesh; they actually *become* one flesh, and God doesn't want them severing that: "What therefore God hath joined together, let not man put asunder" (Matthew 19:5-6). Yet sometimes married couples divorce. Oh, yes, even when one partner doesn't want to. So it is with our relationship with Christ. His Church is His Bride. He doesn't want that broken, but we can divorce Him, and for adultery on our part, He can divorce us. Friend, if the natural father/son relationship can be used in this debate, so can the natural husband/wife relationship, because the Scriptures use *both* metaphors—our being sons of God, and our being the bride of Christ—to portray our relationship with the Divine. But while their father/son example doesn't prove this doctrine true, because sons who die are no longer sons, the husband/wife example does prove we can cease to be Christ's Bride, because marriages can, and often do, end in divorce.

Look at what God said in Jeremiah the 3rd chapter about Israel's backsliding:

6 The LORD said also unto me in the days of Josiah the king, Hast thou seen that which backsliding Israel hath done? she is gone up upon every high mountain and under every green tree, and there hath played the harlot.

7 And I said after she had done all these things, Turn thou unto me. But she returned not. And her treacherous sister Judah saw it.

8 And I saw [Pay attention here], when for all the causes whereby backsliding Israel committed adultery I had put her away, and given her a bill of divorce; yet her treacherous sister Judah feared not, but went and played the harlot also.

12 Go and proclaim these words toward the north, and say, Return, thou backsliding Israel, saith the LORD; and I will not cause mine anger to fall upon you: for I am merciful, saith the LORD, and I will not keep my anger for ever.

14 Turn, O backsliding children, saith the LORD; for I am married unto you . . . .

Friend, did you read what God said? His people had forsaken Him, and He called their backsliding playing the harlot and committing adultery. No matter how God pleaded with Israel, through His prophets, she would not return, so He finally *gave her a bill of divorce.* Not because He desired it, but because she refused to forsake her whoredom. In verse 14, He told her that, although they were divorced, *for His part,* they were still married. That's how much He loved His people. But, on her part, their relationship was severed.

Yes, in spite of His undying love, He still divorced her and, in verse 12, He said that, *if she returned,* and *stopped playing the harlot,* He would not pour out His anger on her. Clearly, if she did not do this, His anger would be poured out, and His love would *not* get it its way. God went on to say, in verse 20, "Surely as a wife treacherously departeth from her husband, so have ye dealt treacherously with me, O house of Israel, saith the LORD." Then, in Chapter 4, verse 1, he wrote, "If thou wilt return, O Israel, saith the LORD, return unto me: and if thou wilt put away thine abominations out of my sight, then shalt thou not remove."

What does all of this tell us, friend? Let's take it point by point and see. In verse 6, God told Jeremiah that Israel had been playing the harlot by forsaking Him and worshiping other gods. In verse 8, He reached the place where, because of her obstinance, her defiance, He actually gave her a bill of divorce. This did not change the way He felt about her! He longed for her return. Yet, *she* was the one who departed, and *she* was the one who had to do the returning. You see, God *will not* force us to follow Him; if we turn from following Him, He will let us go.

In verse 12, God said that if Israel returned, His anger would not fall upon her. Remember, she had been given a bill of divorce, and to ever reunite with God, she had to *return* to Him. She was not still married to Him. And if she did not return from her spiritual whoredom, God's anger, not eternal life, would be poured out on her. Verse 20 says that Israel had *treacherously departed from* her husband. Then 4:1 says that to return required her to put away her abominations, and *only* if she put them away would she then *remain with Him.* This lets us know that, while committing those abominations, she *did not* remain with Him.

Dear one, remember what we learned about loving the world? James 4:4 calls those who do, adulterers and adulteresses. Backsliders, today, who turn back to "the beggerly elements of the world" (Galatians 4:3, 9), and think nothing of what they are doing to God, are just like old

Israel, and doing so will sever their relationship with God just as much as it did Israel's. And, do not cry, "Yes, but today we're under grace. Today we can play the harlot and still enjoy God's favor." My dear reader, I'd be ashamed to say, or even think, anything close to that! Surely claiming that God's grace only aids and abets our breaking His heart is nonsense and blasphemy! And, again, it is extremely selfish, which does not fit in with our *having to deny ourselves* to be Christ's disciples! Remember, Paul said the things that happened to Israel of old were to serve as *examples* to us today. Of what good is an example, then, if it does not mean that we need to give heed to it (1 Corinthians 10:6-12)? And Paul warned the Corinthians, in that 12th verse, "Wherefore let him that thinketh he standeth take heed lest he fall." By referring to Old Israel, the Apostle very clearly brought what happened to them up to our time, and he said *"Wherefore,"* or *because of what happened to them*—because we can fall just as they did—we need to earnestly labor *not* to fall as they did. The writer of Hebrews warns of the same possibility of *our* falling, as did Israel of old, in Hebrews 4:11.

So, what have we learned? First, the idea that backsliding Christians can never cease to be sons, is not biblically supported. Sons can die, no matter how much we love them, and therefore they are not sons forever. And spiritual sons *do* cease to be sons when they sin and, thereby, die. Second, the metaphor of the husband/wife relationship is just as valid for our study as is that of the father/son relationship. Husbands and wives can, and do, end their marriages. *God divorced His people once before, because of their unfaithfulness*, and He will do it again today if we are also unfaithful. Third, even though the Dispensations changed with Christ's advent, God's *moral principles* did not.

All right, what's another argument used to support this once saved, always saved, doctrine? Well, no matter what people do after they've once been converted, it is taught that God will receive these "believing sons" into Glory because their sins—past, present, and future—were covered, *in advance*, when Jesus died on the cross.

Is this biblical? No, dear reader, it is not. Look again at Romans 3:25: "Whom God hath set forth [Christ, verse 24] to be a propitiation through faith in his blood, to declare his righteousness for the remission of sins that are past, through the forbearance of God." Let me repeat that Jesus blood only covers *sins that are past*. Here we read about faith in Christ's blood, and how it secures for us remission of sins. But, though Paul mentions past sins, there is no mention whatsoever of present or future sins being included in this remission.

Solomon wrote in Proverbs 28:13 that "whoso confesseth and forsaketh [his sins] shall have mercy." There's no way we can confess the sins of the future, friend, and we certainly can't forsake them or we wouldn't go on and commit them. And this verse clearly lets us know that sins which are not *forsaken*, as well as those which are not confessed, *are not offered mercy*. When we sin, and come to God confessing our sins, rather than trying to hide them, we'll only find pardon if we forsake them as well. This refutes the idea that we sin day by day and ask for forgiveness day by day, and it also rebuts the idea that once we're born again and go back to sin, our present and future sins are still covered by the Blood. You can confess sins continually, but you cannot forsake them continually. The very fact that you go on sinning shows that you have not forsaken sin. Just so, a once-saved person who goes back to a life of sin has abandoned his forsaking of it. Anytime one goes back to something he had forsaken, the forsaking ceases. When sin ceases to be forsaken, therefore, there is *no mercy* for the new sins. "Future sins" are not covered by Jesus' blood, and present sins are only covered when we, at that point, forsake sin anew.

What else do these once-saved-always-saved folks teach? They claim that, since nothing can separate Christians from the love of God—*nothing*—then we ourselves cannot even do so. Do they use Scripture to support this? Oh, yes. Or I might say they *mis*use Scripture to support it. Here's the text:

Romans 8:35 Who shall separate us from the love of Christ? shall tribulation, or distress, or persecution, or famine, or nakedness, or peril, or sword?

36 As it is written, For thy sake we are killed all the day long; we are accounted as sheep for the slaughter.

37 Nay, in all these things we are more than conquerors through him that loved us.

38 For I am persuaded, that neither death, nor life, nor angels, nor principalities, nor powers, nor things present, nor things to come,

39 Nor height, nor depth, nor any other creature, shall be able to separate us from the love of God, which is in Christ Jesus our Lord.

The phrase, "nor any other creature," these teachers say, must surely include ourselves, and "therefore, since we cannot be separated from the love of God, we will most assuredly go to heaven and not to hell, which, we are often told, means 'eternal separation from God.'"

All right. If Christians can't possibly be separated from the love of God, this argument may seem valid—but only when you don't look deeper into these, and related, verses.

"Oh, come on," you may say, "you're always talking about 'looking deeper.' Don't the Scriptures just mean what they say?" Surely they mean what they say, but you have to pay attention to *all* that they say. For example, this text doesn't just say that nothing can separate us from the love of God. It says something more. What it actually says is that nothing can separate us from the love of God *which is in Christ Jesus our Lord*. Did you get that? The love of God is in Christ Jesus. Nothing can separate us from God's love as long as *we* are in Christ Jesus, but sin will separate us from Christ Jesus. Paul was in Christ, and so were those he was writing to, when he said "nothing shall separate *us* from the love of God that's in Christ." Let me say it this way—nothing can separate *those who are in Christ Jesus* from the Love of God, but those who forsake Christ have no such promise!

Look at Isaiah 59:1-2:

1 Behold, the LORD'S hand is not shortened, that it cannot save; neither his ear heavy, that it cannot hear:

2 But your iniquities have separated between you and your God, and your sins have hid his face from you, that he will not hear.

Notice that the prophet did not say God *cannot* hear those with iniquity, but that He *will not*. Sin separates from God; not only in eternity, as these teachers acknowledge, but in this life as well. He has not changed His mind about sin, just because we're now under the New Covenant and not the Old. He changed what could be done about sin, in the transition from Old to New, but not sin's consequences or the way He feels about it. First John 1:6 confirms that we cannot be in Christ and in sin at the same time: "If we say that we have fellowship with him, and walk in darkness, we lie, and do not the truth." And look at what John added in 2:3-5:

3 And hereby we do know that we know him, if we keep his commandments.

4 He that saith, I know him, and keepeth not his commandments, is a liar, and the truth is not in him.

5 But whoso keepeth his word, in him verily is the love of God perfected: hereby know we that we are in him.

Hereby, or by this, we know that we are *in Him*. We can only know we are in Him when we keep His Word. *He that says he is in Christ and does not keep His commandments is a liar.* Friend, no matter how saved someone may have been at one time, he can only know he is in Christ when he presently keeps His Word. Those who cease to keep His Word are not *in Him*, and only those *in Him* are in, and inseparable from, the love of God. These verses just quoted tell us that *the love of God* is perfected in those who obey God's Word, and only those can know they are in Him, because they do obey. As you can see, I'm not making up the connection between being in Christ and being in His love.

Those who teach eternal security may argue that the love of God is *in* these wandering "Christians," but it is only *perfected* in those who continue to keep the Word. That is a misinterpretation, my friend. Jesus, Himself, clinched this point in John 15:9-10:

9 As the Father hath loved me, so have I loved you: continue ye in my love.

10 If ye keep my commandments, ye shall abide in my love; even as I have kept my Father's commandments, and abide in his love.

Here, Christ plainly said, *"Continue* (or *abide*) in my love." It's not automatic, but *up to us*! And He added, "If you keep my commandments, you shall." Conversely, then, if you do not keep His commandments, or if you cease keeping them, *you shall not* continue in His love. Although nothing else can separate us from Christ, and therefore from God's love, most assuredly our failing to keep His commandments can, and it does. It separates us from Christ, and God's love is in Christ. Abiding, or not abiding, in His love is an action on our own part; it is the result of our own choice. The claim that "nor any other creature" includes ourselves is false, friend. If we could not alter our being in God's love, if nothing we did or failed to do could affect that, why did Jesus prompt us to "continue in His love"? Jesus never spoke idle words. In fact, He told us that any idle words *we* speak will meet us at the Judgment (Matthew 12:36). Let's go over Jesus' words again: *If ye keep my commandments, ye shall abide in my love.* He could just as easily have said, "Ye shall abide in my love *if* ye keep my commandments." Or, He could have said, "If ye do not keep my commandments, ye shall *not* abide in my love."

These plain words of our Savior simply cannot, and do not, support this eternal security doctrine. Clearly, while nothing can separate us from God's love, which is in Christ Jesus, we *choose* to no longer abide in *that love* when we *choose* to no longer abide in Christ by keeping His commandments. This once saved, always saved doctrine *is not* what Romans 8:35-39 is teaching.

Are you still not convinced? Okay. Let's read 1 John 5:18. It says, "We know that whosoever is born of God sinneth not; but he that is begotten of God *keepeth himself,* and that wicked one toucheth him not." Then read Jude 21: *"Keep yourselves in the love of God,* looking for the mercy of our Lord Jesus Christ unto eternal life." [Emphasis added.] Here we learn that we can keep ourselves in the love of God, but we can also *fail* to keep ourselves in His love. This proves that "nor any other creature" does *not* include ourselves! It also proves that, once we are saved, we do not lose our ability to determine our own destinies! Whether or not we are, or remain, in the love of God is entirely up to each individual. Jude had been referring in his epistle, as already shown, to many who had ceased to follow Christ. They had surely failed to keep themselves in God's love, and Jude was exhorting us to take care to keep ourselves in it. Having once been in the love of God, friend, is in no way a guarantee that we will forever be there. *We can fail to keep ourselves in His love!*

John said that those who are born of God keep themselves. And look at what this means: when they keep themselves, *that wicked one toucheth them not.* Obviously, then, when the wicked one works, again, in our members, *we have failed to keep ourselves in the love of God!* So, nothing external can separate us from the love of God—but we can fail to keep ourselves in it.

"How," you may wonder, "do we keep ourselves?" This just means that, as Christians, we either *choose* to continue to serve God, or we *choose* not to serve Him. Our part in our salvation—whether to receive it or to retain it—is exercising our choice. Remember, God said, "I've set before you life and death; choose life." He cares very much what we choose, but He still leaves it up to us. When we choose, each day, to continue to obey Him, we stay in His love; when we choose, at some point, to cease obeying, we *separate ourselves* from *Him* and, consequently, from His love. Paul was assuring those who *obey Christ* that *life*, in all its ups and downs, cannot separate us from our loving

Lord. He, in no way, said we couldn't *choose* to abandon God's love. It is just that simple!

Finally, this argument that even we cannot separate ourselves from the love of God, is clearly destroyed right there in that same 8th Chapter of Romans. I repeat, *right in the same chapter*, Paul clearly teaches the opposite! Let's read it. Verse 13 says, "For if *ye* [the brethren, verse 12] live after the flesh, *ye* shall die: but if *ye* through the Spirit do mortify the deeds of the body, *ye* shall live." (Emphasis added.)

What did you say, Paul? "I said that if the saved continue to crucify their flesh, and walk in the Spirit, they shall continue to live spiritually. However, if they turn again to living after the flesh, they—the saved—shall die again spiritually. They shall not continue to live!" Friend, get this, and get it good: *there is no eternal security* except with continual obedience!

These false prophets also claim that eternal security is promised in Romans 10:9, 10, and 13, so let's examine these verses:

Romans 10:9 That if thou shalt confess with thy mouth the Lord Jesus, and shalt believe in thine heart that God hath raised him from the dead, thou shalt be saved.

10 For with the heart man believeth unto righteousness; and with the mouth confession is made unto salvation.

13 For whosoever shall call upon the name of the Lord shall be saved.

Dear reader, did you see anything in these verses that teach *eternal* salvation? Certainly they show how to be saved, but *being* saved and *staying* saved are two different things. Let's look at their argument: "According to these Scriptures, if a person once truly believes in his heart that God raised Jesus from the dead, and if they actually confess with their mouth that Jesus is Lord, they are irrevocably born again and can never be lost, since the promise clearly states concerning such people, 'you will be saved.' Again, Romans 10:13 tells us that whoever calls upon the name of the Lord will be saved. This is a promise or guarantee of salvation to all who truly call upon the name of the Lord. No conditions can be added to this promise."

Dear friend, did you read *that* in these verses? Surely they tell us that confessing Christ as Lord and believing with the heart will save us, but nowhere is it even implied that this will be irrevocable. God *does* promise to save such, but *maintaining* our experience is up to us. Jesus said, plainly, in Matthew 24:12-13:

12 And because iniquity shall abound, the love of many shall wax cold [people can lose their love for God].

13 But he that shall endure unto the end [emphasis added], *the same shall be saved.*

We could use these false teachers' reasoning with this text. They claim that "whosoever shall call on the name of the Lord," and then "believes" and "confesses," will be saved, because God gives a promise, or a guarantee, that he will. I won't argue with that, although I most certainly disagree that this "saved" is irrevocable. But we could use this same line of reasoning and claim that only those who will endure until the end can ever be saved. Those who would eventually stop obeying God could not even get saved to begin with. Look at it again:

"If thou shalt confess, and believe, and call on the name of the Lord, thou shalt be saved."

"He that shall endure unto the end shall be saved."

Clearly, friend, anyone who confesses, believes, and calls on the Lord *will* be saved when he does so; but *only those who endure unto the end* will be saved *in the end.* In Jesus' own words, we see that those who *do not* endure unto the end are *not* included in this "saved in the end" condition. It makes no difference how saved they were at one time; clearly they must endure unto the end to be saved in the end. And, consider this: their argument included these words, "they are irrevocably born again and can never be lost, since the promise clearly states concerning such people, 'you will be saved.'" Friend, *this* is a really flimsy foundation for a doctrine! "You will be saved" has to mean you will be that way forever? Remember, Paul was telling the Romans *what would happen* when they met God's conditions; in *no way* did he say, or infer, that their salvation would continue if they *stopped* meeting God's conditions. Neither Jesus nor Paul taught any such thing. While Paul said "thou shalt be saved," he did not say "forever," and Jesus plainly taught that no one will be saved in the end except those who endure to the end. I hope that truth is now indelibly imprinted upon your hearts.

By the way, when you tell your friend, "I will be late," does that mean you're going to be late forever? If a salesman says, "I will give you a 15 percent discount," when you buy an item from him, does that mean you will get a 15 percent discount as long as you buy from him? Or, if someone says, "You'll never guess . . ." does that mean you can never try to guess anything again, as long as you live? If your friend says, "You will be surprised," are you going to be surprised forever? Of course not; these expressions only apply to a particular situation at a particular time. Likewise, those who repent and believe will be saved at the time they repent and believe, and for as long as they continue in obedience, but he that turns back will not be saved in the end! That isn't even implied in the Scriptures, let alone stated. It never ceases to amaze me how people can build doctrines out of what the Bible does not say!

"No conditions can be added to this promise," they say. Well, I am not adding conditions to God's promise; I am merely pointing out what His promise actually says. Besides, certainly *we* can't put conditions on God's promises, since He has told us not to add to or take away from His Word, but what authority do they have to challenges God's sovereignty and say that *He* can't put conditions on His promises? He certainly can, and He certainly *does.*

I will leave it to you to study about God's promises and see whether or not they are conditional, but let me give you just one or two examples:

Deuteronomy 28:1 And it shall come to pass, if thou shalt hearken diligently unto the voice of the LORD thy God . . . that the LORD thy God will set thee on high above all nations of the earth:

2 And all these blessings shall come on thee, and overtake thee, if thou shalt hearken unto the voice of the LORD thy God.

3 Blessed shalt thou be in the city, and blessed shalt thou be in the field.

4 Blessed shall be the fruit of thy body, and the fruit of thy ground . . . . (Read on through verse 13.)

These wonderful blessings were only theirs *if* they hearkened to the voice of the Lord. But verses 15-46 tell us a different story; if they disobeyed, they would receive only curses. Following their history shows that when they ceased to hearken to God's voice, the blessings did, indeed cease, and the curses came.

Old Israel's history shows *cycles* of obedience and disobedience. While they were obedient, God blessed them abundantly, but when they turned to other gods and forsook the Lord's commandments, He brought many curses upon them. Finally, with the rejection of God's Son and the "last chance" offered through the Apostles' ministry, their "house was left desolate." God moved out (Matthew 23:37-38). All the promised blessings, being based on their obedience, were forfeited through their disobedience. And, remember, they are our *ensamples*!

Are New Testament promises conditional as well? Yes, friend. God's promise that the devil will flee from us (James 4:7) is only valid when we *resist* him. (But this means we *can* resist him, and when we do, he *has* to flee!) His promise that "we shall reap bountifully" (2 Corinthians 9:6) won't work if we do not sow bountifully. When Peter preached on the Day of Pentecost, and the people were "pricked in their heart," they asked, "what shall we do?" Then Peter told them, "The promise is unto you, and to your children, and to all that are afar off, even as many as the Lord our God shall call" (Acts 2:37-39). Yes, the promise was offered to all people, but to *obtain* the promise, they had to meet the conditions: repent and be baptized.

Lastly, God gave us a conditional promise in Romans 8:28, when Paul said, "And we know that all things work together for good to them that love God, to them who are the called according to his purpose." Certainly those who do not love God, or serve His purpose, cannot claim this promise.

Let's look at one more argument in favor of being once saved, always saved. Those who promote that doctrine teach that, "John wrote his letter that we may know that we have eternal life" (1 John 5:13). God wants us to *know* we have eternal life, they argue, but if it's conditional and we can lose it, we cannot know for sure that we have it. "If our eternal life was depending on our faithfulness, we could never *know* if we have been faithful enough, or good enough," they say.

What's wrong with their position on this? Well, first of all, eternal life is in the Son and he that hath the Son hath life. Can't we know that we have Christ in our lives? The writer of "Blessed Assurance" believed we can, and since truly having Christ gives us victory over sin, we *can* know, for we know if we have victory in our daily lives or not. Remember, sin requires both knowledge and will. If we choose to do wrong, we know it, and if we choose *not* to do wrong, we know it.

First John 2:3 tells us we can *know* we're saved, and *how* we can know; again, it's very simple:

3 Hereby we do know that we know him, if we keep his commandments.

Now look at verses 4-5:

4 He that saith, I know him, and keepeth not his commandments, is a liar, and the truth is not in him.

5 But whoso keepeth his word, in him verily is the love of God perfected: hereby know *we that we are in him.* (Emphasis added.)

Of course, those who stop keeping His commandments can't know that they know Him, because they don't. But we *can* know. These false prophets claim John's letter as proof that once saved, a person is saved forever, but John taught the opposite! Reread verse 4. These words are present tense: if you say you know Christ (now) but you do not keep His commandments (now) you are a liar, no matter how saved you may have been in the past. Assurance comes from obedience. Likewise, peace comes from knowledge, not from "feelings"—knowledge that we have obeyed God. That's the only way to have assurance and peace! Dear reader, when we do not obey, we have no assurance. This once saved, always saved, doctrine does not give people assurance; it only gives them a delusion. When they come up before God, their false "security"—their refuge of lies—will fail, and they will sink in eternal woe, no matter how much they "knew" they were eternally saved! "Eternal security" is a damnable heresy!

Please, dear one, let me say it once more: *This once saved, always saved, doctrine does not give people assurance; it only gives them a delusion.*

This same John attested that *he* knew *he* had eternal life:

1 John 3:2 Beloved, now are we the sons of God, and it doth not yet appear what we shall be: but we know [know!] *that, when he shall appear, we shall be like him; for we shall see him as he is.*

3 And every man that hath this hope in him purifieth himself, even as he is pure.

Friend, if *every man* that has this hope keeps himself pure, surely those who turn back to sin *do not have this hope.*

1 John 2:5 But whoso keepeth his word, in him verily is the love of God perfected: hereby know [know!] *we that we are in him.*

How can we *know* we have eternal life? It's simple, dear one. We can know because we obey Him.

Paul certainly knew he was saved and he was sure of Heaven:

2 Timothy 4:6 For I am now ready to be offered, and the time of my departure is at hand.

7 I have fought a good fight, I have finished my course, I have kept the faith:

8 Henceforth there is laid up for me a crown of righteousness, which the Lord, the righteous judge, shall give me at that day: and not to me only, but unto all them also that love his appearing.

2 Corinthians 5:1 For we know that if our earthly house of this tabernacle were dissolved, we have a building of God, an house not made with hands, eternal in the heavens.

4 For we that are in this tabernacle do groan, being burdened: not for that we would be unclothed, but clothed upon, that mortality might be swallowed up of life.

5 Now he that hath wrought us for the selfsame thing is God, who also hath given unto us the earnest [or pledge] *of the Spirit.*

8 We are confident, I say, and willing rather to be absent from the body, and to be present with the Lord.

2 Timothy 1:12b . . . for I know whom I have believed, and am persuaded that he is able to keep that which I have committed unto him against that day.

Stephen knew without a doubt that he was going to be with Jesus: "And they stoned Stephen, calling upon God, and saying, Lord Jesus, receive my spirit" (Acts 7:59).

These saints' words are words of assurance and confidence. We can know we are saved. I know I am, and you can know, as well, friend. Listen to the confidence Paul felt when he wrote to Titus:

Titus 3:5 Not by works of righteousness which we have done, but according to his mercy he saved us, by the washing of regeneration, and renewing of the Holy Ghost;

6 Which he shed on us abundantly through Jesus Christ our Saviour;

7 That being justified by his grace, we should be made heirs according to the hope of eternal life.

Also, Paul's words, there in 2 Corinthians, Chapter 5, apply to all believers, giving us just as much assurance of hope as Paul had.

Dear reader, close scrutiny of these so-called "proof texts" positively reveals that they do not teach what these eternal security proponents claim they teach. These leaders merely *say* the Scriptures teach "once saved, never lost," when they do not. It is only by lifting verses out of their contexts that these teachers can "prove" their once saved, always saved, doctrine! *Nowhere* does the Bible teach that, but in my next chapter I will give you Scriptures that *do* plainly teach the opposite: those who turn back to sin are lost unless they repent anew and then finish their lives with victory over sin.

Remember, the Gospel is simple. We do not have to strain and twist Scriptures to support the truth. Peter said those who "wrest the Scriptures" do so to their own destruction (2 Peter 3:15-16). Friend, when any Scripture is properly interpreted, it will never cross up any other Scripture. The Bible is in complete harmony with itself—*all* of itself. It is the perfect work of a perfect God. There are no contradictions in God's Word. We have just covered a number of conflicting ideas, all claiming to have a Scriptural basis; but all of these supposed contradictions vanish *when properly interpreted in the light of their contexts.* You saw how a proper explanation did away with the so-called "contradictions" between Romans 6, 7, and 8.

This false doctrine appeals to those who want to live after the flesh, those who love sin, but do not want to suffer its consequences. It appeals to those who don't want to expend the diligence, the fervor, the earnestness, that it takes to maintain an up-to-date experience with Christ. On the other hand, the truth appeals to honest hearts who truly want to live for God. They are thrilled to learn the truth. I trust that you are one of these, and I pray that I have helped you in your effort through this book. If I can help one soul find true saving faith, and the victory it brings, my labor will be well repaid.

Let me sum up this examination of eternal security's "supporting arguments and Scriptures" by quoting John again. He said, "If that which ye [those early Christians] have heard from the beginning shall remain in you, ye also shall continue in the Son, and in the Father" (1 John 2:24). That's quite explicit, is it not? It's easy to see that if what was preached in the beginning of this New Testament Dispensation—what the Bible actually teaches—does not *remain in us*, we do not *continue in Him.* That word *if* is a conditional word. Whatever follows the *if* happens only when the condition, or conditions, are met. Again, when John said "*if* what you've heard remains in you," there was necessarily an "*if not.*" This very "equation" excludes forsaking the obedience of the Word and still continuing in Christ. And it's only *in Him* that we have eternal life. So it is very clear that it is possible for a person, although once genuinely saved, to backslide and be lost.

Do not say, "Well, what we've heard remains in us; we're just not obeying it anymore." No, no, no. Remember, Christ was the Word made flesh. The Word cannot remain in us unless Jesus Christ remains in us, and we will prove beyond any shadow of a doubt, in the next chapter, that *Jesus does not remain in a heart that returns to sinful living.*

CHAPTER ELEVEN

"Well, I Was Saved, So I'm All Right"— The Bible Does Not Teach This!

Well, now that we have found that the texts used to support the once-saved-always-saved doctrine do not actually support it at all, and that those arguments are, in fact, out of harmony with the Scriptures, I am going to give you other Bible texts that positively and absolutely prove this doctrine is false. The verses I have already used to refute "eternal security" are, unlike the opposing view, in total harmony with the verses I am now going to call your attention to.

We'll start with Romans 11:17-22:

17 And if some of the branches be broken off, and thou, being a wild olive tree, wert graffed in among them, and with them partakest of the root and fatness of the olive tree;

18 Boast not against the branches. But if thou boast, thou bearest not the root, but the root thee.

19 Thou wilt say then, The branches were broken off, that I might be graffed in.

20 Well; because of unbelief they were broken off, and thou standest by faith. Be not highminded, but fear:

21 For if God spared not the natural branches, take heed lest he also spare not thee.

22 Behold therefore the goodness and severity of God: on them which fell, severity; but toward thee, goodness, if thou continue in his goodness: otherwise thou also shalt be cut off.

Here Paul shows how being in "the olive tree" no longer depended on one's being born a Jew (read verses 1-15). Because of the Jewish nation's unbelief and rejection of God's Son, they, *as a people*, were cut off and the believing Gentiles were "graffed in." But look at Paul's warning to those grafted-in ones: *continue in His goodness or, likewise, you will be cut off.* Notice that God's goodness does not get in the way of His severity toward those that fall!

We learn at least the following from these verses:

1) we are able, through God's grace and mercy, and by faith, to be grafted into Christ;
2) it is possible to be cut off after being grafted into Christ;
3) God is balanced and fair, so while His goodness grafts in, His severity cuts off when one falls;
4) we should never be highminded, but have godly fear, whereas this eternal security doctrine robs of that fear, for "I'm safe, no matter what I do," and actually makes people gloat, or become highminded, in their "safety."

The Bible is replete with warnings and exhortations regarding steadfastness and fidelity, and the earnestness and diligence it takes to maintain these. Such texts as we are sharing with you here clearly confirm to us what Paul, under the inspiration of the Holy Ghost, taught: that those who do not earnestly exercise themselves to steadfastness and obedience can and will fall from grace. And those who fall will be cut off!

Let us look at some more of Paul's words, in 1 Corinthians 9:27. It reads, "But I keep under my body, and bring it into subjection: lest that by any means, when I have preached to others, I myself should be a castaway." *Strong's Greek Dictionary* says that this term *castaway* is translated from ***adokimos*** (ad-ok'-ee-mos) and means, "*unapproved, i.e. rejected*; by impl. *worthless* (lit. or mor.) . . . reprobate."[1] *Webster's* tells us that *reprobate* comes from "Late Latin" and means, "unprincipled or depraved."[2] Being *rejected* cannot possibly mean the same thing as being *accepted*, and being *unprincipled* and *depraved* cannot mean the same as being *saved!* Friend, surely when you step before God's Judgment Throne, you will want to be accepted, not rejected, and Paul made it clear that, if we do not keep our bodies under, *we can be rejected.*

The very fact that Paul wrote these words proves he fully believed he could end up being rejected and cast away if he did not daily practice "bringing under his body"—that self-denial that Jesus said was required for discipleship. And this was even after he had been saved and preached the Gospel. Just think of those words *rejected* and *cast away*. They just cannot describe ones who abide under God's approval and redemption. Too, the fact that he wrote this to the Corinthians proves that he knew *they* could fall as well.

In 2 Peter 2:12-13a and 15a, we find this:

12 But these, as natural brute beasts, made to be taken and destroyed, speak evil of the things that they understand not; and shall utterly perish in their own corruption;

13a And shall receive the reward of unrighteousness . . . .

15a Which have forsaken the right way, and are gone astray . . . .

I'm not pulling a fast one by leaving out some of this text; I'm just quoting the main parts that are needed to prove my point. You can read this whole portion of Scripture and see that it's all referring to the same people. It certainly shows that it is possible to forsake the right way, and doing so is an act of one's choice. Just as certainly, those who did forsake the right way and go astray in this text *did not* end up in Heaven. Peter said they did not still reap the reward of righteousness; they reaped that of unrighteousness. He said these were brute beasts that would be taken and destroyed; they would utterly perish! Would you say Peter believed in "eternal security"? Did he believe that, no matter what we might do or how we might fail God, we can never be lost? For certain, he believed, and preached, the very opposite. For the "knock-out punch," look at verses 20 and 21:

20 For if after they have escaped the pollutions of the world through the knowledge of the Lord and Saviour Jesus Christ, they are again entangled therein, and overcome, the latter end is worse with them than the beginning.

21 For it had been better for them not to have known the way of righteousness, than, after they have known it, to turn from the holy commandment delivered unto them.

These verses hardly need any commentary or explanation. I'm just going to say that this text is specifically speaking of those who had forsaken the right way, those who had gone astray (verse 15), those who had lured others that had escaped error (preachers or teachers; verse 18), those who had been "overcome" and "brought in bondage" again (verse 19), those who had "escaped the pollutions of the world" through Christ but were "again entangled therein" (verse 20), and those who had "known the way of righteousness" but had turned "from the holy commandment" (verse 21).

Friend, Peter makes it altogether clear that it would have been better for these not to have known, not to have escaped, than for them to *turn from* Christ and again become entangled. But they *had* known. They *had* escaped. They *had* been saved. No one can deny this! Then they *forsook* the right way (verse 15). Did they still go to Heaven? *NO! A million times NO!* That which faced them when they died was not reward; it was not eternal bliss; what faced them was worse than if they had died without ever having been saved in the first place. It was *punishment.* "It had been better for them not to have known the way of righteousness, than, after they have known it, to turn from the holy commandment"! I must say again, what they found at death was so terrible that they would have been better off to have just remained in sin all along and never known the Way. There is no way anyone can read these words of Peter, with an honest and open heart, and still believe in eternal security.

By God's sweet grace, I have been able to "explain away" the Scriptures used by those who promote this false doctrine, but there is no way they can "explain away" Peter's unmistakable words. Through God's mercy, I have shown that when the Word of God is rightly divided, these teachers' supposedly Scriptural "strongholds" crumble to dust. However, they certainly cannot crumble these words of the Apostle Peter. Oh, they may "explain them away" by resorting to more wresting of Scripture, but they cannot do it by the pure Word of God.

Remember when we studied the origin of the devil? In that chapter, we saw how both Peter and Jude spoke of ministers who had failed to be steadfast in proclaiming the Word of God (Peter's version is from this same 2nd Chapter). In very graphic terms, they described the judgment awaiting these "fallen angels": they would be "reserved in everlasting chains under darkness" unto judgment (Jude 6). And Jude 11 says, "Woe unto them!" It is evident that these preachers who had failed God would not be saved in the end, just because they once had been.

Up for our consideration next is that Jesus taught that we could cease to abide in Him. Keeping in mind that He is talking to, and about, His disciples (see the context), look at His stirring words in John 15:1-9:

1 I am the true vine, and my Father is the husbandman.

235

2 Every branch in me that beareth not fruit he taketh away: and every branch that beareth fruit, he purgeth it, that it may bring forth more fruit.

[Wait. Hold everything. These teachers say that, because God gives the saved to Jesus and it's not His will that Christ should lose any of them, no saved person can ever be lost. But here we learn differently. Christ's own words teach us that these branches were "*in me*"—they were saved—yet if they did not bear fruit, it would be the Father, *Himself*, that would *take them away!*]

3 Now ye are clean through the word which I have spoken unto you.

4 Abide in me, and I in you. As the branch cannot bear fruit of itself, except it abide in the vine; no more can ye, except ye abide in me.

[These were clean, but they were told to abide in Jesus. They were told that they could not bear fruit if they didn't abide. Hey, friend, they could *cease* to abide in Him! Our *Lord* said this! If this false doctrine were true, Christ would have said something like, "You are clean, and you'll always abide in me, but please bear fruit." But this is not what He said.]

5 I am the vine, ye are the branches. He that abideth in me, and I in him, the same bringeth forth much fruit: for without me ye can do nothing.

[Here He said we *will* bear fruit, *if we abide in Him*. This term, *abideth*, from the old-time English, is the same as *abides* in modern English, and it indicates that the abiding continues. We are only fruitful if we continue to abide. Once again, dear one, this *if* indicates an *if not*. The next verse tells us what happens if we do not abide in Him and bear fruit.]

6 If a man abide not in me, he is cast forth as a branch, and is withered; and men gather them, and cast them into the fire, and they are burned.

[Here our Lord says plainly that any branches who are in Him but "abide *not*," or do not *stay* in Him, and thereby become unfruitful, are cast forth, withered, gathered, and burned.]

7 If ye abide in me, and my words abide in you, ye shall ask what ye will, and it shall be done unto you.

[Why would Jesus say, "*If* ye abide," if doing otherwise were impossible?]

8 Herein is my Father glorified, that ye bear much fruit; so shall ye be my disciples.

[Remember, He is talking, here, about branches in Him, verse 5. "So shall ye be my disciples" tells us that continuing to be disciples

236

is not automatic, or guaranteed, or irrevokable. It depends on our continually abiding in Him and bearing fruit, *much* fruit.]

9 As the Father hath loved me, so have I loved you: continue ye in my love.

Dear one, it is *up to us* whether or not we continue in His love. Surely no one can reasonably assert that "I am the vine, ye are the branches" does not refer to saved people's relationship with Christ. And this text very definitely lets us know that our relationship with Him is entirely conditional, and it is conditioned upon *our behavior*. Jesus did not say branches that cease to bear fruit will merely cease to be blessed; He said they will *no longer be in Him*.

Someone may say, "Oh, He didn't mean we'd no longer be in *Him*. He just meant that if we stopped bearing fruit, we'd no longer be in His perfect will." No. I'll have to burst your bubble; He said branches that don't bear fruit get *taken away*, they are *cast forth*, they are *gathered and cast into the fire*. There is no way the branches can be taken away and cast forth, and then gathered and burned, and still be in the Vine! Since He is the Vine, it is certain that we can cease to be in Him.

Verse 6 uses the verb phrase *cast forth*. This sounds very much like what Paul said about being *cast away*. Friend, be honest with your own soul. How can one be cast forth, or cast away, and still be in the Vine? And what do those who claim that Christians can never get outside of Christ's love do with verse 9? Surely our Lord would never have urged us to continue in His love if we could not fall out of it no matter what we did. Jesus did not say, "As the Father hath loved me, so have I loved you: and ye shall forever continue in my love." The words "Continue ye in my love" constitute an imperative sentence, which is, "A sentence that expresses a command or a request. (The subject *you* is understood if it is not expressed.)"[3] Since Jesus said, in reality, "*You* continue in my love," He put the ball in our court, as the saying goes.

John's words absolutely prove that saved people are not "eternally secure"; if they go back to sin, they are lost:

1 John 1:5 This then is the message which we have heard of him, and declare unto you, that God is light, and in him is no darkness at all.

6 If we say that we have fellowship with him, and walk in darkness, we lie, and do not the truth.

1 John 3:5 And ye know that he was manifested to take away our sins; and in him is no sin.

6 Whosoever abideth in him sinneth not: whosoever sinneth hath not seen him, neither known him,
7a Little children, let no man deceive you . . . .
Just what do these verses teaches us? Just this:

1) John said what he was declaring to the Church was what he had heard from Jesus. These truths came straight from the Incarnate Word, Himself. This was not John's opinion. It was Jesus Who first declared these truths.
2) God is light and *in Him is no darkness at all.*
3) If we say we have fellowship with Him, and walk in darkness, *we lie.*
4) In Him is no sin.
5) Since whosoever abides in Christ (the Vine) *does not sin*, then whosoever sins, does not abide in Christ (the Vine); if he ever did abide in Jesus, he ceases to abide in Him when he turns again to sinning.
6) Such a one does not know Christ. If he ever did, he knows Him no longer.
7) Believing otherwise is to be deceived.
8) Jesus places the burden of making sure we are not deceived in our own hands. Let me remind you that the way to do this is to stay humble and honest, stay willing to obey whatever He shows you, and to *earnestly seek God's face* that the Holy Spirit may lead you into truth.

Quite simply, friend, anyone who is presently sinning cannot and will not *be in, or abide in,* Christ Jesus. *If we say we have fellowship with Him, and walk in darkness, we lie!* Friend, in this verse, as well as the others just quoted, John totally crushes the eternal security doctrine. Do you remember what we learned about *darkness* being the same as sin? Those who say they still have fellowship with Christ although they go back to walking in darkness, John said, are liars. That means such a doctrine is a lie. This once-saved-always-saved doctrine *is a lie!* Please, dear one, take John's counsel and "let no man deceive *you*"!
Ephesians 5:5-8 and 10-11 instruct us:

5 For this ye know, that no whoremonger, nor unclean person, nor covetous man, who is an idolater, hath any inheritance in the kingdom of Christ and of God.

6 Let no man deceive you with vain words: for because of these things [found in verses 3-5] *cometh the wrath of God upon the children of disobedience.*

7 Be not ye therefore partakers with them.

8 For ye were sometimes darkness, but now are ye light in the Lord: walk as children of light . . .

10 Proving what is acceptable unto the Lord.

11 And have no fellowship with the unfruitful works of darkness, but rather reprove them.

Here, again, we see the incompatibility of the kingdom of darkness and that of light. There is *no fellowship* between the two. Paul asked, "What communion hath light with darkness" (2 Corinthians 6:14)? Verse 6, above, mentions the children of disobedience. This false doctrine (as well as the sin-you-must-from-day-to-day teaching) claims that God can have consistently disobedient children, but that is a lie! But, hey, even if it were true, Paul said that God will have nothing for them but wrath. Not Heaven, not eternal security, but *wrath.* Verse 8 says that "ye *were* sometimes darkness, but *now* are ye light in the Lord." (Emphasis added.) These two conditions cannot coexist in the same heart! Lastly, verse 5 says, "For this ye know . . . ." Evidently it was common knowledge among the early Christians that no one could inherit the Kingdom of God if these conditions were in their lives. How sad, dear one, that today's "Christians" aren't hearing the same Gospel that was preached by our Lord Jesus Christ and the Apostles.

There are many other Scriptures which prove this "once saved, never lost" doctrine is not true. See John 3:19, John 8:12, John 12:35, Acts 26:18, Romans 13:12, and 1 John 2:8.

Now look with me at Ezekiel 18:20a and 21-29. These verses read:

20a The soul that sinneth, it shall die.

21 But if the wicked will turn from all his sins that he hath committed, and keep all my statutes, and do that which is lawful and right, he shall surely live, he shall not die.

22 All his transgressions that he hath committed, they shall not be mentioned unto him: in his righteousness that he hath done he shall live.

239

23 Have I any pleasure at all that the wicked should die? saith the Lord GOD: and not that he should return from his ways, and live?

24 But when the righteous turneth away from his righteousness, and committeth iniquity, and doeth according to all the abominations that the wicked man doeth, shall he live? All his righteousness that he hath done shall not be mentioned: in his trespass that he hath trespassed, and in his sin that he hath sinned, in them shall he die.

25 Yet ye say, The way of the Lord is not equal. Hear now, O house of Israel; Is not my way equal? Are not your ways unequal?

26 When a righteous man turneth away from his righteousness, and committeth iniquity, and dieth in them; for his iniquity that he hath done shall he die.

27 Again, when the wicked man turneth away from his wickedness that he hath committed, and doeth that which is lawful and right, he shall save his soul alive.

28 Because he considereth, and turneth away from all his transgressions that he hath committed, he shall surely live, he shall not die.

29 Yet saith the house of Israel, The way of the Lord is not equal. O house of Israel, are not my ways equal? Are not your ways unequal?

The Hebrew word translated as both *equal* and *unequal*, here, is **takan** (taw-kan'), and *Strong's Hebrew Dictionary* defines it as "to *balance*, i.e. *measure* out (by weight or dimension); fig. to *arrange*, *equalize*, through the idea of *levelling*."[4] To balance, to measure out in a way that equalizes, means to be just and fair. The Israelites were accusing God of being unfair. What was the equation God drew here? That sin brings death; however, if a man considers his ways and turns from his sins, he shall find mercy (Proverbs 28:13). His sins will never be mentioned. He shall live and not die. But, *by the same fairness*, if a righteous man turns from his righteousness and commits sin, *that sin will bring death to him*. Friend, if God did not handle both of these "turners-from" the same, His way would *not* be equal, but He made His claim to fairness, or justice, on the ground that He *did* treat the two the same. Can I say that again? God made His claim to fairness, or justice, on the ground that He *did* treat the two the same. If a wicked man turns from sin to righteousness, he shall not die, and if a righteous man turns from righteousness to sin, he shall not live. *Webster's* says *equal* means, "**1** of the same quantity, size, value, etc. **2** having the same rights, ability, rank, etc. **3** evenly proportioned."[5]

Are not my ways equal? Are not your ways unequal? Dear one, God is just. When people, yet today, say that He will forgive the unrighteous one who turns to righteousness, but He will not condemn the righteous one who turns back to unrighteousness, God, Himself, says, "Are not your ways unequal," or unjust? This is very clear, and Ezekiel, in 33:9-20, repeated this important truth. Let's read the part that deals with righteous people turning again to sin:

12 Therefore, thou son of man, say unto the children of thy people, The righteousness of the righteous shall not deliver him in the day of his transgression . . . neither shall the righteous be able to live for his righteousness in the day that he sinneth.

13 When I shall say to the righteous, that he shall surely live; if he trust to his own righteousness, and commit iniquity, all his righteousnesses shall not be remembered; but for his iniquity that he hath committed, he shall die for it.

[These teachers claim that when God, through Paul, said "thou shalt be saved" (Romans 10:9), nothing could alter it; it was forever. However, God, Himself, said, here, that *even though He says the righteous shall live*, that living ends when the righteous one commits sin.]

18 When the righteous turneth from his righteousness, and committeth iniquity, he shall even die thereby.

20 Yet ye say, The way of the Lord is not equal. O ye house of Israel, I will judge you every one after his ways.

God said, there, in direct response to Israel's charge that He was unfair, that judging *every one after his ways* (not after what he was in the past) makes God's way equal, or fair and just. Conversely, to judge anyone for what he has been, rather than for what he presently is, would clearly render God unequal, or unjust. Friend, this is so clear! And this is God speaking. "In my view," He the same as said, "justifying the wicked one who turns from his sin, and not condemning the righteous one who turns from his righteousness, is not just." And God will never be unjust. Allow me to say it again: His rule, stated in Ezekiel 18:20, is, "The soul that sinneth (present tense), it *shall die*"! Past righteousness will mean nothing in the day a soul turns back to sinning!

Someone may say, "Well, that's from the Old Testament. It doesn't apply in this New Testament Dispensation. Since Christ came, we're under a different standard."

Are we? Study the writings of the New Testament. All N.T. writers, as well as Jesus, Himself, referred often to Old Testament Scriptures, making our use of them in the Gospel Dispensation altogether valid. That is all the Scriptures they had. And may I remind you? The N.T. Scriptures, which came later, especially the Book of Hebrews, let us know that the only Old Testament things that changed with the coming of Jesus Christ were the *ceremonial* and *symbolic* things that pointed forward to Jesus' work on earth for mankind. The reason these changed is because Christ fulfilled them. Once the fulfillment came, the types and shadows were no longer needed. But God's *moral Law* never changed. It never will.

A good example of this is found in the very dawning of time. God condemned and punished Cain for killing his brother, Abel, long before Moses received the Law that said, "Thou shalt not kill." Also, God destroyed the whole world in Noah's day, because their thoughts were only evil continually. This, too, was long before Moses was given God's Law spelling out the things "thou shalt" and "thou shalt not" do. "Thou shalt not steal" and "Thou shalt not commit adultery," as well as "Thou shalt not kill" (among others), are still in force. We know this for sure because Jesus and the Apostles condemned adultery, murder, and stealing in the New Testament. In fact, the coming of Christ made these demands even stricter; under Moses' Law, the *outward deed* brought punishment, but under the Gospel, murder or adultery, etc., *in the heart*, even if the deed is never done, brings condemnation and the wrath of God.

"Equality," or justice, is a part of God's nature, just as are love, mercy, compassion, anger, jealousy, etc., and God's nature did not change when the Dispensations changed. The New Testament is full of references to God's being just. Every bit as much as He was "equal," or just, in Ezekiel's day, He is, in our day. If the wicked can turn and find life, and thank God, they can, then the righteous that turn will find death. This is *justice*, and just as God can never be unholy, He can never be unjust. God hates sin, no matter who commits it. The way modern Christendom acts, though, one would think that God doesn't hate sin, but that He's almost in partnership with it: He and the devil share the same hearts and souls and somehow work side by side. *Not so!* They have no communion, no agreement, no fellowship, no concord. Paul went on to say that we, Christians, as the temple of God

(2 Corinthians 6:14-16), have no communion, agreement, fellowship, or concord with Satan either. It is impossible for God and Satan to share the same temple. I want to ask these once-saved-always-saved folks something: was God *fair* under the Old Testament, but *not fair* under the New Testament? Friend, that is utter nonsense! "For I am the LORD, I change not" (Malachi 3:6). "Jesus Christ the same yesterday, and to day, and for ever" (Hebrews 13:8).

Look at John 5:30 (this is Jesus speaking, in the New Testament): "I can of mine own self do nothing: as I hear, I judge: and my judgment is just; because I seek not mine own will, but the will of the Father which hath sent me." *It is the Father's will that Jesus render just judgment in New Testament times.* Dear reader, please read also Acts 3:14, Acts 7:52, Acts 22:14, Romans 2:2, Romans 3:26, Colossians 4:1, and 1 Peter 3:18.

Let's look at some other texts showing that God's attitude has not changed toward those who turn away from Him. Second Chronicles 15:1-2 reads:

1 And the Spirit of God came upon Azariah the son of Oded:

2 And he went out to meet Asa, and said unto him, Hear ye me, Asa, and all Judah and Benjamin; The LORD is with you, while ye be with him; and if ye seek him, he will be found of you; but if ye forsake him, he will forsake you.

This is an example to us, remember? What does this example teach us? That we reap what we sow! If we forsake God, God will forsake us! The Holy Spirit moved Azariah to say this; it is absolutely true. Let us now look at Deuteronomy 31:16-17:

16 And the LORD said unto Moses, Behold, thou shalt sleep with thy fathers; and this people will rise up, and go a whoring after the gods of the strangers of the land, whither they go to be among them, and will forsake me, and break my covenant which I have made with them.

17 Then my anger shall be kindled against them in that day, and I will forsake them, and I will hide my face from them, and they shall be devoured, and many evils and troubles shall befall them; so that they will say in that day, Are not these evils come upon us, because our God is not among us?

Second Kings 21:14-15 says this:

14 And I will forsake the remnant of mine inheritance, and deliver them into the hand of their enemies; and they shall become a prey and a spoil to all their enemies;

15 Because they have done that which was evil in my sight, and have provoked me to anger, since the day their fathers came forth out of Egypt, even unto this day.

Second Chronicles 7:21b-22 states:

21b Why hath the LORD done thus unto this land, and unto this house?

22 And it shall be answered, Because they forsook the LORD God of their fathers, which brought them forth out of the land of Egypt, and laid hold on other gods, and worshipped them, and served them: therefore hath he brought all this evil upon them.

Ezra 8:22b says this:

The hand of our God is upon all them for good that seek him; but his power and his wrath is against all them that forsake him.

Isaiah 1:28 reads:

And the destruction of the transgressors and of the sinners shall be together, and they that forsake the LORD shall be consumed.

All right. Does the New Testament bear the same witness? It does; remember what Peter said? Let's look at it again in this context: "Which have forsaken the right way . . . . The latter end is worse with them than the beginning. For it had been better for them not to have known the way of righteousness, than, after they have known it, to turn from the holy commandment delivered unto them" (2 Peter 2:15, 20-21). The record is clear, dear one. We can forsake God, and when we do, and because we do, He forsakes us.

Peter definitely taught that backsliders are lost: "Wherefore, beloved, seeing that ye look for such things [the second coming of Christ and its blessings, verses 10-13], be diligent that ye may be found of him in peace, without spot, and blameless (2 Peter 3:14). Here, Peter urges the "beloved"—those who were saved and *looked forward* to Christ's coming—to diligence in order to be found of Christ in peace at His coming. After being saved, they could still miss Heaven. And this lends yet another proof that we're not made blameless after this life, but that we must be found that way when Jesus comes, for he certainly informs us that being found in peace is to be *without spot and blameless.* Once-saved-always-saved advocates defy this Scripture when they claim that Christians can go back to sinning, being no longer without spot, and still be found of the Lord in peace. There is just no way that can be!

Peter had already told the church this, in 1:10-11:

10 Wherefore the rather, brethren, give diligence to make your calling and election sure: for if ye do these things [verses 4-9], *ye shall never fall:*

11 For so an entrance shall be ministered unto you abundantly into the everlasting kingdom of our Lord and Savior Jesus Christ.

Here we learn that the *brethren's* calling and election are not automatically and eternally sure. They (we) must give diligence to *make* them sure. If, and only if, we give diligence to the instructions Peter gave in verses 4-9, and, indeed, to all the Word of God, will our souls be secure and find an abundant entrance into Heaven. Again the "if" renders to us an "if not." *If* we do *not* give diligence, we *shall* fall; we will lose our calling and election, and we will lose that hope of Heaven.

Hebrews 12:15 says the same thing: "Looking diligently lest any man fail of the grace of God . . . ." The clear lesson here is that if we do not look diligently to it, we *can* fail of God's grace. False teachers say God's grace covers the "believer," and the "once saved," even though they sin, but the Hebrew writer said these can fail of the grace of God. Grace *won't* always be there for us, unless we're diligent not to fail of it. Why would God, through the inspired writers, urge us to this diligence to make our calling sure, and lest we fail of His grace, if these were forever secure once we believe? Again, this teaching mocks every Scripture that spurs us to diligence.

Someone may say, "Well, of course, the Bible warns us to be on guard lest we fail. That way we bear fruit, help the lost, and further the Kingdom. God wants us be diligent and watchful, surely, but if we aren't, we're still saved." My friend, if you believe that, I'm sure it's dear to you, but it simply will not stand up to the test of Scripture. Hear, again, Jesus' words in Matthew 24:12-13:

12 And because iniquity shall abound, the love of many shall wax cold.

13 But he that shall endure unto the end, the same shall be saved.

For love to "wax cold," it had to have been hot once. The fact that some people's love will wax cold is undeniable. However, look at the next point. When it does, that soul is not saved! Jesus said, "*But,*" and this "but" sets the rest of His point directly counter to the first part. To paraphrase Jesus, it says, "Some will lose their fire, but those who don't will be saved in the end." Without a doubt, those whose love waxes cold do not endure to the end, and they are not saved in the end.

Remember Jesus' words, "If ye love me, keep my commandments." Whenever a saved person stops obeying Christ's commandments, for sure his love has waxed cold. In verse 13, Jesus set those whose love waxed cold *against* those who endured unto the end. There is no way a person can fit both descriptions, and, friend, take this to heart: he that does not endure to the end, *shall not be saved* in the end. The word translated *saved* here is the same as that in our opening Scripture, Acts 16:31, the Greek word *sozo* (sode'-zo). Anyone who does not endure to the end in loving, and therefore obeying, Jesus, will not continue to possess the "saved" promised to those who believe in the Lord Jesus Christ. *It's just that simple!*

Galatians 6:7-8, which we have already studied, clinches this truth:

7 Be not deceived; God is not mocked: for whatsoever a man soweth, that shall he also reap.

8 For he that soweth to his flesh shall of the flesh reap corruption; but he that soweth to the Spirit shall of the Spirit reap life everlasting.

Soweth, again, is the same as *sows*, and is a present-tense, continuing, verb. It does not refer to what one sowed in the past, but what he is presently sowing. Again we have a "but" that sets the two independent clauses of verse 8 contrary to each other. They are directly opposed to one another. So, to say one can sow to the flesh and reap everlasting life is to call God a liar! To say that is *to mock God*, but God is not mocked! We will reap exactly what we are sowing at the time we are called into eternity. Past righteousness is lost whenever one turns again to sin. Ezekiel said it will not even be mentioned! And in these verses, Paul used the terms "a man," "he," and "his." "*He* that soweth to *his* flesh," and "whatsoever *a man* soweth." There is absolutely no distinction, here, between saved, once-saved, or unsaved, men. But if you will read the context, you'll see that Paul was addressing *the saved* in this Chapter, both before and after these verses. Since this is the case, and he doesn't indicate any change of focus in these statements, it follows that, whatever a *Christian* sows, he will reap. If a *Christian* sows, again, to his flesh, he will reap corruption, *not* life everlasting. Friend, I'll take the teachings of the Apostle Paul over the teachings of modern, failed, Christendom in a heartbeat—and for as long as my heart beats. Please hold on to the fact that Paul said, "*Be not deceived*" about this!

We already studied Romans, Chapter 6, but there are divine truths there that also prove the "eternal security" teaching to be false. Look with me, again, at verses 14-16:

14 For sin shall not have dominion over you: for ye are not under the law, but under grace.

[Paul was talking to the saved.]

15 What then? shall we sin, because we are not under the law, but under grace? God forbid.

[God forbids that the saved go back to sinning.]

16 Know ye not, that to whom ye yield yourselves servants to obey, his servants ye are to whom ye obey; whether of sin unto death, or of obedience unto righteousness?

When Christians yield again to sin, it brings death. The followers of this false doctrine are directly contradicting God when they say that these still have life. Friend, they are calling God a liar. Think of the audacity of these people! But *they* are telling the lie. Paul asked, "Shall we sin, because we are under grace?" Then he answered his own question: NO! Friend, God's grace was *never* intended to merely shield us from the consequences of our sins! It was given to deliver us from sin's power and influence, and only then from its consequences.

Paul said sin *shall not have dominion* over those who are under grace (verse 14). *Shall not* is not the same as *should not*; it means sin *will not* have dominion over those who are under grace. And Paul tells us that yielding to sin makes us servants, or under the dominion, of sin (verse 16). Therefore, when a saved individual yields again to sin, he is no longer under the grace of God. Don't forget that Jesus said *we cannot serve two masters* (Matthew 6:24).

This text makes it obvious that believers (verses 14 and 17) still have the right of choice; they don't lose it when they get saved. He is talking, here, to the Church, and he says that, after salvation, we can still control whom we yield to, and through our yielding, whose servants we are and what has dominion over us. And, yielding again to sin does not find us yet under irrevocable eternal life, or eternal security, but under spiritual death (verse 16). This is, indeed, a devilish doctrine, and it will cause many, many, souls to perish in a lost eternity.

Does it shock you that I call "eternal security" a devilish doctrine? Well, friend, *the Bible* calls false teachings damnable heresies (see 2 Peter 2:1-2). That's pretty much the same as devilish doctrines. What would *you* call a teaching that deceives men and women into a false security? Because people believe this heresy, they freely sin without any concern about it, and they will land in hell's fire when they expected eternal bliss. That's very devilish, if you ask me, and when I see people being seduced by this delusion, it raises my righteous indignation. I *have* to cry out against it! Do you remember the story, in 1 Kings, Chapter 13, of the disobedient prophet who was told by God not to eat or drink "in this place" (verse 8), but who was seduced by an older, *lying*, prophet? Because he esteemed the old prophet, he disobeyed God—and it cost him his life. Friend, the old prophet *lied*, and the young prophet *died!* If you allow these false, these *lying*, prophets to seduce you, you too will die!

Can you see, now, how this false interpretation of the Bible is contrary to sound reasoning, as well as to the pure Word of God? Remember that when God set the choice before mankind, there in Deuteronomy, it was not merely between the *results* of good and evil, but between good and evil, themselves. When these teachers say we can choose to sin if we want to, but we still *have* to be God's children, whether we want to be or not, they are speaking foolishness. When they say our choice to sin doesn't cover whether or not we will reap the wages of that sin, they are speaking nonsense. We have seen that God does not want any such "service"!

There is absolutely no way this doctrine of eternal security can pass Scriptural muster. Friend, if you are committing sin from day to day, you are *not* saved, and you have no spiritual security, eternal or otherwise. The only ones who have eternal security are those who are continually obedient to God's Word, those who maintain their calling and election, those who endure unto the end. May God help you to receive His divine truth.

The Hebrew writer certainly disproves this teaching. Let's read Hebrews 2:1-3 and Hebrews 10:26-29:

2:1 Therefore we ought to give the more earnest heed to the things which we have heard, lest at any time we should let them slip.

2 For if the word spoken by angels was stedfast, and every transgression and disobedience received a just recompence of reward [under the Mosaic Law];

3 How shall we [under the Gospel] *escape, if we neglect so great salvation . . . ?*

10:26 For if we sin wilfully after that we have received the knowledge of the truth, there remaineth no more sacrifice for sins,

27 But a certain fearful looking for of judgment and fiery indignation, which shall devour the adversaries.

28 He that despised Moses' law died without mercy under two or three witnesses:

29 Of how much sorer punishment, suppose ye, shall he be thought worthy, who hath trodden under foot the Son of God, and hath counted the blood of the covenant, wherewith he was sanctified [hagiazo; to make holy], *an unholy thing, and hath done despite unto the Spirit of grace?*

Oh, this is so powerful, and it tells us this:

1) we, as Christians, can let the Word of God slip from us;
2) doing so is referred to as neglect of our salvation experience;
3) if we neglect our salvation, we cannot escape a just punishment, any more than those under the Old Testament could;
4) if those believing Hebrews sinned wilfully after they got saved, the Law's animal sacrifices would no longer be accepted for their remission; likewise, when we sin wilfully, we're not still covered under Christ's sacrifice without renewed repentance;
5) that which does "cover" us is judgment and fiery indignation which will devour us;
6) this will be *sore punishment*, much sorer than what offenders under the Law received;
7) sinning willfully after conversion is treading the Son of God under our feet;
8) sinning willfully after conversion is counting the precious blood that sanctified us an unholy thing;
9) sinning willfully after conversion is doing despite to the Spirit of grace.

How can anyone suppose that trampling the Son of God under our feet, and counting His sacred blood as unholy, and doing despite to the Holy Spirit of grace will leave us still under that grace? Oh, my precious reader, there is no way! That's why God said, there, that such people will fall under the wrath of God. God is loving, yes, but giving a heavenly reward to such as this would be a tremendous miscarriage of justice, and He *is still as just*, in these New Testament times, as He is loving.

This passage in Hebrews was definitely written to God's children; the writer repeatedly used the term *us*. Also, he was addressing those who had received the knowledge of truth, those who had been sanctified. If *we*, the saved, go back to sin, *we*, the once-saved, will receive judgment and fiery indignation that will devour *us*. Oh, friend, can you read these Scriptures and believe any longer that Christians who turn back to sin are eternally secure?

Someone may say, "When you say those born of God *cannot* sin, it sounds like *you're* teaching that God takes away the believer's free right of choice."

Well, first of all, I didn't say this; John did. But he wasn't taking away the believer's free moral agency. You know as well as I do that it's possible for believers to sin. What God, through John, is teaching here, I repeat, is simply that we cannot be born again *at the same time* we're willfully sinning. As Christians, we are still free to choose which we want, but we cannot have both. There is just no way!

To conclude this study on being once-saved-always-saved, let's turn again to the very words of Jesus, Himself. He is Truth, friend, and He said, in Luke 6:46-49:

46 And why call ye me, Lord, Lord, and do not the things which I say?

47 Whosoever cometh to me, and heareth my sayings, and doeth them, I will shew you to whom he is like:

48 He is like a man which built an house, and digged deep, and laid the foundation on a rock: and when the flood arose, the stream beat vehemently upon that house, and could not shake it: for it was founded upon a rock.

49 But he that heareth, and doeth not, is like a man that without a foundation built an house upon the earth; against which the stream did beat vehemently, and immediately it fell; and the ruin of that house was great.

Jesus does not want people claiming Him as their Lord when they are not doing what He says. He won't *be* Lord to any who do not do what He says. And He lets us know beyond a shadow of a doubt that those who hear but do not obey are headed, not for Heaven, but for a fall and *great ruin*. Why? Because their "house," or life, does not meet the test. Once again, the words *heareth* and *doeth* are present-tense, continuing, verbs, and they do not refer to anything done in the past, friend! Hearing or hearing not, doing or doing not, right now, today, determines our spiritual success or failure right now, today. And Jesus clearly set forth the results of both choices. Some people backslide and later get back to God, but while backslidden, their lives are on the sand and headed for destruction. When they cease to hear and do God's will, *they are not on the Rock*! And if they die that way, they will experience destruction and not safety.

Absolutely no one knows the truth as Jesus does, for Jesus *is* truth, and in John 8:31-36, we find these profound words:

31 Then said Jesus to those Jews which believed on Him, If ye continue in my word, then are ye my disciples indeed;

32 And ye shall know the truth, and the truth shall make you free.

33 They answered him, We be Abraham's seed, and were never in bondage to any man: how sayest thou, Ye shall be made free?

34 Jesus answered them, Verily, verily, I say unto you, Whosoever committeth sin is the servant of sin.

35 And the servant abideth not in the house for ever: but the Son abideth ever.

36 If the Son therefore shall make you free, ye shall be free indeed.

Here He confirms, once more, these truths:

1) those who *commit* sin (present tense) are *in bondage* to sin (present tense);
2) He cannot be our Lord, or Master, at the same time we're servants of another (sin);
3) truth sets free;
4) since the Jews were in bondage to sin, when Jesus said He would set them free, He meant *free from sin*;
5) He is *able* to set us free, from sin, indeed;

251

6) but, what is most important at this point, He clearly stated that *only those who continue in His Word, continue to be His disciples.*

Additionally, He set forth these facts of interest:

1) like many today, those Jews thought their religious experience was good enough, in spite of their disobedience, and they didn't need anything more;
2) one can be a *believer* and yet not believe unto salvation. Read the rest of Jesus' discourse with those Jews; He called them sons of the devil.

Finally, friend, our precious Lord puts this matter of eternal security to rest as false and destructive doctrine. In Revelation 3:5 and Revelation 20:12 and 15 He says this:

3:5 He that overcometh, the same shall be clothed in white raiment; and I will not blot out his name out of the book of life, but I will confess his name before my Father, and before his angels.

20:12 And I saw the dead, small and great, stand before God; and the books were opened: and another book was opened, which is the book of life: and the dead were judged out of those things which were written in the books, according to their works.

15 And whosoever was not found written in the book of life was cast into the lake of fire.

Did you really catch what these verses say? Without a doubt Jesus *blots some out* of the Book of Life, but overcomers have His promise that He will not blot *them* out. Conversely, those who do not overcome, do not have any such promise. To be blotted out of the Book of Life, friend, one's name had to be there at one time. Jesus also said He would only confess the names of those who *overcame* before His Father. We can know, therefore, that those who did not overcome, but rather were themselves overcome, were not confessed to the Father by Christ. Again verse 12, being written to the *Church*, says our judgment will be according to *our works.* By these words of the Bible Jesus we see that those not found in the Book of Life—including those who have been blotted out of it—will be cast into the lake of fire. Dear one, this is a *strong* proof that no one who goes back into sin, after being saved, is going to Heaven, and these are the words of the very Savior that "once saved, always saved," people claim will receive them into glory no matter what they do.

If you haven't been made free from sin, dear one, it wasn't the true Son of God who "saved" you. And if you were once saved, but you have returned to living in sin, you failed to overcome Satan and were overcome yourself, by Satan; therefore, your name has been blotted out of the Book of Life. Jesus will not confess you before His Father. *Please give heed!* I know that's hard to take. But the Bible Jesus wants His truth to *set you free!*

CHAPTER TWELVE

Conclusion

As we begin to wrap up our study, having established that the Word of God is absolute authority with absolute truth, may I encourage you to read and study your Bible. If you're saved, you need to do this often. When the flesh draws back from this, and it will, bring the body under. It is Satan's deep desire to keep you from your Bible, because he knows that's where you will find the path that leads to salvation and Heaven. And you will find that the more you get into the Word, the more you'll want to be in the Word. The treasures you will find there are beyond description! But as you gain deeper understanding, be watchful that it doesn't cause you to think more highly of yourself, dear one, than you ought to think (Romans 12:3). Remember, God resists the proud but gives grace to the humble (1 Peter 5:5). And the revelation of God's Word is not something we get because of anything we are or do, except for being genuinely humble and wholly given over to God and His will, then being willing to study and dig it out.

If you're not saved, you still need to read the Bible, friend. And you need to ask Him to show you His ways. Although God's deep truths are reserved for His children, you will find within the Word of God enough understanding to get saved, to repent and believe, and to find true salvation.

It has not been my intention, in this book, to hurt or trample on anyone. But I have tried very hard to trample the false theories that drag people to hell under a false hope of Heaven. That thought really breaks my heart! I trust you have been able to feel the compassion I have for those souls. For *your* soul. I truly love the souls of men and women, and I just cannot sit idly by and watch them being thus seduced and misled into hell without crying "*foul*"! After all, if I saw someone conning you out of your life's savings, knowing his scheme was a fraud, wouldn't you want me to warn you? Well, these false prophets are conning you out of your *soul's saving*, and perpetrating upon you a most heinous fraud, the results of which will last forever. Friend, you soul is at stake. False religious spirits are out to get you. Thank God, Jesus said the truth will set you free. But you must *hear* truth if it is to set you free. I want to say again, and emphasize, that this and this alone is the motive for this book.

I'm not saying that every preacher or teacher who tells people they can't be holy in this life is deliberately deceiving them. Some may be simply deceived themselves and think they are right. Also, many fight holiness because their "faith" was directed to a false concept of Christ, and since they didn't find real deliverance from sin, they think it isn't possible to do so. And, since they have never been truly saved themselves, they cannot discern spiritual things but live under sin's blindness. But there are very many who fight holiness because they are not willing to have Christ reign over them, because they're not willing to pay the price for ruffling their people's feathers, because they love the praise and honor of men more than that of God, and because they love their sins and want to believe that God will overlook them. But whatever the case may be, you do not want to follow these teachers! They only hinder you from gaining the real experience God wants you to have, and they lead you, not to Heaven's door, but to eternal damnation. *There is no greater tragedy.* How sad it is to see someone conned out of the results of years of laboring and planning, losing tens of thousands of dollars or more. But how much worse it is to see never-dying souls being seduced into relinquishing their eternal welfare to Satan's deceptive scheme, who is the most malicious con artist ever.

It amazes me how people can claim to believe the Word of God, yet instead of accepting what it says, they explain it away. Second Corinthians 5:17 is a prime example of this. Again, the verse reads, "Therefore if any man be in Christ, he is a new creature: old things are passed away; behold, all things are become new." It's certain that these "old things" and "new things" refer to the manner in which this *new creature* had lived and is now living. So, the way he used to live passes away, and he is living a new life. That's very simple. But, again getting away from the simplicity that's in Christ, religious leaders say that *some* of one's old life passes away, and *some* things become new. They say that the *inner man* is new, but the *outer man* won't become new until eternity, so some of the old life hangs around; we can't get away from all of it.

This is not believing the Bible! Paul said *all* things change. All things *are become* (present tense) new. Someone may argue, "He just said 'old things pass away.' He didn't say *all* old things." Yes he did. When "*all* things become new," that means that nothing old remains; *all* old things go. My question to you is, do *you* believe the Word of God? If you do, you'll accept that when one gets in Christ, all of the old life passes away, and all of the life as a Christian is new. The next verse says even more: "And all things are of God." Sin is not of God, so if all things in the new creature's new life are of God, there is no sin in it. And for any who still want to argue that, yes, our *inner* man is new, but our *outer* man is still under the power of sin, I'll let the Apostle Paul reply. Once again Romans 6:12-14a says:

12 Let not sin therefore reign in your mortal body, *that ye should obey it in the lusts* thereof.

13 Neither yield ye your members *as instruments of unrighteousness unto sin: but yield yourselves unto God, as those that are alive from the dead, and* your members *as instruments of righteousness unto God.*

14 For sin shall not have dominion over you . . . . (All emphasis added.)

Our physical members are only instruments of the inner man: "Don't *you*—the inner man—yield your *members*—the outer man—unto sin." Dear one, if the inner man is all new, it won't act out anything from the old life in its members. This is so crystal clear! I repeat, it amazes me that these holiness fighters claim to believe the Word of God, yet try to explain it away. If you show most of them the above paragraphs, they will do exactly that. If you don't believe me, try it. Tell them what this Scripture means, and they will come back with all sorts of "explanations" why it doesn't mean what it says. But no matter how much they try to explain it away, it will stand. God's Word is eternal, and it is "forever settled in heaven" (Psalm 119:89). I pray that you will be honest of heart and really believe these *simple* words of God.

Remember what Alexis de Tocqueville found when he visited America in the 1830s? It was righteousness, and it affected every area of American life. He said the pulpits flamed with it. Certainly not every person was saved, but society in general had a healthy respect for God's Word, and practically everyone lived, and taught their children, the principles contained within the Holy Bible. Sadly, today's pulpits reek, instead, with sin-protectionism. *What a contrast!* Instead of sin-trampling, blazing, truth, we find Christendom coming up with all kinds of "new paths" that they claim are "just as good as" the time-honored righteous principles that defined the early Christian Church and early America. God, Himself, addressed the thought of "ways" and "old paths," through the prophet Jeremiah. Let's read it: "Thus saith the LORD, Stand ye in the ways, and see, and ask for the old paths, where is the good way, and walk therein, and ye shall find rest for your souls" (Jeremiah 6:16).

Let's break this down, friend:

First, "stand ye in the ways, and see." *You* are standing in the many ways false Christianity is setting forth for men to travel today. Take a good look at it all. Then,

Second, "ask for the old paths." *Ask for them.* Again, it is *our* responsibility to seek after truth and to make sure we find it. Living for God requires diligence, friend. It takes earnest endeavor. Just going along, trusting this one or that one to lead us to Heaven, without any proving on our part, is very foolish and extremely hazardous. How many times does the Bible say, "Let no man deceive you"? It is up to you and I to make sure no man deceives us.

Third, the old paths are "where the good way is." All of the wonderful things the Word of God brings into the lives of men and women—the peace, the deep, boundless joy, the comfort and strength for meeting life's demands, the sweet fellowship, the tender bond, and that real, true salvation Christ died to bring us, with much, much more—can only be found in the old paths. What worked for the Apostles and early believers will still work today. Just as true, these modern "ways" will never produce true salvation!

Fourth, since all of this is true, God instructs us to "walk therein." This is what He foreordained for us, this is what Jesus brought to us, and God reasonably expects us to embrace it. He will not accept anything less. Why? Because this is the good way, the only good way. It is what is good, and right, for us.

Fifth, when we walk therein, "ye shall find rest for your souls." Remember Jesus' tender invitation, there in Matthew 11:28-29:

28 Come unto me, all ye that labour and are heavy laden, and I will give you rest.

29 Take my yoke upon you, and learn of me; for I am meek and lowly in heart: and ye shall find rest unto your souls.

Dear one, any way of living other than these "old paths" will wear you out, leave you heavy laden, and keep you under the yoke of Satan. He is a hard taskmaster. I urge you, walk in the old paths, those old time-tested, and time-proven, principles of holiness and righteousness, and you will find everything your soul longs for, and more!

It breaks my heart that modern Christendom has left the old paths. America once walked the good way, and her light shined brightly when her pulpits flamed with righteousness. But, today, her pulpits are silent—no; they are hostile—concerning righteousness. Look around in all of the confusion and chaos that professes to be Christianity, and take hold of the truth of God's Word, the old paths, the good way. There is only one good, or right, way, friend; Jesus said "I am the way" (John 14:6). Not the "Jesus" that is heralded all over the land today, but the *Bible Jesus.* You are at a crossroads. You must decide whether to "go with the flow" or stand against the current. God does not provide us with "multiple choice"—go to the church of your choice—but with the edict, "This is the way; walk ye in it" (Isaiah 30:21). Will you take the old paths? Will you heed the warnings we have set forth in this book, taken from God's Book? Please do not be like Israel of old. When Jeremiah gave them this command from God to seek and walk in the good way, they rebelled: "But they said, We will not walk therein." Please! Don't do that.

Throughout this book, I've endeavored to show that there is a false Jesus, a false faith, and a false hope, through false Christianity. But there is also a false peace. True peace is not a feeling; it is not an emotion. It is a knowledge. A knowledge that, because one has followed the Bible Plan, he is clear before God. A knowledge that one is living in obedience to everything God has revealed to him. A knowledge that there is no sin in his life. This is a far cry from the "peace" one obtains in Christendom today, where he is told that *he is sure of Heaven because he "believes,"* no matter how he falls short in obedience. Such "peace," such "believing," may lift the *awareness* of condemnation somewhat, dear one, but it will not lift the condemnation itself! It is, I repeat, a false peace. Jesus told Nicodemus, "He that believeth on him is not condemned: but he that believeth not is condemned already, because he hath not believed in the name of the only begotten Son of God" (John 3:18). You now know what it really means to believe in His Name. If you do not believe what the Scriptures testify of Jesus, you do not actually believe in His Name, and if you do not believe, biblically, you are still under condemnation. Jesus added, "And this is the condemnation, that light is come into the world, and men loved darkness rather than light" (verse 19). Friend, I beg you! Receive the light God has revealed to you through this book. Please do not prefer, do not love, the darkness of "sin-you-will-and-sin-you-must," the darkness of "no one can live holy," or the darkness of "once saved, always saved." Please embrace the light! Please realize how blessed you are to have found that light amidst the prevailing darkness that false Christianity has spread over the religious landscape. If you have this false peace, having been given a false hope, I urge you to trade it off for true peace. This is my whole burden and my earnest prayer.

As we wrap things up, I want to leave the truths covered in this book indelibly imprinted on your minds, by the power and mercy of God, and I trust that you will let Him write them in your hearts. So, in conclusion, we have learned:

1) We have a horrible dilemma in our world today. Millions of people are claiming a promise that, if they believe in Jesus' Name, they will be saved. This is a very faithful and true promise, and it will be kept with every single believer *who believes in the Jesus of the Bible and receives the Bible experience*. However, modern Christendom is directing the masses around the true Savior and presenting them with false Jesuses who cannot save. Because of this, many, many, souls are expecting Heaven when they are actually headed for a lost eternity in hell. *This is worse than disastrous!*

2) True believing on the Bible Jesus does not produce an experience that leaves the believers under the power of sin, where they can't help but do wrong now and then. What it does produce is a thriving, victorious, life above sin in this present world!

3) The grace of God was never given, never intended, to "cover" sin in Christians' lives, to give them, as it were, sin "licenses" whereby they are allowed to sin without any penalty, while those without the "license" are punished severely for doing

the same things. What the grace of God *was* given for is to provide divine strength and power that enables believers to overcome sin every day. And grace, itself, teaches us this (Titus 2:11-12).

4) The Apostle Paul was *not* a sinning Christian. He had, from day one, total victory over sin and the devil, and was soon preaching what he had found to others. The 7th Chapter of Romans must be read within the context of Chapters 6 and 8. Taking Scriptures out of their context can completely reverse their meanings. You can lift the words, Judas "went and hanged himself" from Matthew 27:5, and, "Go, and do thou likewise" from Luke 10:37, and build a "Bible-based" doctrine supporting suicide. "Now, that's extreme," someone may say, and I agree; but it gets your attention, and it does show how lifting Scriptures out of their settings can leave the true meaning behind and make them appear to support a lie. In our chapter on Paul's so-called testimony, we have shown how that is exactly what these false prophets have done. They lift Romans 7 right out of its setting and say it teaches something it absolutely does not teach.

5) The oft-repeated, "Try to be more and more like Jesus; do your best to emulate Him" is nowhere found within the holy Scriptures. Not even a trace of that idea exists. God always says, "Do it," not "*Try* to do it." And God commands us to "be holy, for I am holy."

6) The devil was never in Heaven. Again, to teach this, church leaders have totally lifted verses of Scripture out of their settings. Satan has always been a devil; he was created a devil by God in order to give us a free choice and to test and exercise our faith, and he is totally under God's authority. It is only through our yielding to him, initially or after conversion, that he takes control of us. By the power of God, living and reigning in us through the Holy Spirit, we can have daily victory over him. We must never take Satan lightly, of course. We are constantly exhorted to be diligent, earnest, and watchful or vigilant. It is *only* by the power of God that we can overcome him, and carelessness hinders our connection with that divine Power.

Satan was never an angel, never a "day star." The term *day star* certainly has a pleasant ring to it. "Day star" refers to the sun, as the sun is the only star that can be seen in the day time. Jesus is called the Sun of righteousness in Malachi 4:2. The term "day star" is used in 2 Peter 1:19 to describe when Christ, or light, comes to an individual. Jesus is the Light of God (John 1:9-13). The Savior said, in Revelation 22:16, "I am . . . the bright and morning star."

No one would ever use the name *Lucifer* to refer to Jesus, although, literally, it would surely apply. But false religion has so used the term as a name for Satan that, although it means something beautiful and brilliant, and was never in any way connected with the devil, himself, it has only negative meaning in the minds of the masses today. Satan no doubt started his horrid "rumor" about having been an angel, with the intent of exalting himself, all right, and he *has* exalted himself. He has given millions the impression that he is a power almost equal to God, one that God can only barely handle, and one that even God Himself cannot give real and complete victory over. What nonsense! But Satan loves to propagate it. He loves to exalt himself in the minds of people. He loves to make people think there's no way they can overcome him.

By the way, Satan does a lot more damage when he takes on an "angel costume" than when he appears as he is. Did you know that Paul talks about Satan wearing an angel costume? We'll look at it in a minute, but, first, consider that Satan's reason for spreading this lie about himself is *to deceive souls*. That's his goal. He wants to deceive, and then destroy, souls like you.

Satan wears an angel costume. We read about it in 2 Corinthians 11:13-15:

13 For such are false apostles, deceitful workers, transforming themselves into the apostles of Christ.

14 And no marvel; for Satan himself is transformed into an angel of light.

15 Therefore it is no great thing if his ministers also be transformed as the ministers of righteousness; whose end shall be according to their works.

Friend, here we find one of Satan's favorite devices: convincing people that he is something he is not, and that his ministers are something they are not. Paul was referring to those who claimed to be Christ's ministers while in truth they were the ministers of the devil. Paul said that they were *transformed as ministers of righteousness*. We know he did not mean they were *actually* transformed into something righteous. But they were so deceptive that people *thought* they were Christ's righteous ministers. People really believed they were. The transformation took place in people's minds when they were deceived. Oh, friend, the Bible is full of warnings about false prophets, and they are still with us today. It says *many* would come, but, remember, we can tell who they are by their fruits. Although they are in sheep's clothing, although they *look* like sheep, they are still wolves, and they leave *wolf tracks*. My precious reader, anyone who claims to be a minister of Christ (a sheep) while leaving "tracks," or fruits, other than those of a holy life is a dangerous person to follow (a wolf)!

Satan loves to parade about as something greater than what he is. He loves wearing the garb of nominal Christianity—claiming to be Christ Himself, actually, and being lauded as Christ Himself—while all the time he is a sneaking, low-down deceiver, and murderer, of souls. (Remember, Jesus said he was a *murderer* from the beginning.) The devil is wreaking a much, much greater destruction on the souls of mankind through what claims to be Christianity than he ever did through any other means. Dear reader, I want to say something in this book that I have expressed many times verbally: *false religion is the greatest curse on earth!*

7) In deceiving the masses into a false hope—where they sincerely believe they are saved, yet are not, and where they really trust that they'll live with Christ in eternity, yet will not—nominal Christianity, as a whole, has horribly failed souls. Their "faith," their "worship," their "remedy," their "hope," their "salting" of the watching world, their "soul winning," their "great campaigns," and the "experience" they offer, are all an exercise in futility. For certain, some do get saved under these, but that "sin-more-or-less" teaching will only kill these precious souls unless they find their way out of the system in time. No matter how beloved these teachers and preachers are to you, friend, "they shall not profit you at all"! They are "telling their own dreams," and not the pure Word of truth (Jeremiah 23:30-32).

Certainly, it takes more than a false doctrine to make one a false prophet; it also takes a wrong spirit. Perhaps your preacher is, himself, deceived, and is honest is what he is doing. In spite of the false doctrine(s) he's giving out, he may have a right spirit and be teaching the wrong thing honestly. If this is the case, all he needs to do is hear, study, and accept, the truth. Lend him this book, or buy him a copy as a gift. It will be the best gift you can give him. But don't be surprised, friend, if he gets angry, acts ugly, and shows that, after all, his spirit is wrong. I've heard it said that people don't fight something they don't see. They may disagree because they don't understand and have been taught against it, but they will never act ugly and mean-spirited toward something they do not understand. They will never want to "wring the necks," or anything similar, of those who seek to enlighten them. It is when God has shown them truth and they don't want to line up with it that their reactions are ugly and blasphemous. When they do react in a wrong way, you can know that they do not have the Spirit of God.

8) The idea that Jesus is too good to send a soul to hell is 100 percent contrary to fact. The thing He is too good to do is to take sinning souls to Heaven and, thereby, reward them for their sinning. Our society has so plummeted from right principles and standards of conduct these days that criminals are pitied and victims are ignored. Parents, teachers, judges, and politicians, may talk "tough," but how many actually carry out true justice? Instead, they "pity the poor offender," and the offender blames everything and everyone else for his behavior. What about pitying the one or ones who suffered at the offender's hands? Cold-blooded murderers, who showed absolutely no mercy on, or remorse over, their victims, get in the court room and sob and wail about how they were abused or deprived or harassed, and people think they should be "let off easy." But there have been multitudes of people who have been abused, deprived, and/or harassed, that never turned into violent criminals. We are not products of things that are out of our control; we are the product of our own choices! We cannot always control others' actions, but we *can* control our *re*actions. Since Christ came, no one has been more persecuted than the Christians, and yet they do not become evil in return.

How many parents do you know that tell their child, "Now, if you don't stop it, you're really going to get it," but when the time comes, they don't do anything except coddle them. It seems that no one gets justice for his actions anymore. Well, friend, you need to be "deconditioned" from thinking that God is the same way. God is not a warped Being; He is balanced. Just as He is good, loving, and merciful, He is also holy, righteous, and just. He will never condone sin, and He certainly will never reward it. His love and mercy, instead, deliver from it.

9) Although holiness fighters have an "arsenal" of Scriptures that they claim prove no one can be holy in this life, they are all taken out of context and misinterpreted. As we have shown, by God's mercy, when left in their settings, and when rightly interpreted, they do not in any way condone, but rather very definitely condemn, sin in believers' lives. All biblical "objections" to holiness are shown to be no objections at all.

10) Those who believe, or claim to believe, that once they've been truly born again, they can never be "unborn" and lost, are, again, misusing the Scriptures. We showed you how definitely they are misinterpreting their favorite texts and defying the true meaning of the rest of the Bible. But to reemphasize that truth, in this, our conclusion, look again at what Paul said in Romans 8:13: "For if ye [the saved] live after the flesh, ye [the saved] shall die." Paul went on in that verse, however, and said that if one keeps the deeds of the body mortified, through the power of the Holy Spirit, "ye shall live." It's only when we continue to live holy lives, through mortifying our flesh, that we can continue to be saved. The Bible *does not teach* that born-again believers can turn back to sinning and still remain saved and have hope of Heaven when they die.

11) The Bible *does* teach, and that very emphatically, that backsliders lose their relationship with God here, and their hope of being with Him after death. What awaits these, instead, is fiery indignation and wrath and eternal destruction. God is as just as He is loving, and He will never reward unfaithfulness. Only those who endure unto the end will be saved in the end.

Friend, I haven't relied, in this book, on commentary by great religious thinkers or on the consensus of well-known theologians, to prove my position. I have based my arguments solely on the Word of God. Why? Because, friend, it is the final authority; in fact, it is the *only* authority when it comes to matters of religion and faith (or anything else). And, of course, this, my book, is not the authority on holy living; it merely brings attention to the biblical stance on holiness and emphasizes the Bible's authority. Remember what Paul said, in 2 Timothy 3:16-17:

16 All scripture is given by inspiration of God, and is profitable for doctrine, for reproof, for correction, for instruction in righteousness:

17 That the man of God may be perfect, throughly furnished unto all good works.

The Scriptures are inspired by God, Himself. They, and they alone, form a safe foundation for our beliefs, our doctrines. They are profitable for this; anything else is unprofitable. Basing doctrine merely on what some church organization or body of theologians decrees, is, indeed, foolish, for man can, and usually does, get it wrong. We should always, always, *always*, check what the preacher says by the immutable Word of God. My pastor often asks us, when he gets up to preach, if we have our Bibles with us, and he encourages us to hold the Word right on him. You see, a truly honest minister, trying to be honest with God and with the people, is open to scrutiny, and he should be. But a preacher who is preacher-factory-tooled usually has an agenda other than that of finding and teaching what is actually God's truth; he is more interested in forwarding "what our church teaches."

Many years ago, divine revelation caused our ministers to realize that they were teaching a false doctrine. It was a "foundational" doctrine that defined us, we thought, and therefore we held it sacred and very dear. But, one day, one minister had a "lightbulb" moment; he began to realize that the Bible did not, in fact, support it. It had come down to us through centuries of tradition and a mistaken interpretation of Scripture. After much study and prayer, he was convinced of the right interpretation and shared what he'd learned with the Church. In turn, other ministers, through study and prayer, then changed their position on the matter as well. Why? Because the Word of God is the final, and the only, authority. And because they recognized that truth marches on and we need to walk in light as it comes to us. This new revelation

265

of truth made our experience of holiness more practical and satisfying, but no less *holy*. Indeed, it made holiness shine in an even greater way. It also brought persecution.

I personally had a problem, at first, with the "new light." I was a "dyed-in-the-wool" believer of the former teaching. My first impulse was to find somewhere else to worship. But God spoke to me. He told me not to make any rash moves. So, I stayed, but I cried out to God to not let me be deceived. Then, as I very cautiously studied the Scriptures related to the teaching—both the "old" way and the "new"—God opened my understanding. Friend, when the Holy Spirit "guides us into truth" (John 16:13), we know it. Truth just has a certain "ring" to it that finds an "echo" in the honest heart. *When God opens your eyes, you can clearly see!* By walking in the light as it shined on my pathway, I found a far greater liberty to obey God's Word than I'd had before. Light *always* makes us more like Christ and less like the world!

When religious leaders close their minds to greater Light, preferring their "official" position, or "what we've always believed," or when they're too proud to admit they are wrong, they render themselves unfit to lead and instruct others. And when religious bodies get their marching orders from "headquarters," rather than from the Holy Spirit, they're not Christ's body. Unfortunately, most of the "new light" these false leaders get only quiets even more their voice for righteousness and takes people farther from God's standard for life. You know, "greater enlightenment" such as that pride, adultery, fornication, white lies, homosexuality, worldly entertainment, lack of true self-denial, and a host of other sins, are not really so bad after all.

Jesus said, "He that rejecteth me, and receiveth not my words, hath one that judgeth him: the word that I have spoken, the same shall judge him in the last day" (John 12:48). Not "the words," but "the *word* I have spoken." Since the Word of God will judge us in the last day, doesn't it make sense to base our beliefs—and our day-to-day living—on it alone? Almost every denomination in existence bases its doctrine on the beliefs of its founder or its headquarters. And when we talk with its members, and show them what the Bible says, so often we hear something like, "Yes, I can see the Bible says that, but our church doesn't teach it." They go away, then, holding to what their church teaches and ignoring what the Bible says. Please, I beg you, don't do that if God has revealed His truth on holiness to you through this study! If you turn away from revealed truth, you will never get one step further in your spiritual walk, dear one. Jesus warned us about this in John 12:35-36:

35 Then Jesus said unto them, Yet a little while is the light with you. Walk while ye have the light, lest darkness come upon you: for he that walketh in darkness knoweth not whither he goeth.

36 While ye have light, believe in the light, that ye may be the children of light.

Friend, I am not trying to offend, but neither what your church teaches, nor what you, yourself, believe, is going to matter on that day. I feel a keen desire to line up with the rule God is going to measure me by at the Judgment, and I trust that you do too!

When godly ministers rely solely on the Holy Spirit and get the Word at God's mouth (instead of being told what to preach, and sometimes when to preach it, by "headquarters"), you will not find confusion. We can *trust* God—it is frail and faulty man that we need to beware of. On the contrary, modern Christendom is full of confusion. You can find pre-millennium, post-millennium, and a-millennium adherents. When it comes to the simple matter of being saved, you find those who teach that joining church is what you need. Others say baptism saves. Many say, "Just believe." If an ignorant person asked a dozen denominations how to get saved, he could very easily get a dozen different routes set before him. It is certain that he would get more than one. This very book was written for the sole purpose of examining true faith and true salvation by the Word of God alone. God's teachers do *not* confuse, friend. Those who are truly called and anointed of Him, preach a clear and powerful message from God's own mouth, and God tells them all the same things. Confusion comes when people aren't willing to take what the Bible teaches, but try to use it to back up what *they* teach. This gives people the many conflicting ideas we find in Christendom today. Jesus promised that if we read the Word with a deep and genuine desire to know God's will, in order to obey it, He will open it up to us. Whenever teachers and preachers try to tell you that you can't understand it and must have them interpret it for you, beware! Check history and you will find that darkness reigned when the Bibles were kept from the people and the religious leaders, alone, had the "right" to say what it taught. On the other hand, the precious

Word of God striking some open, honest heart has brought mighty revivals and reformations about.

Do you have trouble with the thought that God tells all of His ministers the same things? I know that boggles the minds of people today—they're so used to there being thousands of beliefs, and of being instructed to "go to the church of your choice." But think about it. How could God do otherwise? Seriously, how could the God of truth tell different preachers that opposing ideas are somehow all true? Throughout the Old Testament, covering thousands of years, and written by many different writers, God told them all the same things! Malachi did not cross Jeremiah up. David's prophesies lined up exactly with Isaiah's. Even the lessons learned, and taught, by the patriarchs fit hand-in-glove with later revelations given to the prophets and sages. Then, in the transition from the Old Covenant to the New, all the types and shadows that God gave Moses and the prophets lined up perfectly with what Christ did while on earth. Friend, they all got it right, exactly right, and *it is no different today*. Those who *get the Word at God's mouth* get the same doctrine, the same *truth*! God is not the author of confusion (1 Corinthians 14:33), and this applies to all the confusion in Christendom today. That confusion is the result of fleshly minds, that have no spiritual discernment, trying to interpret spiritual things. It is because men without the code key are trying to unlock the code.

All right. The Word of God is profitable for doctrine. What else is it profitable for? For instruction in righteousness. Isn't it amazing how the masses of "Christian" ministers and teachers use it, rather, for instructing that no one can be righteous? Again, Bible righteousness is to be righteous as Christ is righteous. Are you aware that using the Bible to teach that no one can be holy, when the Bible was given to teach us *how* to be holy, is nothing less than perverting the Gospel? It is going 100 percent contrary to God's purpose in giving us the Word. Friend, modern "Christianity" does not actually teach the Word of God; rather, it *uses* the Word to teach *against* the truth of the Word and to support the ideas and doctrines of men. I hope this study has helped you to see this, but let me give you yet another example. Romans 12:2 says, "And be not conformed to this world: but be ye transformed by the renewing of your mind, that ye may prove what is that good, and acceptable, and perfect, will of God."

Be not conformed to the world, but be transformed, in order to prove the perfect will of God. This divine transformation enables us to do that. But, according to anti-holiness doctrine, which almost all of Christendom preaches, we're transformed, yet still conformed to the world, and as we sin day by day, we're somehow proving what God's perfect will is. *This is utterly ludicrous!* All that these so-called believers "prove" is that God's will, supposedly, *cannot be done,* rather than proving *what His perfect will is.* The only way we can *prove* what God's will is, is by *living* it.

Let's take a last look at 2 Timothy 3:5: "Having a form of godliness, but denying the power thereof: from such turn away." Please really grasp what the power of godliness is—the power to live godly, as Paul told us we are taught to do, by God's grace, in Titus 2:11-12. The Apostle was condemning those who denied this power. Friend, if your minister, and your church, deny this power, as most do, please don't let them deceive you any longer. *From such turn away!* This is God's command! If you obey it, and everything else you know is God's will, you can find blessed deliverance and have a sure hope!

Even though these religious leaders deny the power of godliness, they certainly do not abandon that *form* of godliness Paul said they have. They earnestly proclaim their form. They talk a lot about God, about their love for God, about how God is working in their lives, about the great things God is doing and how He can do *anything.* Yet, all the while, they insist that sin is greater than He is. With all God's power, He can't work godliness in their lives. They say He is mighty, even *al*mighty, then they turn around and say He's not mighty enough to enable them to live without sin. That's rather contradictory, don't you think? That *is* actually saying that Satan is greater than God! Oh, yes it is. Although they cry, "Our God is greater than any other power. He can conquer any foe. There's nothing He cannot do," they still proclaim, "Oh, sin is so rampant. Sin is so great. Sin is so 'everywhere.' We just can't escape its power and influence here in this life." Talk about inconsistency! Talk about professing to be wise while becoming fools! (I didn't call them that; the Word does.) When they claim that sin is so great that even God cannot handle it, that's exactly what they are doing! These leaders claim to be lifting up Christ in their lives and ministries, but, dear one, no one can lift Christ up by heralding what He *"cannot do."* These "prophets" draw near to God with their lips, but their hearts are far from Him (Isaiah 29:13, Matthew 15:8-9). Based on their message, what, may I ask, *is* God able to do?

"Well," someone may say, "He can make us better." Oh, just *better*. Satan is so powerful, and sin so prevalent, that the best God can do is make us *better*. And you doubt that these false prophets are saying Satan's power is greater than God's? Is that being made "better" what *you* believe? My friend, the God I serve is greater than that. He is greater than Satan. He is greater than sin. Remember how the Apostle John said, "Greater is he [Christ] that is in you, than he [Satan] that is in the world" (1 John 4:4)? I don't know about you, but *I believe John. I believe the Bible*! If your "God" is not greater than Satan (if he, living in you, cannot give you daily victory over he who lives in the world), you are serving a false god. You are trusting a false "Jesus." In actuality, you are no better off than someone who worships a hunk of stone, wood, or iron. *That is the terrible state false Christendom has banished you to.*

No doubt many, if not most, of those who deny holiness in a Christian's life will say, "Oh, it's not the power of God that's not able. He *is* almighty. He *can* do anything. The problem is that we humans are too weak. We're too earthbound and fleshly, and therefore we just can't escape the influence of sin."

Dear one, the Word of God soundly and completely disproves any such notion! Throughout this book, we've studied many clear and irrefutable Scriptures that prove that we do not live for God in our own strength, ability, or wisdom. The *miracle* is done by God alone. It is an *inside* work, where our very hearts and spirits are changed and we are *made new creatures*. We do not do any of this ourselves. *God does it all.* The change is wrought by the Holy Ghost, and the power to live godly comes from His dwelling within us. When a "believer," a "Christian," pleads his human weaknesses as an excuse for his sinning, he only shows that he does not have the "saved" promised to true believers—those who believe, according to the Scriptures, in the true Jesus of the Bible. The Scriptures say that *Christ's* strength is *made perfect* in our *weakness*. Our frailties do not hinder our ability to live holy, godly, lives; they only perfect Christ's strength in us. You see, as the world looks on, they realize that only God can work holiness in a human being, and He is thereby glorified. His strength and power are magnified. This is God's plan, but so-called Christianity doesn't set this powerful witness before the world. Instead, they negate it, and tell the world that there is no such experience. Oh, friend, these false prophets are in terrible trouble with God!

Let's look at something else the Apostle John said. In the 17th verse of that 4th Chapter of his first epistle, he said, " . . . because as he is, so are we in this world." Reading the context of this verse will show plainly that the "he" John is referring to is Christ. We are just like Christ *in this world.* Could John really mean that? Well, look at what he said in Chapter 2, verse 6: "He that saith he abideth in him ought himself also so to walk, even as he walked."

Do you recall our three key points from the first chapter of this book? They were these:

1) where sin abounds, grace does much more abound;
2) greater is He that is in you than he that is in the world;
3) the weapons of our warfare are mighty through God to the pulling down of strongholds and the bringing of every thought into obedience to Christ.

Whenever anyone tells you how strong sin is all around us, and, therefore, how impossible it is to live without sinning in this world, measure their words against these three principles taken directly out of the pages of God's unfailing Word. You can search the contexts of all these Scriptures and you will not find anything contrary to what I have set before you in these pages. I have *not* lifted them out of their settings. Friend, the entire Bible proclaims holiness!

May I say it again? I'm trying to indelibly impress these truths on your mind, friend, before I leave them with you. Therefore, let's remind ourselves about King Saul's "partial obedience." Saul, literally, did about 90 percent of what God had commanded him to do. Wow! Most of today's pastors would love to have someone like him among their members! They would consider him a prime example for their flocks, and they would probably make him chairman of several committees. But did God take his 90 percent into account? Absolutely not. Were his "good works" weighed against his "evil works" and given a final "score" based on which outweighed the other? Not at all. God said he was rebellious, and that his sin equaled being in witchcraft and idolatry. You see, he disobeyed. In God's eyes, Saul was *100 percent* disobedient. Why? Because he did *not* do what God told him to do.

It's just that simple. God said destroy all, and Saul did not destroy all. Because he did not destroy all, he did not obey. The 90 percent that he did destroy did not count for obedience at all. *Not at all.* This idea of getting credit for the part we do obey is modern day heresy! It is not found within the pages, or tenor, of God's Word.

But, like Saul, today's professed Christians *think* that because they keep *most* of God's Word, they'll be accepted. Dear reader, if you disobey *any* of God's Word, you are *disobedient.* You are *not* an obedient child. Remember, James said that if we keep the whole law and yet offend in one point, we're *guilty of all.* I want to press into your consciousness that "partial obedience is disobedience." Samuel told Saul that his disobedience amounted to *rejecting* the Word of the Lord. Friend, whatever part of God's Word you do not obey, you are rejecting, and rejecting one part is rejecting it all. Do you think you can reject any of God's Word and be accepted of Him? Saul couldn't, and neither can you.

Some think that God is easier on our disobediences in the New Testament era—the age of grace—but this is not only a false concept, it is a very dangerous one. Why? Well, class, it's time for another review. Turn to Hebrews 10:28-31 and read:

28 He that despised Moses' law died without mercy under two or three witnesses:

29 Of how much sorer punishment, suppose ye, shall he be thought worthy, who hath trodden under foot the Son of God, and hath counted the blood of the covenant, wherewith he was sanctified, an unholy thing, and hath done despite unto the Spirit of grace?

30 For we know him that hath said, Vengeance belongeth unto me, I will recompense, saith the Lord. And again, The Lord shall judge his people.

31 It is a fearful thing to fall into the hands of the living God.

Now we'll have a quiz. It's an essay question. Please explain what "sorer punishment" means? Okay, ready to self-grade your papers? Sorer punishment tells us assuredly that disobedience under the New Testament is not more tolerable, but even less so, than it was under the Law. Why is this true? Because God has brought us so much more than people had under the Old Testament. He now saves us from sin and gives us power over it, something those people did not receive. Because of this, there's no excuse for our failing to live right. They were punished for their disobedience, but we will be much more sorely punished for ours, because disobedience under the age of grace and full redemption means *we trample Jesus and His blood under our feet.* That is exactly what one is doing who "sins more or less, day by day," while professing to be a Christian! This is a serious offense in the eyes of a God Who sacrificed His Son to provide for our deliverance.

Again, in wrapping up our study, let me remind you of what the Bible says about if a Christian *does* sin. In such a case, 1 John 2:1-2 tells us what to do. But did you notice, again, that tiny word *if?* John used it in this text. He didn't say *when* a Christian sins, he said *if* a Christian sins, we have an advocate. So, here, yet again, there has to be an *if not;* no one who has been born again *has* to sin. If a Christian does sin, however, it is usually the result of growing careless and neglectful. It is usually not "wickedly departing" from God (Psalm 18:21), a deliberate act of rebellion. It is not a matter of knowing something is wrong and just doing it anyway. When it's that kind of disobedience, it is *backsliding.* That is *turning one's back* on Christ. The true Christian who sins is immediately filled with extreme remorse, ready to fix it right now. And when he comes to the Father, broken and sorry, he has an Advocate. But to get forgiveness, he must repent, and that means he's determined, by the grace of God, not to fail again.

Also, in parting, let's look once more at 1 John 5:4: "For whatsoever is born of God overcometh the world: and this is the victory that overcometh the world, even our faith." Friend, this text is so plain that I don't know how anyone can attempt to refute it, yet modern Christendom says the opposite: "The world even overcomes those who are born again." That's a lie! If you are born again, you *overcome the world!* And the rest of this verse tells us that the thing that gives us victory over the world is our *faith.* Today's nominal Christian says he has faith, and because he "believes in Jesus," he is saved, yet he cannot overcome the world. The Apostle John said *his* faith was that by which he *did* overcome the world. What a difference! Oh, how far today's "church" has fallen from the Church of the Apostolic era! Well, the true Church hasn't. God still has a people who preach, teach, and live, what Jesus and the Apostles taught and lived, and I choose to have the faith that John had, friend. It *gives us victory that overcomes the world.* Any believing that does not produce victory over sin *is not Bible believing!* Any "Jesus" that does not bring this victory to the believer *is not the Bible Jesus*! By promoting this deception, these "pastors and teachers" are doing nothing less than engaging in a wholesale massacre of souls. If that sounds harsh, dear reader, think for a moment how harsh you will think these words are when you plunge into hell, instead of being welcomed into Heaven, because you are one of those souls.

Hebrews 12:14 says, "Follow peace with all men, and holiness, without which no man shall see the Lord." Dear one, the nominal "Christian" church is, by its own admission, without holiness, and without holiness, no man shall see the Lord! This verse confirms what I've tried to set forth throughout this book: *that people are not seeing the LORD Jesus in sinning religion. They are seeing, and believing in, a FALSE Jesus.*

Notice how we are expressly told to follow holiness. Paul said this is our *calling* (1 Thessalonians 4:7). I know sin abounds in this world. The Bible says it does. I know the world is wicked. The Bible says it is. But please "hide this word in your heart" (Psalm 119:11): *whatsoever is born of God overcometh the world.* How? By true faith in the true Savior, and by the salvation He came to bring. Any faith that does not bring you this *victory over the world* will leave you short of the salvation you were told believing would bring to you. But, praise God, He has burdened my heart to bring you the truth, my precious reader, about what saving faith really is, and for only one reason: that you might be saved!

Jesus said sin springs up out of the heart (Mark 7:21-23), and Paul said the true believer obeys from the heart (Romans 6:16). What happens in salvation is that we get a *new heart* (Ezekiel 36:26). Beloved, sin and salvation simply do not dwell in the same heart! Do not be as the Jews of Jesus' day, who talked a good talk, but of whose hearts Christ testified, remember, in Matthew 15:7-8:

7 Ye hypocrites, well did Esaias prophesy of you, saying,

8 This people draweth nigh unto me with their mouth, and honoureth me with their lips; but their heart *is far from me.* (Emphasis added.)

I know a lot of religious leaders are going to hate this book and fight its message. They are going to hate me and call me a deceiver. They are going to tell you to throw this book away. They are going to warn others to avoid reading it like the plague. But, dear one, the things I've presented here are based on the pure Word of God, not the ideas and opinions of men, and when left in their contexts and rightly interpreted, they are not hard to grasp. Paul told the Galatians that he didn't get his Gospel from men, but from God (Galatians 1:11-12), so every word that I've quoted from Paul's writings is straight from God (as are all the other Scriptures), and I didn't get what's in this book from men, either. I got it from the holy Word of God. After preaching to them, Paul asked those Galatians, "Am I therefore become your enemy, because I tell you the truth" (4:16)? I trust you will not consider me an enemy because I have told you the truth—a very unpopular truth today, to be sure, but still the truth. I know you love your pastor, your youth leader, your Sunday School teacher, and believe that he or she loves you, but "Little children, let *no man* deceive you [emphasis added]: he that doeth righteousness is righteous, even as he [Christ] is righteous. He that committeth sin is of the devil" (1 John 3:7-8a). I beg you not to let *anyone* persuade you to reject these irrefutable biblical truths. Remember, this is an individual matter. When you stand before God at Judgment, you will not be able to call your pastor, your denominational leaders, or anyone else, to stand up in your defense. If you do not accept God's Word, you will have to stand there, alone, with full responsibility for rejecting it. That's why we dare not risk our souls on *anyone's* word but God's! And, if you love your leaders, do your best to help them see the truth.

If any of your church leaders bring an argument that I have not covered, or if I've said anything you still do not understand, I welcome your calls and/or letters. I will do my best, by God's help, to give you the Word of God on it. If I don't know the answer, I'll prayerfully seek it. But in any case, I will be honest with you. You'll find how to contact me in the front of this book.

Paul closed his letter to the Ephesians with these words, and I feel it is very appropriate to close this book with them:

Ephesians 6:10 Finally, my brethren, be strong in the Lord, and in the power of his might.

11 Put on the whole armour of God, that ye may be able to stand against the wiles of the devil.

12 For we wrestle not against flesh and blood, but against principalities, against powers, against the rulers of the darkness of this world, against spiritual wickedness in high places.

13 Wherefore take unto you the whole armour of God, that ye may be able to withstand in the evil day, and having done all, to stand.

14 Stand therefore, having your loins girt about with truth, and having on the breastplate of righteousness;

15 And your feet shod with the preparation of the gospel of peace;

16 Above all, taking the shield of faith, wherewith ye shall be able to quench all the fiery darts of the wicked.

17 And take the helmet of salvation, and the sword of the Spirit, which is the word of God.

These verses are chock full of victorious, overcoming, living! Verse 11 says that God has provided us with a *whole armour* that enables us to *stand against the wiles of the devil.* Certainly a *whole* armour leaves nothing lacking that's needed for our complete success in battle. Verse 12 tells us that our enemy is not the false preachers or teachers, themselves, but the devil who is working through them; *our enemy* is spiritual wickedness in high places, wrought by the rulers of the darkness of this world. For sure, this includes false Christianity, which has a *high* place (that ecclesiastical heaven) in the minds of multitudes of "believers" and nonbelievers alike, but which keeps them in darkness. And the massacre of souls by this mass deception is certainly spiritual wickedness.

Verses 11 and 13 let us know that all of these powers and principalities, as dreadful as they are, can be *resisted* by wearing this armour, and verses 14-18 tell us what it is comprised of: truth, righteousness, the Gospel of peace, faith, salvation, the Word of God, and vigilant prayer. In connection with this study on holiness, these three stand out: truth, righteousness, and faith. It is the truth that sets (and keeps) us free, and we absolutely can possess righteousness (just as Christ is righteous), for we are told, here, to put it on. Then there is faith, which is our victory that *overcomes the world.*

Let's break that 16th verse down. I like to do this, as it really enhances one's understanding. Paul said, "Above all." What Paul is about to exhort us to do is *all-important.* It is *top priority.* It is *vital* that we do not fail in it. Then he said, "taking." Again, this is something practical that we can *do.* What do we take? "The shield." Here we see that we have protection from the powers of Satan; we're *shielded*—not *in* our sins, but *from* sin. We can know for sure this is true when we continue dissecting this verse. The next words we'll focus on are "of faith." Grasp this, dear one: it is our *faith* that shields us; and any faith that does not shield us is not Bible faith. Let's read on. "Wherewith" is the next word, and it means "with which," so there is something this shield of faith equips us to do. What is that? "Ye shall." Not "ye might," not "ye possibly can," and certainly not "ye cannot"! This term removes all doubt. With the shield of faith, *ye shall!* Shall what? "Be able." While today's "Christian" leaders unceasingly cry, "we're unable," Paul said, "Ye shall be able!"

All right, we're down to where the rubber meets the road; what does our shield of faith make us able to do? "Quench all." My friend, all means all. Again, the simplicity of the Gospel can be seen in this verse. When God says *all*, He means *all*. And when we quench *all*, nothing is left unquenched. *Quench* means "to extinguish."[1] What do we extinguish with this shield of faith? "Fiery darts!" Remember, God said, "No weapon that is formed against thee shall prosper" (Isaiah 54:17). Since this glorious armor is ours, today, this promise is for us, today, as well as for the Hebrews in Isaiah's day. Indeed, the Prophet closed that verse with these wonderful words: "This is the heritage of the servants of the LORD, and their righteousness is of me, saith the LORD." Then, finally, in our break down of this text, we find that we shall be able to quench all the fiery darts "of the wicked." My friend, be assured that *you* can quench every fiery dart Satan hurls your way, if you have true faith in the Jesus of the Bible. This is *your* heritage if you are a real believer. Don't let anyone cheat you out of your rightful inheritance!

Well, dear one, we've reached the end of our study. I have greatly enjoyed it—I love the Word of God—and my earnest prayer is that you have received help from it. As we part company, please remember how Paul said we are "called unto holiness" (1 Thessalonians 4:7). My purpose in this book has been to *reissue this call* that modern Christendom refuses to sound forth. In Christ's stead, I'm calling *you* to this beautiful and sweet experience of living with victory over sin and Satan each and every day of your life! Will you answer this call? If so, I'd love to hear from you. I long to see souls delivered through the truth, and learning that you were, will make my labor of love even more satisfying. Now, good-bye, my friend. Let me leave you with *this final word* from a heart of love: *"Believe on the Lord Jesus Christ, and thou shalt be saved"* (Acts 16:31).

APPENDIX A

Further Reading

I am going to give you an "assignment." On the following pages is a list of other Scriptures that deal with the subjects and main theme of this book. This is "further reading" for those who want to learn more about holiness; there are sixty-nine references given here, but I don't claim this list to be complete. Friend, the Word of God is "chock full" of holiness. So, please, read these texts. It will take you a little time, and you may have to do it over a few days, but it will be well worth it! Here, then, is the list:

Colossians 3:23-24	2 Peter 3:11	Isaiah 55:7
Philippians 1:10-11	James 2:14-20	Isaiah 1:21
1 John 4:1 and 5-6	1 John 2:3-6	Hebrews 7:19
Jeremiah 6:13-17	Ephesians 4:8	Titus 2:3
2 Timothy 1:9, 12	Matthew 28:18	James 4:7
Philippians 1:9-11	1 John 3:10	James 1:27
2 Corinthians 7:1	Ezekiel 33:12	Romans 14:17
1 Peter 2:5, 9, 11	Matthew 12:50	Hebrews 3:1
2 Corinthians 5:17-18	Revelation 14:5	Luke 10:19
1 Timothy 6:5-6, 11	Ephesians 1:4	Hosea 10:12
1 Corinthians 15:34, 57	Galatians 5:5	1 John 2:29
Colossians 3:9-10, 12-13	Hebrews 12:10	Titus 1:1, 8
2 Corinthians 5:6 and 8	2 Peter 2:1-3	Isaiah 33:5
1 Corinthians 3:16-17	James 3:17-18	Matthew 5:8
2 Timothy 2:19, 22	1 Peter 2:21-24	1 Timothy 1:5
2 Corinthians 2:14	2 Peter 1:6-7	1 Timothy 5:22
Revelation 3:12-14	Revelation 19:8	2 Timothy 3:12
Revelation 20:14-15	1 Timothy 2:2, 10	2 Timothy 4:2-4

Colossians 1:9-23, 28	Philippians 2:13-15	Isaiah 32:17-18
1 Peter 1:14-16	Philippians 2:15	Philippians 4:13
1 Thessalonians 5:27	2 Corinthians 1:12	Matthew 25:37, 46
Galatians 2:19-21	Ephesians 6:10-17	1 Thessalonians 4:7
1 Corinthians 1:17-21	Colossians 2:2-3	Colossians 4:12[b]

---

[b] *Strong's* says this *perfect* [**teleios**, tel'-i-os] means "complete" regarding "*moral character*."[1]

APPENDIX B

Joyful Praise for Holy Living!

I want you to see how grateful the human soul is for deliverance from, and victory over, sin, so I'm going to share some of our song lyrics with you. I hope you enjoy these selections, and that they cause you to long for what these writers—and generations of saints—have possessed, if you have not yet found it.

These songs are now in the public domain, so feel free to share them with others. May God bless you as you read these lyrics!

—

The Blameless Church
by Barney E. Warren

1. Without spot and blameless, O Savior,
       What a glorious church thou hast built!
    For this thou didst patiently suffer,
       For this was thy blood freely spilt.

Ch. Without spot and blameless, my brother,
       She lives 'neath the all-cleansing blood;
    In heaven and earth is no other,
       Her builder and maker is God.

2. Without spot and blameless, so holy,
       See the church in her beauty sublime;
    She lives on the bright hills of glory,
       She reigns over sin all the time.

3. Without spot and blameless, He bought her,
   In the likeness of Heaven above,
   From depths that were sinful He sought her,
   And filled her with infinite love.

4. She's blameless, without spot or wrinkle,
   From the last stain of sin she is free;
   With blood from the cross He doth sprinkle
   Her altars of cleansing for me.

—

The Church Triumphant
by Daniel S. Warner

1. Men speak of a "church triumphant" as something on earth unknown,
   They think us beneath the tyrant until we shall reach our home.

Ch. Thank God for a church triumphant, all pure in this world below!
   For the kingdom that Jesus founded does triumph o'er every foe.

2. O cannot the great Redeemer prevail over Satan here?
   Or must we remain yet under confusion, pressed down in fear?

3. He built on a sure foundation, and said that the gates of hell
   Against her divine munition can never indeed prevail.

4. 'Tis not in the church of Jesus that people yet live in sin;
   But in the dark creeds they're joining, and vainly are trusting in.

5. God's church is alone triumphant, in holiness all complete;
   And all the dark pow'rs of Satan she tramples beneath her feet.

—

More Than a Conqueror
by D. Otis Teasley

1. More than a conqueror thro' the mighty God,
   More than a conqueror by the cleansing blood;
   Kept by a pow'r divine, walking in the light,
   More than a conqueror, reigning day and night.

Ch. More—more—More than a conqueror thro' my Lord;
    More—more—More than a conqueror, standing on
    His Word.

2. More than a conqueror by the living Lord,
   More than a conqueror, standing on His Word;
   Mine is the victory, happy on the way,
   More than a conqueror till my dying day.

3. More than a conqueror in the battle's din,
   More than a conqueror over every sin;
   Ready to meet the Lord at the trumpet call,
   More than a conqueror, victor over all.

4. More than a conqueror while I live below,
   More than a conqueror over every foe;
   And by the grace of God ever shall I be
   More than a conqueror thro' eternity.

—

I Am From Sin Set Free
Verse lyrics by John Newton; Chorus & music by H. R. Jeffrey

1. Let worldly minds the world pursue, It has no charms for me;
   Once I admired its trifles, too, But grace hath set me free.

Ch. Free—! Free—! Free—! I am from sin set free!
    This world has now no charms for me, For Christ has set me free.

283

2. Its pleasures can no longer please, Nor happiness afford;
   Far from my heart be joys like these, Now I have seen the Lord.

3. As by the light of op'ning day The stars are all concealed,
   So earthly pleasures fade away, When Jesus is revealed.

4. Creatures no divide my choice, I bid them all depart;
   His name, His love, His gracious voice, Have fixed my roving heart.

—

Reigning in This Life
by Daniel S. Warner

1. Do you triumph, O my brother, Over all this world of sin?
   In each storm of tribulation, Does your Jesus reign within?

Ch. I am reigning, sweetly reigning, far above this world of strife;
   In my blessed loving Savior, I am reigning in this life.

2. One we hail as King immortal, He did earth and hell subdue;
   And bequeathing us His glory, We are kings anointed too.

3. Shall we then by sin be humbled? Must we yield to any foe?
   No, by heaven's gift we're reigning Over all this world below.

4. Oh, what grace and high promotion, That in Jesus I should be
   Raised from sin to royal honor, Even reigning, Lord, with thee.

5. Then we'll sing and shout the story, Of the wondrous blood divine;
   Full salvation, glory, glory! I am reigning all the time.

REFERENCE NOTES

Chapter 1

1. *Webster's New World Compact School and Office Dictionary*, Macmillan, New York, 1995, p. 212.

Chapter 2

1. *Webster's Compact Dictionary*, p. 381.
2. James Strong, S.T.D., LL.D., *Strong's Exhaustive Concordance of the Bible, Greek Dictionary of the New Testament*, World Bible Publishers, Inc., Iowa Falls, IA, 1986, p. 94.
3. *Webster's New World Dictionary of the American Language, Second College Edition*, Simon & Schuster, New York, 1980, p. 1267.
4. *The System Bible Study, Zondervan Book of Life*, Zondervan, Chicago, 1978, p. 273.
5. *Webster's Compact Dictionary*, p. 220.
6. Ibid., p. 16.

Chapter 3

1. *Webster's Dictionary, Second College Edition*, p. 605.
2. *Webster's Compact Dictionary*, p. 243.
3. Ibid., p. 320.
4. Ibid., p. 362.
5. Ibid., p. 411.
6. *Webster's Dictionary, Second College Edition*, p. 1511.

Chapter 4

1. *Webster's Compact Dictionary,* p. 291
2. Ibid., p. 217.
3. Ibid., p. 34.
4. *Webster's Dictionary, Second College Edition,* p. 702.
5. *Strong's Greek Dictionary,* p. 86.
6. Ibid.

Chapter 5

1. *Strongs' Greek Dictionary,* p. 12.
2. *Webster's Compact Dictionary, p. 39.*
3. *Strong's Greek Dictionary,* p. 53.
4. Ibid., p. 96.

Chapter 6

1. *Strong's Greek Dictionary,* p. 41
2. James Strong, S.T.D., LL.D., *Strong's Exhaustive Concordance of the Bible,* World Bible Publishers, Inc., Iowa Falls, IA, 1986, p. 638.
3. *Webster's Compact Dictionary,* p. 274.
4. *Strong's Hebrew Dictionary,* p. 156.
5. *Strong's Greek Dictionary,* p. 87.
6. *Webster's Compact Dictionary,* p. 399.
7. Ibid.
8. Ibid., p. 451.
9. *Strong's Greek Dictionary,* p. 5.
10. *Webster's Compact Dictionary,* p. 158.
11. Ibid., p. 302.
12. *Strong's Greek Dictionary,* p. 61.
13. Ibid., p. 86.
14. *Strong's Hebrew Dictionary,* p. 152.
15. Ibid., p. 144.

Chapter 7

1. *Webster's Compact Dictionary*, p. 19.
2. Ibid., p. 340.
3. Ibid., p. 461.
4. Ibid., p. 155.
5. *Strong's Hebrew Dictionary*, p. 165.
6. Ibid., p. 112.
7. *Strong's Greek Dictionary*, p. 29.
8. Ibid., p. 9.
9. Ibid., p. 34.
10. *Strong's Hebrew Dictionary*, p. 147.
11. *Strong's Greek Dictionary*, p. 23.
12. Ibid., p. 6.
13. Ibid., p. 95.
14. William J. Federer, *America's God and Country Encyclopedia of Quotations*, Amerisearch, Inc., St. Louis, 1994, p. 204.
15. Ibid., pp. 204-205.

Chapter 8

1. Reb Bradley, *Born Liberal, Raised Right*, WND Books, Los Angeles, 2008, p. 18.
2. *Webster's Dictionary, Second College Edition*, p. 766.
3. Ibid., p. 1188.
4. *Strong's Hebrew Dictionary*, p. 152.

Chapter 9

1. *Strong's Greek Dictionary*, p. 5.
2. Ibid.
3. Ibid.
4. Ibid.
5. Frank Charles Thompson, D.D., PH.D., *The Thompson Chain-Reference Bible*, B. B. Kirkbride Bible Co., Inc., Indianapolis, 1988, p. 1272.
6. *Webster's Compact Dictionary*, p. 473.
7. Ibid.

Chapter 10

1. *Webster's Compact Dictionary*, p. 329.
2. Ibid., p. 406.
3. Ibid., p. 388.
4. *Strong's Greek Dictionary*, p. 17.
5. Ibid.
6. Ibid., p. 57.
7. Ibid.
8. *Webster's Compact Dictionary*, p. 319.
9. Ibid., p. 110.
10. Ibid.

Chapter 11

1. *Strong's Greek Dictionary*, p. 6.
2. *Webster's Compact Dictionary*, p. 365.
3. William A. Sabin, *The Gregg Reference Manual*, Ninth Edition, The McGraw-Hill Companies, Inc., New York, 2001, p. 560.
4. *Strong's Hebrew Dictionary*, p. 164.
5. *Webster's Compact Dictionary*, p. 146.

Chapter 12

1. *Webster's Compact Dictionary*, p. 351.

Appendix A

1. *Strong's Greek Dictionary*, p. 96.

BRIEF AUTHOR BIOGRAPHY

Who in the world is Marie York? Well, it's no wonder you haven't heard of her before. She is not well known, and she says, "I don't need to be," but she has achieved a bit of recognition among the Churches of God around the world through the books, articles, tracts, and songs, that the Lord has inspired her to write. With this latest book, God burdened her to reach beyond her "circle" to Christendom as a whole. "Becoming 'famous' is not my goal," she said. "This effort is for *you*, dear reader."

Marie got saved when she was eight years old and spent several years searching from church to church for real substance to feed her soul, while living at times an up-and-down experience for lack of it. But God led her to a place where she could enjoy the depths of the unsearchable and boundless riches of His Word. Having a real yearning for understanding, and being, still, a very young woman, Marie was able to "grow up" while she grew in the grace and knowledge of God.

Marie studied Computer Programming in college, where she carried straight A's, but with only four quarters to go, she dropped out due to her husband's health. Some may wonder, because of the depth of this book's subject, whether she ever went to a seminary. Her answer is, "No. I don't know of a seminary that doesn't make room for sin in the lives of Christians." She has, however, been tested on her Bible knowledge and scored "Ministerial Level."

Over the years, Marie has worked for God in many capacities: in the Church's bus ministry, music and Sunday School departments, tape and CD ministry, camp meetings and revivals, and she is a regular part of the prayer ministry. She has written and edited, as well as other tasks, for *The Gospel Trumpeter*, a Church of God holiness journal that is sent around the world without subscription price.

By the grace of God, Marie has published two books before this one—a Christian novel entitled *To Walk Alone*, and a book of poems,

Echoes From Zion. She is also the founder and manager of SonShine Publications (www.sonshinepublications.com).

Marie knows well that "if a man think himself to be something, when he is nothing, he deceiveth himself" (Galatians 6:3). "No one knows better than I, just how *nothing* I am," she says, "but it's such a joy to be 'nothing' in the hands of my Heavenly Father. You see, He has chosen the things which are naught, or nothing, and He has done so, so no flesh should glory in His Presence (1 Corinthians 1:26-29). Truly I give God *all the glory* for this effort, for He, alone, is worthy!"

Marie can be reached for questions or comments through the contact form on her website, by e-mailing her at marie@sonshinepublications. com, or in care of the Church of God, 675 N. Cedar St., Newark, OH 43055.